THE TEMERITY OF HOPE

THE TEMERITY OF HOPE

Beverley Boissery

Wesbrook Bay Books

Vancouver

Published by Wesbrook Bay Books, 3338 Wesbrook Mall, Vancouver. www.wesbrookbay.ca;

www.boissery.com;

https://www.facebook.com/boissery

Editor: Valerie Gray

Cover Design: Mila Perry, Mila@Creative Motions.com

Interior Design: BDG Lewis

ISBN: 978-1-928112-54-9

FOR

Lois Wark

Evelyn Thorsen

and, Gloria in exclexis Deo etc.

CONTENTS

PART V. THE QUESTION OF FAITH

PART I

LEARNING TO BE INVISIBLE

CHAPTER 1

A AND R

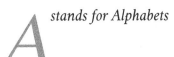

stands for Alphabets

Alphabets are astounding.

From the moment someone takes our chubby little finger and traces it over a shape and then connects it with the picture of a fruit, we learn that *A* is for apple, and a pulsating, ever-changing world of hundreds of thousands of words opens up for us.

A is also for Adam, our Biblical and genetic forefather. *A* is for adventure; such as the first time we deliberately splash in puddles because we like the sound of the water. *A* is for anxious as we trudge home in sodden clothes to the inevitable scolding. *A* is for adamant when we promise not to do such a thing again, and *A* stands for abuse when we dishonour that promise when the next rainfall arrives.

The alphabet, when its letters are grouped into words, enhances our experiences. A bird on a bush becomes, to T.S. Eliot, "A purple bullfinch in a lilac tree". Words express emotions, such as John Donne's exasperation with his talkative lover: "For God's sake, hold your tongue and let me love." The Foo Fighters use them to evoke memories about the time "we built these paper mountains and sat and watched them burn".

Letters and words define. S.P.Q.R., for example, identified the Roman Republic throughout the ancient world. They also refine – René Descarte's "I think, therefore I am."

How unfortunate, then, that the alphabet can also confine, as it did with my grandmother. Her alphabet began with *R* and skipped through every other letter until she came back around to *P*. That was it, an alphabet of just two letters – *R* and *P*.

Evelyn Cunningham was born in 1893 at a time when everything was changing. Indoor toilets were replacing outhouses. Charles Darwin's theory of evolution was converting many from their Christian faith. For thousands and thousands of English people, change meant coming to the cities in vain searches for work and living a precarious day-to-day existence. Queen Victoria clung to life, although to her frustrated subjects it seemed that she'd given up on both them and her reign. Someone even put a "For Sale or Rent" sign up outside Buckingham Palace.

Britain, the mother country, had always governed Australian attitudes up to this point. In her remote colonial outpost of Sydney, local politics ruled the day. People didn't particularly care what changes Edward, Prince of Wales, might make to English life when his mother finally died. They were more concerned with the future of their fledgling country. The six Australian colonies were about to amalgamate into one nation. Its future citizens wanted their new constitution to reflect a forward-looking country rather than a colonial past, and vigorous debate was the order of the day as the citizens discussed what their future might be like. The lawmakers looked across the Tasman Sea to a radical New Zealand that allowed its women to vote in parliamentary elections. Not to be outdone, Australia extended the same right to its female citizens in 1901 and went even further, making voting compulsory with significant fines for non-compliance. The Suffragette movement in England could only observe from afar with envy.

This was the world into which my grandmother was born and the world in which she lived her early life. James, her father, worked for a famous brewery's temperance division. The family lived in Redfern, a notorious inner-city suburb of Sydney. As the second oldest in the family, she was expected to help Olive, her elder sister, with the younger children, and together they took over the management of the house during their mother's frequent pregnancies. Both girls probably missed a lot of school as a result and, although education was prized in the family, neither went to high school.

The new constitution emboldened Australia so that when Britain went to war in 1914 men immediately enlisted in the Australian Army Corps, motivated not so much by the desire to defend England, but by the necessity to prove their nationhood on the world stage. Like all Australians, Evelyn was shocked by the horrific death and casualty rates suffered by the new army at Gallipoli in the Dardanelles, and then later in France. However, an exciting development in her life dulled the pain and worry of wartime when a young man, Victor Lionel Thorsen, began to court her.

The Thorsen family had emigrated from Denmark in the 1850s, settling first in the Maryborough district of Queensland and then moving to the inner west of Sydney shortly after Lionel was born in the 1890s, the fourth of nine children. Lionel was popular, attracting friends like a magnet. He had the most amazing knowledge and asked questions about things nobody else thought about.

One afternoon in 1915, Lionel took Evelyn to a library and showed her pictures of famous artists' works. Time and again he returned to one book, telling her to look at the portraits. She dutifully studied them, choosing one of a girl with a blue and white headscarf and a pearl earring as her favourite. She left the library thinking that all the houses in the book had black and white tiled floors exactly like those in her father's new house in the northern suburb of Hornsby. Just before they said goodbye, she told Lionel about this similarity. He laughed. "If I had all the money in the world, I'd take us to Holland, and we'd go to that artist, and I'd beg on my knees for a chance to learn from him."

"Vermeer is dead, Lionel," my pragmatic grandmother scoffed.

"I know, and I know it's only a dream. But I keep wondering if time could ever become elastic, and if I *could* study under Vermeer," he replied.

Another time he took her for a great treat – day tripping across Sydney Harbour to Manly Beach with a few of their friends. On the way back, he manoeuvred things so that they were alone on the ferry's outside deck. On the pretext of protecting her from the wind, he pulled her close to him and then pointed to the sky. "See the Southern Cross?"

After Evelyn pointed it out, he told her the names of the main stars — Acrux. Becrux. Gacrux and Delta Crucis. This was typical Lionel, knowing all sorts of obscure information, but he became pure Lionel when he added, "Do you know that Jesus probably saw them too? From what I've read, astronomers lost the Cross for hundreds of years and then found it in our hemisphere. Funny, isn't it? First it was north and now it's our southern icon."

That was exactly what she loved most about Lionel. Although he knew the most interesting bits of information, he didn't go on about them like some other people. He just said things and left her to think them over. Then, as the ferry ploughed its way through the heavy swells guarding the entrance to Sydney Harbour, Lionel tugged her even closer. "In Job, God talks about a time when the morning stars sang together."

"But, there's only one morning star," Evelyn protested.

"That's true now," Lionel said. "But think, Evie. Dream a little. If the Southern Cross used to be a northern cross, surely things aren't necessarily as black and white as those tiled floors. Things change. God says there was a time when morning stars sang together and angels shouted for joy. Wouldn't it have been wonderful? To see singing stars and everyone shouting for joy? I wish for that even more than the chance of learning from Vermeer." They sat in silence with Evelyn imaging the wonder of singing stars and joyous shouts until Lionel whispered, "You're the star that brings me joy. Shall I stand right now and shout it across the harbour?"

They married a few months later in October of 1914 and the children came quickly –Victor, joyous and full of wonder; and little Evelyn whom they called Girlie. Lionel loved his children. He tossed them high into the air and cuddled them every night while Evelyn read Bible stories to them. They seemed to be the happiest of families. Lionel worked as a cobbler during the day, and at night he channelled his artistry into beautiful furniture and wooden sculptures for his home and for special clients. They were a popular couple and the *de facto* leaders for their group of friends and their young families. Life was full and good and blessed.

Thinking about that time, particularly the World War I era, I've come to realize that Boxing Day, December 26, 1917 would prove to be a seminal date not only Evelyn, but also for my mother and myself.

When Evelyn's father asked that she and the family come to Hornsby for Christmas 1917, Lionel suggested that their friends come up for a grand picnic on Boxing Day. The most adventuresome would join him at the Hornsby railway station and then cycle down the fearsome, yet spectacularly beautiful Galston Gorge. Evelyn and the others would be driven down in a relatively new invention – a utility truck that someone promised to commandeer. Evelyn's younger sisters were thrilled for the chance to babysit young Victor and Girlie, so she could organize the food and ride down in the truck. Plans made, everyone celebrated Christmas with much love and laughter.

As a Christmas gift, Lionel gave Evelyn a white lacy dress with beautiful embroidery. It was perfect for the hot summer and when she tried it on, she realized it was also a perfect fit. "Don't tell me this came from a shop. It's too beautiful. How did you get the measurements right?"

"Olive made it," he told her. "I traded the cedar cabinet for it. Will you wear it tomorrow for the picnic?"

Evelyn knew her elder sister had longed for that cabinet as soon as she had seen it. Both Olive and Lionel would have spent long hours working on the cabinet and dress and she felt more cherished than she had ever been. The next morning she hummed to herself as she made crust-less sandwiches, then wrapped them in dampened linen napkins and packed them into wicker baskets for transport down to the gorge.

An up-country Thorsen cousin had arrived just in time for Christmas dinner the day before bringing two dozen bottles of ginger beer with him. Evelyn knew how temperamental the homemade brew was and she treated the bottles as though they contained liquid dynamite. As she swaddled them with straw Jack, the cousin, laughed, "It won't matter if they go off. It will be good training for my nerves. I'll have to get used to more than a few ginger beer bottles exploding if I'm to be any good in France."

This was the only blemish on their lives. Jack, the newly met and fun loving cousin, was on his way to the western front. The newspapers predicted that the war would be over before he even reached France, but no one believed them anymore. They'd been predicting an armistice since 1915.

The utility truck arrived, as promised, full of friends, and while they packed the food and picnic supplies into it Evelyn hurried back to the house to change into Lionel's dress. Jack carried the ginger beer out to the truck and, once Evelyn settled herself on the front seat, he handed the box to her. She would be responsible for its contents.

Evelyn had always loved the sheer excitement of going down the Galston Gorge. It dropped more than one hundred meters in little more than a kilometer. The road had six tight hairpin bends, and if horses or vehicles went just a tad too fast, or if they met someone coming up at the wrong place, disaster was inevitable. And, with people being people, everyone pushed their speed to the limit. Today was no exception. When the utility truck passed the cyclists about half way down, Evelyn noticed that Lionel looked anxious. She assumed he was worried about their speed, and she shouted to him to say that she was making sure they didn't drive too fast.

When the truck reached the valley floor everyone jumped out and Evelyn couldn't help feeling exhilarated. The men marked out their spot—the one with the best view, of course. While the women began setting up the picnic, laying cloths on the ground, the men foraged for kindling, and Evelyn carried the ginger beer to the small creek that tumbled over rocks on its way to the distant Hawkesbury River. By the time the cyclists arrived, they had their choice of jugs of fresh water, hot tea, and cold ginger beer.

Jack took charge of the fire and, with the help of a couple of unmarried women, cooked sausages in its flames. Evelyn and the rest of the women unpacked the sandwiches, laid out plates and cutlery on the table together with table linen. Someone started singing the grace: "For health and strength and daily food." All the jobs finally done, Evelyn sat down beside Lionel.

He wasn't singing. "You're pale," she whispered. "Are you all right?"

"Shush. It's just a headache."

While the last "Amen" echoed through the clearing, she studied him. "Is it a migraine?"

"I'm just tired, love. Enjoy yourself and let me be. I think I'm too old to ride the gorge anymore."

"Old? You're only twenty-four."

She brought over some food and felt somewhat cheered when Lionel nibbled on a couple of cucumber sandwiches and drank some water. He sat against a rock while talk around the *al fresco* table became boisterous as their friends debated what they'd do after Jack single-handedly won the war.

"I'm going to set up a dress shop," one declared. "With all those soldiers coming home, and all us unmarried women, there'll be babies galore."

"If that's so, they'll need houses. Anyone interested in joining my brand new construction company?"

"Well, I know what I'll want when I come home," Jack announced. "First, a hero's welcome and then some entertainment. I'll be sick of blood and guts, doom and gloom. So, why doesn't someone get a dance band up and running?"

A dance band? Entertainment? That was an unusual thought. The picnickers looked at each other. All, except Jack, were members of a Christian sect known as the Plymouth Brethren. For most of them, entertainment usually meant a lively Bible Study, or attending a talk given by an interesting missionary. In any case, the church leaders, known as Elders, probably could not even spell the word "dance".

Jack sensed that he'd said the wrong thing so he pulled out his mouth organ. "Bah. Enough of that. Let's sing a few songs before we trek home." He started playing "Billy Boy" and, after some hesitation, a few joined in. Then one person after another added their voices, and the music swelled throughout the picnic ground. When other picnickers joined in, everyone grinned. Jack took them through "Men of Harlech", "The Ash Grove", and "Bound for Botany Bay", and then called for requests. "Onward

Christian Soldiers" roused everyone, and although "It's a Long Way to Tipperary" brought on a few frowns, they vanished in the roar of the chorus.

Then someone from another group suggested one of the current hit songs, "Pretty Baby". Jack began playing it but stopped when no one sang. "We can't," someone told him. "Tipperary's one thing but common, hit songs are another. If someone here reported us to the elders, we'd all be in huge trouble."

"Trouble?" Jack laughed and made a show of looking up into a couple of fern trees and then high into the gum trees. "Do you think an elder might be sitting up there, cuddling a koala, and making notes on what your doing?"

A few people nodded and Lionel spoke up. "We're supposed to be "part" of the world, but not "of" it."

Confused, Jack scratched his head. He went to a tolerant Anglican church. "So, what's the worst that could happen? A lecture on your sins? They wouldn't excommunicate you, would they?"

"At Lionel's church, probably not. At mine, almost certainly," someone said quietly.

Jack looked rattled. "I thought the enemy was in France."

"Tell you what," Lionel said. "Evie? Why don't you give us a solo? 'The Holy City'?"

Evelyn stood immediately and walked closer to Jack. She'd been trained to sing whenever asked. Today, however, she worried about the hemline of her dress. It was above her ankles and all the talk about elders made her wonder if it was too risqué. She smiled at Lionel, hummed the first bars to Jack, and then began singing in her clear soprano, *"Last night I lay a-sleeping, there came a dream so fair."*

Her voice soared up into the gorge and silenced everyone. When she reached the last chorus, and encouraged people to join in, the resulting roar was one of triumph. Who knew what 1918 would bring? Maybe peace was possible, after all, with 1917 ending on this magnificent level.

After being thanked by everyone for her solo, Evelyn walked over to Lionel. "How's the headache? You still look pale. Why don't you come back in the truck with us? Someone can tie your bike onto the roof." She bent down and took his hand. "Come on, love, you can snuggle next to me up front."

"I rode down, I'll ride back."

"Victor Lionel Thorsen, don't be a hero. You've got a headache, your hands feel clammy, and it's such a long way."

"Then I'll sing Tipperary," he said with a grin as he walked over to the cyclists. As they set off, the rest of the group started cleaning up. Evelyn threw some leftovers to a hovering magpie, but she made up her mind that when they passed the cyclists on the way up the gorge, she would look hard and long at Lionel. If he seemed to be struggling, she'd make the truck stop and insist he get in, even if it meant treading on his manly toes.

As she turned her attention back to the packing up, she found a debate raging. Some of the women advocated putting the empty ginger beer bottles in the truck for later disposal. Others sided with Jack and thought they should be left by the fireplace in the picnic area. Evelyn imagined little Victor paddling in the creek one day and cutting his feet on broken glass. "We'll bring them back along with the leftover cakes. The birds can have what's left of the sandwiches."

Jack packed the empties into the back of the truck and helped scatter the edibles. "Come along then," he ordered. "Get in. I'll drive."

The truck set off and was only part way up the gorge when a

couple of cyclists raced towards them, coming back down the hill. "Hurry," they shouted. "Lionel's fallen off his bike."

Terrified, Evelyn sat on the edge of her seat. The truck, labouring because of the steep climb, was going faster than it should. More importantly, what had happened to Lionel? Five long minutes later, they found the rest of the cyclists.

One of them ran over to the truck. "Hurry. Fast as you can. A car's taken Lionel to Hornsby Hospital."

Jack drove with every ounce of his expertise. The truck valiantly took the dangerous hairpin curves, but by the time they reached the hospital it was too late. Somewhere along the road out of the gorge, Victor Lionel Thorsen had died.

In that one afternoon, Evelyn lost her own morning star and, I think, her dreams and a lot of her laughter. She had two children under three who somehow had to understand that the marvellous man who tossed them into the air was gone. They must have felt something of her devastation, as her shouts of joy became distant memories. In the madness of grief, she tore her white dress from top to bottom and wore black for the next two years.

I have no idea how my grandmother survived. She had no marketable skills. Life must continue, but how? Her father had nine other children to raise and care for. If the church gave her anything, I'm sure she was made to understand that it was charity. Her friends must have helped as much as they could, but they were all so young themselves, all of them just trying to make ends meet.

All I know for sure is that at some point during this time, as Evelyn worked out her formula for living, her alphabet became confined to the two letters R and P.

R stands for Rules and Righteousness.

It also stands for Rigidity.

The world changed for everyone in the Thorsen family that Boxing Day of 1917. Two-year-old Victor was just old enough to go to the funeral where various well-meaning people shook his hand and told him that he was now the man of the house. It took him a while to understand what they meant, but he never stopped feeling responsible for his mother and sister. His father's death changed him from a toddler who had exulted in his happiness to a serious, rather stolid youngster who understood two things: helping his mother and working hard at school.

Months passed before Evelyn recovered any kind of equilibrium after Lionel's death. As a second daughter she would have had child management skills given the number of younger siblings she'd cared for, and she had probably gained some monetary management knowledge from Lionel's small after hours business. Maybe she took in washing. Later in life, she only spoke of these years as being those of survival through which her Christian beliefs sustained her, but no longer was Christianity a joyous faith where morning stars sang together. Now it became like the Old Testament version of Godliness, with its reliance on obeying the "Thou shalt not" rules.

Little Girlie, my mother, suffered the most. Her nine-month life was destroyed. Before Boxing Day 1917, she had been part of a small but extraordinarily happy universe. She'd been cuddled and caressed. After Lionel's death, she became almost unimportant. When she cried, her weeping mother or brother would look after her basic needs, but they had little else to give her at the time. As the months and years went by, all she knew was that her father and mother had gone on a picnic and only her mother had returned.

In Girlie's mind, Evelyn was responsible for Lionel's death. A few years ago, Girlie, then in her nineties, told me that her mother had murdered her father. Factual evidence to the contrary was irrelevant. Her childish conviction had hardened into a corrosive certainty that governed her life. Facts establishing natural causes as the cause for Lionel's demise were irrelevant to her.

But, as the saying goes, life goes on. Five or six years after Lionel's death, the Thorsen family's fortunes changed again.

Evelyn had a suitor – a teenage plumbing apprentice named Allan. At first, Evelyn didn't take him seriously. But a certain charm went with his good looks, and he was not deterred by the thought of bringing up Victor and Girlie.

Their courting became the Thorsen version of an irresistible force meeting an immovable object. In this case, the immovable moved. Allan wooed her with flowers and picnics and brought back a little of the family's almost forgotten sense of fun. More importantly, he made sure that Evelyn knew of his unwavering desire to do anything to make her happy.

However, there were problems.

One was his age. He was nine or ten years younger than Evelyn who, at the time, was thirty-one. A brilliant cricketer, he was expected to be on both the New South Wales and Australia teams. But more important than those was the fact that he was Anglican, not Plymouth Brethren.

Evelyn and her children went to morning service, evening service and prayer meeting every Sunday, Allan played cricket. This religious difference was the major stumbling block for Evelyn. She could live with her friends' jeers that she was cradle robbing, but she could not marry outside her church. But she needn't have worried–Allan joined the Plymouth Brethren and told the selectors for the New South Wales and Australian teams that he would not play on Sundays. They married in 1924 and he never played serious cricket again.

Evelyn finally had the security she and her family needed, and she would never know want again. Economic want, that is. But when her new husband spoke of black and white tiles, he meant those in the hardware store, not the ones painted by Vermeer. He couldn't give her morning stars and he had to be taught that angels sang. But he made her the queen of his world and he called her Regina.

She called him Boy.

In an echo of Evelyn's first marriage, they had two children by 1927: Boy Junior and a little girl called Vera. But this was not to be the beautiful blended family that we talk about nowadays. Twelve-year-old Victor realized he could escape a blue-collar life by studying and, somehow, convinced Evelyn to let him stay in school until he was sixteen. He became the best student in his school and passed the necessary exam for entrance into the public service. Eventually, he joined the corporate world and became a senior executive in a large American multinational company's Australian subsidiary.

Once again Girlie was hit the hardest by events she couldn't control. At ten, she put her dolls away to look after the real life babies. While Victor studied, she changed diapers and entertained the newborns. Her friends might consider looking after their younger brothers and sisters as normal; she dreamed of following in Victor's footsteps. Girlie did almost as well as Victor had done at school. A job in the public service, even as a junior clerk, was her idea of heaven. Unfortunately, the apostle Paul had not mandated that girls should be educated, and her mother set great store by the teachings of Paul. Although Girlie fought against it, Evelyn made her leave school on her fifteenth birthday.

At first, she became a full time and unpaid maid in the house. But once Girlie saw her friends working in factories and spending their pay packets, she rebelled. Before Evelyn knew anything about it, she got a factory job. It was her personal fait accompli. In response, Evelyn demanded that she bring her pay packet home unopened every Friday.

In Boy's household, Evelyn had several elevated roles – regina, chatelaine, and comptroller. In the latter function, she took out two-thirds of Girlie's wages for room and board and nothing Girlie could do or say altered that. Girlie could spend the remaining third however she wanted, but she was now responsible for buying her own clothes, and paying for transportation and other necessities. What incensed her was that Evelyn insisted that she still help with the washing, the ironing and looking after Boy's children when she came home from work.

By this time, Girlie's feelings for Junior and Vera bordered on hatred. They had no respect for her. Junior, in particular, went out of his way to make her life miserable. He'd spill milk on floors that she'd just finished washing, tear holes in his socks after she'd darned them. He was a bully who thought he had a soft target. Things came to a climax one Friday when Girlie came home from work and handed over her pay packet as usual.

What happened next can't be known. People always have different memories of traumatic events and, in this case, everyone had a need to throw the blame elsewhere. Girlie swore that when she sat down at the dinner table that Friday night, Junior started kicking her under the table. When she told him to stop, he kicked even harder. This was the proverbial straw. Her temper boiled over and she smacked his face several times, believing that smacks were less painful than kicks. But Boy saw his son's bruised face and his own temper got the better of him. He dragged Girlie from the table to her bedroom, made her strip to her panties, and threw her face down on her bed. Then he straddled her and beat her within the proverbial inch.

After he and Evelyn went to bed, Girlie ran away to a friend's house without money and with only the clothes on her painful back.

Evelyn's version of the story was different. In later years, the incident was held up to me as an example of the wages of disobedience. Evelyn said that because Girlie wouldn't do what she was told to do, that is, stop hitting Junior, she lost her temper and ran away. Boy added that she had become the devil's spawn and was an example to everyone who thought of disobeying his or her parents. Over time, gory details got added to this bare framework.

Girlie told her friends that Evelyn and Boy didn't even bother to look for her. But in later years Victor's wife told me that the whole family, Boy included, scoured every place they thought she might have gone that night and they continued to do so for weeks afterwards. Victor himself had walked through the notorious parts of Sydney in the event she had might have been caught by a pimp. Soon rumors circulated that she had been raped and so traumatized that she had hidden herself somewhere in the countryside.

I have no idea what the truth is. I believe the flogging incident because it tallies exactly with the way Boy would eventually flog me when I failed to measure up. I can also imagine Junior and Girlie fighting. They had an equal truculence, and resentment festered on both sides. I also believe that once Girlie handed over her pay packet, she would have no money from it until the following Sunday and then it was to put in the collection plate. Again, I believe this because it was the way Evelyn operated. But I also believe that Evelyn and Boy drove through the streets of Sydney looking for their daughter for several weeks after she'd run away. Evelyn, in spite of her rules, did care. Her problem was that she rarely showed it.

The net result of that evening must have depressed her.

Rules + rigidity = Running away from home.

Evelyn's life went on and by 1938 she must have thought she'd weathered most of life's disasters. She'd survived the loss of Lionel and the disgrace of Girlie. She'd made an acceptable second marriage to Boy who had proved to be a steady provider. He was now a master plumber, gasfitter and drainer, and had built his family a large brick home in Sydney's working class suburb of Botany. They were respected, especially in their church circles. Vera was obediently plodding her way through school. Junior was about to follow in his father's steps by becoming a plumbing apprentice, and the successful Victor was courting an extremely fine woman. What could go wrong with this world?

Three words. Girlie became pregnant.

Being pregnant in 1938, at the age of twenty-two, was easier than it would have been in 1838, but only marginally so. Girlie, with minimal education and a tempestuous temperament, had few choices. She decided, early in her pregnancy, that she did not want the child, but lacked the connections or, hopefully, the conviction to find a backdoor abortionist. Instead she drank vinegar and other "popular" potions in order to induce labour. But she had met her match in me. I was as determined to be born as she was to rid herself of me.

Finally, it seems, she realized she had only one choice and, like the prodigal son, she returned home to Evelyn and Boy. But she showed no repentance for having left in the first place. Certainly, there was no joy in my grandmother's acceptance of her errant daughter and, in one of life's ironies; I would be the one who eventually ate the fatted calf.

CHAPTER 2

M AND K

M *stands for Momentous, Maestro, Marauder.*
It also stands for Memory.

Defining memories is easy. It's understanding them that's so hard. Memories tantalize, hovering on the edges of our minds. Sometimes they need help to bring them into focus. A smell can remind us of events in the distant past: the first time we went to the beach; the time we drank coffee in a Moroccan souk; or when a baby burped on our shoulders. Music also reminds us of times and places. My husband always remembered jitterbugging after school whenever he heard Louis Armstrong and "Blueberry Hill".

Memories are not always reliable sources of knowledge. Two people can be in the exact same place at the same time but remember things differently. For example, an old cathedral: one person, with an interest in archaeology, might date the crumbling mortar while another might be entranced by the light as it streamed through the stained-glass windows. Afterwards, the archaeologist might say, "Oh, that was the church with the twelfth century mortar," while the other enthused about the way the light had enhanced the blues in the disciple's clothes.

Memories are not necessarily stable and they can change over time. While I am grateful that age is giving me a perspective about my own memories and helping me interpret them with a new clarity, I know that age can also be notoriously unkind, sometimes taking us to faraway lands that no one else can visit. It's ironic, therefore, that memoirs, one of the hardest genres to write, rely on such a variable foundation. Yet, it's a testimony to the human need to understand and explain one's self, to teach through experience, that makes memoirs so valuable.

In 1945, I was six and living with Boy and Evelyn in the Botany house. I called them Father and Mother, believing they were my parents, and that Junior and Vera (then aged about twenty and eighteen respectively) were my blood brother and sister.

I attended Grade 1 at Botany Public School. On August 15th of that year I remember sitting in class. I cannot remember what we were working on, but I know I would have been hard at work, because I loved everything about school. Suddenly, a loudspeaker announcement broke the silence. Everyone in grades one through six was to report to the Great Hall for a special assembly. My teacher's eyes widened. This was an emergency.

We lined up and marched off. We "littles," the first graders, were silent as we led the way into the hall and sat cross-legged at the front, huddling together and blowing on our fingers to keep them warm.

Then, Mr. Wilding, the headmaster strode in, followed by all the teachers, and everyone scrambled up to stand at attention. "Keep standing. It's a special occasion," he began. "But first, we must pray and thank God." We rattled off the Lord's Prayer and, at Mr. Wilding's nod, one of the teachers sat down at the piano and played the opening chords for "Now Thank We All Our God." Everyone sang enthusiastically.

Then we waited. This couldn't be bad news.

And we waited some more, because Mr. Wilding didn't start to speak until the last person stopped fidgeting. "Today is a day you'll remember for the rest of your life. Thanks to God, we have defeated evil. The war has ended, and our boys overseas will be coming home."

Everyone began cheering. I didn't quite know what was happening. World War II hadn't really affected my home and family. Junior had been old enough to join up, but he'd somehow managed to avoid conscription. Mr. Wilding's words puzzled me though. When we'd said the Lord's Prayer, we'd asked God to deliver us from evil. Now that Mr. Wilding said we'd defeated it would the Lord's Prayer change? Would we even say it anymore?

But the news meant more than esoteric questions to my classmates. Around me, kids jumped and cheered until Mr. Wilding put his hand up to stop us. "I have more good news for you. Because this is such a special day, I have declared a special holiday. Go back to your classrooms, collect your things, and go home."

Only a moment before we'd been too hoarse to cheer anymore, but now we managed to break out into even more raucous cheering and laughter. It almost seemed that the rafters were quivering. Some kids stood silently, tears rolling down their cheeks. Peace had come too late for their fathers who had died as slave labourers while working on railways in Burma, or fighting in the New Guinea jungles. But most of us just shouted our happiness while friends pounded our backs in glee.

The war was over. We'd won.

Then one boy tossed a football in the air, "Come on," he yelled. "It's a holiday. Last one to Matthew's field has to set up." And, like everyone else, I raced to the classroom for my hat and school blazer.

The school's entrance gate was not my favourite place. Like most school children today, I was always taken to and from school. Someone always met me – Vera, or Zillah the maid, even Boy on occasion. I hated being met. Nobody else was escorted home, and as I walked through the gate kids jeered, "Cowardly, cowardly, custard; eat your mother's mustard."

I had no idea what they meant. What did eating mustard have to do with anything? I knew, though, that I wasn't the only coward. If Evelyn happened to be in the car waiting at the gate, the kids would bob their heads in some remnant of the feudal touch-your-forelock gesture, and then scatter like slingshot.

By this time, Evelyn was in her early fifties. I think she was only five foot three or four, but nobody thought about height when faced with her truly magnificent bosom. The early lissom elegance that had captivated Lionel had been replaced by indomitability. She scared school kids and made grown men quake. When she said no, it was no.

But this special morning of August 15, no one waited for me. Some kids realized this and a few looked back and beckoned. "Come along," they called. "We're going to Matthew's field. Come on, she won't find out."

Evelyn not find out? They didn't know her.

I wanted to go so badly. This was the first time I'd been asked to play with them. But the consequences would be severe if I was caught out. I'd have to kneel beside the kitchen table for ten minutes confessing my sin until Boy would jerk me to my feet and tug me to my room. There, he'd take off his belt and hit me between six and twelve times. A trip to Matthew's field might even merit twenty-four lashes—twelve for not coming home, and twelve for playing with "them".

Evelyn and Boy had pretensions of grandeur. We lived on the "right" side of Botany Road. Matthew's field, a vacant plot of land and our unofficial playground, was on the "wrong" side of the road, and Boy called the families who lived near it "gutter-trash". Playing with their children would be a sin beyond the pale.

"I can't," I called back. "I'll get belted."

They nodded their understanding. They all knew that savage corporal punishment was the norm. For a moment I felt disconsolate after they left, then I brightened up. Presumably no one at home knew about the holiday, so no one would be expecting me. Not yet anyway. For the first time in my entire life, I was free.

I dawdled towards home – window-shopping, running in one door of a shop and out another. Silly things, but nevertheless forbidden. I even summoned enough courage to cross Botany Road and stare into what I'd been taught was the devil's house – the Captain Cook Hotel.

The Plymouth Brethren talked a lot about the devil. I thought he must be almost as powerful as God himself, and I expected his house would be something like a palace, especially if it was Captain Cook's house as well. James Cook was the first European to chart the eastern coast of Australia and had landed across the bay from Botany in 1770. If Botany were ever to have a saint, it would be Captain James Cook—though what he'd be doing in a devil's house was something I couldn't figure out.

But instead of being glorious, the hotel smelled of stale tobacco and carbolic soap. Even the chairs disappointed me. I'd expected damask or chintz-covered armchairs with gilded armrests. Or, fancy chairs around linen-covered tables with shining silverware and candles. Instead I saw battered stools, so dirty that I couldn't imagine anyone sitting on them.

If the Captain Cook Hotel was the devil's house, the devil didn't know much about keeping a clean house. Ours was so much better. Maybe the devil should have asked Evelyn to get new chairs for the hotel to make it bright and clean, and have Boy check the drains to make the smells go away.

But just thinking about Evelyn made me suddenly queasy. I'd once heard the word omniscient and asked what it meant. God, I was told, knew everything. I'd nodded and added it to my list of words. In my world, Evelyn was omniscient and that meant she would know about the holiday and would have sent someone to collect me. The dawdling stopped. Terror took over and I started sprinting. There was a short cut I could take, forbidden like everything else in my carefully circumscribed life, but that August day I had nothing to lose.

I raced down the lane between the post office and Botany's town hall, my school scarf flying out behind me. When a black car stopped and blocked my way, I didn't worry. I was too young to be wary, and felt more irritated than afraid. Only after a man got out and slapped a smelly handkerchief over my nose did I suspect something might be wrong but, by then, it was already too late.

K stands for Kindergarten, Kopiyka and Klutz.

It also stands for Kidnapping.

The handkerchief must have been soaked in chloroform because when I regained consciousness, I was face down on the dirty carpet between the front and back seats of a speeding car. I'll never forget that mix of smells — stale tobacco, dirt, rotting food and, after a while, my own vomit. Then I wet my pants and added this very personal odour to the mix, and a further layer to my humiliation.

I'd been blindfolded. Rough ropes tied my wrists and ankles together. I had no idea what was happening, and my terror focused itself on Evelyn. I worried that the vomit had ruined my almost new uniform. What she'd say about that, on top of everything else, was beyond my imagination.

Shivering with cold, I wondered if the car ride would ever end. In the blackness of the blindfold, I couldn't tell what time it was, much less where I was. I desperately wanted to clean my mouth, and I was angry. What had I ever done to deserve being trussed like a chicken ready for the roasting pan? Why were the bad men driving me away?

I had no options but prayer, and even that felt futile.

My relationship with Christianity at that stage was extremely pragmatic. Earlier that year I'd been taken to a highly emotional "evangelistic" service. The preacher kept shouting something about being saved. What stuck in my mind was his question about what I'd do if I woke up one day and found that all my family had gone to heaven. That hit a nerve. How would I eat? Who would put my clothes out for me each morning? When the altar call came, I raced down the aisle as fast as I could. I didn't know how many tickets the preacher was giving out, but I wanted to make sure I got one for the heavenly express.

Maybe not exactly the right attitude, and I wondered if God would listen to me now that I really needed his help. And how would I pray? Because I knew he was omniscient he knew where I was and why I needed him to intervene. Eventually, it came down to four words that I repeated over and over: "Lord Jesus, help me."

Eventually, the car stopped and it seemed like nighttime. I felt helpless as I was dragged out of the car and slung over one of the men's shoulders. After carrying me into the house, he dumped me onto a bed and untied my arms and legs. The resulting cramps made the ensuing unconsciousness merciful. I woke to the roar of an argument with one man shouting, "She's a filthy little thing. Hope she's worth the trouble."

A woman answered, "I'll clean her up when I take the soup in."

I froze. I thought I'd known terror already, but I'd been wrong. This was beyond anything I had experienced in my short life. My guts clenched, sweat broke out and any vestige of hope vanished. I recognized the woman's voice. I knew who she was.

It was Girlie.

She had been an infrequent visitor to our house in Botany. Every time she came the atmosphere was akin to fingernails scraping down a chalkboard and, sooner or later, everyone began shouting and fighting. If I had enough warning, I'd grab a couple of books and lose myself in my room, or out in the depths of the back yard. Girlie always tried to be nice to me but she overdid it, and her attentions seemed artificial even to my young mind. When she ran her fingers up and down my arms or back, I wanted to scream. The simple fact was that I didn't trust her.

I didn't trust her at home and I certainly didn't trust her in this strange situation. When she brought me a cup of soup, I pushed it away. I was suspicious; goodness knows what she could have put in it.

Eventually survival won over suspicion. When she brought me hot cocoa hours later, I was so thirsty that I sipped it, and then asked for water. After my thirst was quenched she tied a handkerchief over my mouth and I dozed off again.

I woke to chaos some time later. Men were shouting at each other, and Girlie's shrill voice could be heard over the cacophony. Crockery smashed to the floor; fists and bodies thudded into walls. Someone slapped someone else hard several times, and there was a lot of cursing and swearing, new words that I added to my vocabulary.

I tucked myself into a fetal position, making myself as small as possible. I was convinced that the violence would eventually crash through the walls and into the bedroom. Things calmed gradually, as though someone had turned the volume down and, once everything was quiet, the bedroom door opened.

Normally, I would have screamed my head off. Instead, I thought I'd choke with the effort of remaining quiet. Girlie's whisper only eased my fear a little bit, "If I take the handkerchief off your mouth, promise you won't say a word. Quiet like a graveyard. Ready?"

I nodded. She removed the filthy handkerchief and, as she untied the rope that tied my right leg to a bedpost, I saw her face. She had a cut over one eye and someone had hit her hard many times. Incredibly, she seemed more terrified than I was. I looked at her, trying to work out if I should say something, but she put a clean handkerchief over my mouth and then pushed me into a closet. "Hide yourself in the clothes and don't, whatever you do, make any noise."

As the door clicked shut, I shoved my way through heavy coats to the back wall and, after my heart stopped trying to explode through my chest, and my breathing resembled normality, I explored my new prison touching everything. Its walls were satiny smooth, almost luxurious. I felt a couple of tweed jackets with mothballs stuffed into their pockets.

Why would someone put mothballs into pockets? It was mid-winter, the very time when tweed jackets should be worn, not stored. Was the owner dead? Or, heaven forbid, did they belong to one of the bad men? I had no idea what all of it meant. All I could do was concentrate on what I did know. Muffling my sneezes as best I could, I burrowed my way to the back wall and hunkered down to think.

I was certain that peeking in the devil's house that day on the way home from school, and then taking the short cut through the lane had been disobedience of the highest order, pure and simple. I knew that when Boy found out I would get a special beating, and he would stop after each belt to ask what the Bible said about sin. I also knew that I'd quote the proper text, "Be sure your sins will find you out," but that wouldn't satisfy him. Somehow, I never made him happy and that wasn't fair. Nothing was.

I could accept the consequence of my disobedience resulting in one of Boy's special beltings. But the bad men had made things worse for me, and that was hard to accept—they'd thrown me in a car and had made me vomit all over my school uniform. My uniform was made of wool and it had to be dry cleaned, and dry cleaning was expensive. Once Evelyn found out about it, she would remind me about the dry-cleaning bill every time I was late for a meal, or when she caught me reading in bed. She would say that she wouldn't have had to pay it if I'd only obeyed her rules.

Sleep should have been impossible but it came in snatches, as did other bodily imperatives. The need to urinate made me search the wardrobe for a chamber pot or the semblance of one. In utter shame, I used a shoebox and pretended I was someplace else—heaven, Buckingham Palace, even the lowliest outhouse in the slums. Then I tunnelled back to the nest I'd made and tried to separate myself from that other corner of the closet.

I kept trying to work out what had happened to me. And why? Could it be somehow connected with the end of World War II? But how? And when I thought about the war's ending, I was somewhat sad. The war years had been an era of the Biggles books by W. E. Johns, and I was just old enough to read them. Johns made war into the best possible adventure, and I'd imagined myself in that glamorous world. Sometimes I was a spy, at other times a nurse, flying to help some wounded soldiers. After Japanese Zeros shot me down, I'd evade capture and somehow find my way back home. But now the war was over, and Biggles wouldn't be needed anymore.

I felt much better once I thought about Biggles. I was in the exact same situation that I'd fantasized about. I was captured in alien territory, and I had to escape. With fresh hope, I began searching for a scraping tool, something I might be able to use to jack the door off its hinges like Biggles had once done. I had no luck, but then I wondered if I could slide something through the door and force the clasp of the lock upwards. The first bit of shoebox was too thick and others crumpled into uselessness.

As I worked away on the door, Evelyn's anger gnawed away in the depths of my heart. I wondered what I might be able to do to mitigate it. Would an abject apology work? Would that be enough to ratchet down her wrath? What could I promise? Never to disobey her again? If I escaped, I could promise to stand up in church and talk about being afraid and praying to Jesus to save me. That might work, I thought.

And soon a pattern emerged: scraping, worrying, telling myself Biggles stories, and singing little bits of hymns while fighting an almost insane thirst.

Time had little meaning. I don't know how long I was in the wardrobe. Fifteen, even thirty-five hours? I have no idea. Eventually self-pity took over. I began to believe I'd never get out. I'd shrivel up and die, unmourned, and be forgotten about. But Jesus loved me, I reminded myself. Jesus wouldn't care about my smelly clothes. Then I remembered that Jesus also saves, and I hoped with all my might that he would somehow save me.

But it turned out that my saviour was a kind policeman.

A tremendous commotion broke through my lethargy. The closet trembled and it seemed as if every stick of furniture in the house was being turned upside down and thrown against the walls. Angry men shouted very bad words, and Girlie's sobs rose and fell like a tiny rowboat in an angry pool of cess. I made myself small again and pulled the coats over me.

At long last, the closet door was wrenched open. I was terrified. I cowered behind my pathetic wall of shoeboxes and coats until a long arm reached in and tugged me out. As Girlie's sobs escalated, I tried to stand on legs that had been cramped for far too long. I screamed with the overwhelming pain of pins and needles, my relief and the frustration of not being able to sort things out. The policeman's hand comforted me while his other hand gently smoothed my hair, teasing a few of the tangles out. I wanted to hug him, but my arms wouldn't react.

"May I have a drink, please?" I whispered through parched lips.

He lifted me up and briefly cuddled me as he walked down a

hallway. I heard shouts of "We found her in a closet," and then we entered the kitchen.

Evelyn sat in a chair, her head propped up by her elbows. "How is she?"

"Starved and very thirsty."

Evelyn went to a cupboard, found a glass, filled it from the tap and handed it to me. Then she began clattering her way through a cupboard.

"Sip very slowly," the policeman warned. "Your insides have to get used to water again."

I nodded. Water had never tasted more wonderful, and when I put the half-full glass back on the table, the policeman sat across from me and pulled out his notebook. "Now, while your mother makes some cocoa, I want to ask you a couple of questions. Can you tell me what you remember?"

Remember?

I was just a little girl who had been frightened out of her wits and slung over a man's shoulder like a sack of dung. My stomach had growled until it was too pinched to make noise, my throat had felt like the Great Sandy Desert. The smell of various body discharges still clung me to like a dense tobacco fug.

Remember?

I wanted to forget. But that little girl had stared down the unknown and I had something important to say. I looked at Evelyn's back and then at the policeman. "They were bad men," I pronounced as importantly as I could. I looked at Evelyn again and wondered if I could shift some blame onto them, so my voice was a little louder when I added, "Very, very bad men."

He wanted details, so he gradually and gently took me through what I could remember. Then he asked, "And the woman. Do you know her?"

Evelyn turned at the question. She stood by the stove, ready to pour cocoa into the mugs, but she looked at something far, far away. I'd never seen anyone's face look so ineffably sad.

"Well?" the policeman prodded.

He'd asked the wrong question. I knew he'd meant to ask if I knew who she was, but it wouldn't be a lie if I said I didn't know her, because I didn't. I didn't know her last name, much less why she had been in this house. I didn't know why she occasionally came to my house, or what she thought. I hated her, although didn't know why. So, I looked the policeman straight in the face and with a clear conscience told him, "No. I don't know her, but she's a bad woman. A very bad woman."

He tried other questions, but I'd told him everything I knew. Eventually he nodded to Evelyn. "That's it, for now. She needs sleep and the comfort of her own bed." Someone carried me out to a police car, put me in the back and I stretched out on the back seat and felt strangely at home.

I woke up the next morning when Vera came into my room. "Mother wants to see you."

I sat on the bed. I wasn't ready for another inquisition particularly when my sins would be foremost on the agenda. Vera jerked me to my feet. "She said now, gutter-brat, not when you feel like it."

I pulled on my dressing gown and trudged my way down to the dining room. Evelyn waved Vera out of the room and then looked me over. "You need another bath or two to get all the smells out. But how are you, child?"

"Very well, thank you." It was an automatic reply and meant nothing. But I didn't know what else to say. My conversations with Evelyn were usually limited to my care or behaviour. I looked at her face, saw huge dark circles under her eyes and wondered if she'd had any sleep. She hadn't arrived home by the time I'd gone to bed. Without knowing exactly why, I felt sorry for her for a minute or two. At least, until she spoke again.

"You needn't go to school until Monday. In the meantime, you should rest and think about the consequences of sin. We won't speak about what happened and you're not to tell anyone about your adventure, even Vera. Understand?"

I shuffled my feet and she took that to mean agreement.

But I didn't understand.

I still don't know if Boy knew what had happened. Reason says he must have but, as she said, the entire episode went away and might never have happened. For the longest time, I thought kidnapping was a normal part of growing up. When girls gossiped and giggled together, I thought they were probably telling each other bits and pieces about their abductions. It was only when I read about the Lindbergh kidnapping that I understood it wasn't something everyone had to endure, and that's when Q (for questions) became the dominant letter of the alphabet in my mind. Why had I been I kidnapped? Why was Girlie involved? How did she fit into everything? And, were we so rich that the bad men and Girlie thought they'd get a ransom?

World War II was a time of want for so many people, but not for us. Although we had rationing in Australia, my family always had more than enough gas to go on picnics or long trips to the country to visit friends every Saturday. Boy employed five men and had a fleet of trucks and vans for his business, and we had two Chevrolets (one from 1939, the other from 1941) for family use. This might not mean much today, but several of my well-off relatives didn't get cars until the late 1940s and even then they were rarely new. As well, Australia imposed a punishing luxury tax on imported vehicles. How Boy managed to get a new car, much less two, during the war is inexplicable. Maybe, he used his rental money because, by this time, he and Evelyn owned seven or eight houses in Mascot, the area that adjoins Botany, and is now part of Sydney's Kingsford Smith International Airport.

By the end of World War II, Boy was the dominant plumber in the area with more business than he could handle. His customers were both rich (the Anglican Diocese of Sydney) and poor. People said that I lived in the lap of luxury. Certainly, I've been told over and over that I was the best-dressed child in Sydney.

This so-called luxury, though, didn't extent to Junior and Vera. Both had left school when they turned fifteen. Junior became his father's apprentice and Vera worked in a factory, but that didn't relieve her of duties around the house. She still was largely responsible for making sure that I got up and dressed and, as the Plymouth Brethren didn't allow women to cut their hair, she had to make sure mine was braided every morning. Her litany while she did this revealed her opinion of me: "You came from the gutter. The quicker you go back to it, the better it will be." By the time I understood what she meant, I was beyond being hurt by her words, but her hatred left an indelible mark.

None of this explained the kidnapping. I still don't know if a ransom was demanded and, if so, how much it was. I can't remember going to court or giving additional statements to the police. I don't know if the men were charged or not. I've often wished that I could have had a conversation with Evelyn, or ask her the many questions I had, but that was impossible. I did ask Girlie about it sixty years later, but she claimed she couldn't remember anything about it.

When I got ready for school the next Monday, I found a completely new set of clothes laid out for me. New tunic, shirt and tie, new blazer, new underwear, socks and shoes. They were the only hint, the only suggestions, that something might have happened to me and, with things as they were, I couldn't even tell

Evelyn thank you. It took me several decades before I understood that those new clothes might have been her way of showing love.

It is impossible to overstate how circumscribed my life became. Not only did someone walk me back and forth to school until I was about nine, I knew nothing of popular culture. Comics and movies were forbidden. I didn't know any of the so-called hit songs, much less who Bing Crosby or Frank Sinatra were. Although I took music lessons for seven years, I only learned how to play hymns. The works of Brahms, Bach and Albioni were *terra incognita*. My life was church, school and the world of books.

In retrospect, this seems the only consequence from the kidnapping. I don't know if Girlie was punished or went to jail. The next time I saw her was about five years later and, by then, she was married and had a small daughter. And, it must be remembered that this was a generation when we were constantly told, "not to push ourselves forward" and asking difficult questions was definitely pushing oneself forward.

I only found corroboration and more details about the kidnapping in 2005 when I visited Victor's widow, Eugenie (known as Gene). To my surprise, she told me that I'd actually been kidnapped three times. When she began describing the first, I interrupted her. "I've always had this memory of being pulled through a train window. No one believes me because I think I was about six months old at the time. But my eyes concentrated on the jacket I was wearing." I stopped and drew a design for her. "I remembered this. It's why I learned to knit. I thought if I could knit the pattern, I might remember other things."

Gene laughed. "I made that jacket for you. But, Bev, you weren't six months. You were six *weeks*."

That silenced me. Memories from six-week-old babies weren't supposed to happen. "What happened? Who was pulling me?"

Gene looked sad and shame-faced. "Girlie was never going to

keep you. Vic and I talked about getting married early so that we could bring you up, but we knew people would think you were mine and born out of wedlock and we couldn't stand the shame. Anyway, Evelyn stepped in, paid Girlie some money and took you herself, and that was that. Or it was until Girlie changed her mind because she thought she should get more money."

When Gene told me that Girlie had also tried to kidnap me when I was ten months old, I tuned out. Girlie hadn't wanted me to be born in the first place, and when that didn't work out for her she sold me. Why had she tried to get me back? According to Gene, Girlie was always after money and, unfortunately, Gene was almost ninety at the time of this conversation and very frail. I was too numb to ask more and by the time I'd thought about everything, it was too late. Gene had told me what she thought I should know, that she and Vic had always loved me and wished they'd had more courage in 1939 but, beyond that, things should be left in the past.

Memories can be ephemeral, or they can be as solid as the Canadian Shield. While I can remember the colour of our Chevrolet (green), and the number of its license plate (HS-800), I cannot remember incidents of joy or happiness or love from my very young days. Maybe the kidnapping clouded everything. I simply don't know.

CHAPTER 3

S AND W

S *stands for Solitary, Sadness, and Singularity. .*
It also stands for Sunday school.

In the late 1940s, parents still sent their children to Sunday school—Anglican, Methodist, Presbyterian, Catholic, or other denominations. All children attended Sunday school, especially me.

In my family, Sundays had a special order. We would drive fifteen miles to a Brethren church (called a Gospel Hall) for communion, come home for a lunch of roast beef or lamb, and then drive to Mascot for outdoor Sunday school. We'd come home again; eat a light meal and then drive to various Gospel Halls for evening church.

Sunday school was my family's own cottage industry. In their own way, Boy and Evelyn were descendants of Industrial Revolution Christians, people who taught literacy to the children working in the mills. Every Saturday one of Boy's trucks was loaded with benches, a portable organ, all kinds of sports gear, and boxes of books. Then, after our roast beef lunch on Sunday, we'd drive to a vacant lot in Mascot, the adjoining suburb to Botany, and unload the truck. Evelyn would set up a library, choosing her display books with great care. She wanted to go home with fewer books than what she came with. Boy rounded up forty or fifty children and began playing cricket or footie with them, and sometimes skipping rope with the girls.

Boy thrived in this environment, and the children loved him. At three o'clock Evelyn started the service off by singing. Her voice might have been excellent at some stage but, by then, it was heavy on the vibrato. I used to sit on the backbench and pretend I couldn't hear it. Maybe her voice was still good and I was just too self-conscious. I don't know. Then Boy conducted several choruses, sometimes altering the words to highlight someone the kids knew. For example, a song with the line "Better than ever a sinner could be" would change to "Better than ever Beverley Dawn could be". His reference to me would cause me to squirm on my bench, again pretending I was somewhere else.

My job was handing out texts – little bits of brightly coloured cardboard with a picture and a small quote from the Bible. I cut these up from large sheets of cardboard the preceding Friday night. Once the children recited their quote to Evelyn the following Sunday, I'd paste a new picture into their book. This practice was, of course, was the origin of the word textbook.

Evelyn and Boy truly cared for their flock of inner city children. Every three months, they hired double-decker buses and took the kids and their families to various parks around Sydney that they'd rented for the day. All manner of games would be played—we had the best sports gear outside a sporting goods store—and everyone shared a catered lunch. Afterwards Boy gave out packages of candy, and then everyone piled back into the buses and sang their way home.

Even today, I cannot reconcile the Boy and Evelyn from those times with the people I knew at home. Did their zeal for God ever result in real joy? I don't know, but one thing is certain. They spent a tremendous amount of their own time and money doing what they were convinced was good.

The sports equipment was stored in a huge building at the back of our property. It could have seated sixty people and seemed designed to have been a church. I'd always wondered why we drove to the Rockdale School of Arts each Sunday morning. The churches my school friends attended had real buildings on Botany Road, not rented rooms fifteen miles away. But now, looking back, I wonder if Boy and Evelyn had meant the building to become the Botany Gospel Hall, but their largesse had been rejected so badly that they preferred to drive far away each Sunday.

In any case, once I found the key to the building, it became my private cathedral of delights. In addition to the sports cupboard, it had a blackboard with white and colored chalks and, in a separate alcove, a large library full of children's novels and some theological tomes. If I had a choice between this hoard and Blackbeard's riches, I would have chosen the treasure in our building any day.

It became my favourite place to hide. Sometimes, it was simply a place to escape boredom but, more frequently than I'd like to admit, I also used it as a place to get away from Vera. She was the acknowledged "good" girl in the family and praised as such. But by now she was a woman of twenty with an intense sexual curiosity and, after having endured her fumbling experiments when I was eight or nine, I stayed as far away from her as I could. This became even more necessary after she had mastered several minor forms of torture. If displeased, she'd yank my hair when she plaited it every morning. At other times, she'd twist my arms till they hurt while taunting me with being a "gutter-brat." I knew I should tell someone about the abuse, but who? I remembered the lesson I learned from being kidnapped — never talk about unpleasant things, and Vera's abuse was definitely unpleasant.

But the kidnapping had changed me. Ever since I can remember I've had an occasional, recurring nightmare where I'm trapped. I always seem to be fully conscious, and I try to get people to help me, but they don't hear me. Sometimes, people with Munch-like faces use me in a tug-of-war and, after the kidnapping; I dreamed that the faces were distortions of Evelyn's and Girlie's.

I still endure the nightmare but now I interpret it differently, asking if it's a memory from my distant past in which I'm still an embryo fighting to be born before Girlie manages to kill me. The other scenario is even scarier. Is the nightmare a premonition of senility? Will I ever be unable to communicate my consciousness and fight to make deaf people hear my screams?

Nothing made sense. The only thing to do was to keep my questions to myself and, as the saying was in those days, soldier on.

I got along fine with the kids at school, but there were boundaries. At first, I was invited to every birthday party. Evelyn bought lavish presents for me to give, mainly Christian books with a similar theme — the protagonist sins, get into trouble and ends up accepting Jesus as their own personal saviour. Worse, I'd have to explain to the birthday girl or boy that I wasn't able to attend their party. I'd blush when I handed over their gift, watch them grimace and hear their stuttering gratitude. After a while, my friends simply told me there was a party, but that they couldn't ask me to come. I knew why, of course, but to this day I don't know if Evelyn ever wondered what her "witnessing" for Christ cost me on a personal level.

I hated the Brethren evening church services with a passion. They had a small entertainment factor to them because a visiting preacher usually gave the sermon. Boy somehow got himself added to this list and Evelyn made it into a family show. She would write the sermon for Boy to deliver and I became the prize exhibit. He would call me up to the pulpit and ask me to talk about Jesus. I felt akin to a prize cow on display. Boy would tell everyone my age and add: "If Beverley, at her young stage in life, can see the light and take Jesus as her own personal saviour, why can't you?" Afterwards people clustered round me, and the more praise they gave, the more I'd shrivel with shame. But the shame changed to anger a couple of years later when I found that being a Christian meant that you weren't allowed to think, at least not if you were a member of the Plymouth Brethren.

One morning, I sat in church, listening on and off, while someone preached about the forty days and nights of Christ's temptation. "Christ was perfect, Christ *is* perfect," he declaimed. "He could not, and cannot, sin."

I turned to Evelyn. "But he must have been able to sin," I said in what I thought was a whisper. "Because, if he couldn't, why would the Devil waste all that time?"

This attempt at logic resulted in a stunned silence. A female had spoken, and a young one at that. Boy stood up, grabbed my arm, and marched me outside to the side of the church. He then took off his belt. "Don't you ever say that again," he shouted as he lifted his right arm. "It's heresy." In between blows, he told me that if I had I been born four centuries earlier, I would have burned at the stake for what I'd said. I hurt inside and out. When he marched me back into church, no one would meet my gaze. I kept my head up, tried to stiffen my lower lip so that it wouldn't quiver, and sat down in disgrace. I added Christianity to my list of things that didn't make sense to me and, like the kidnapping, couldn't be talked about.

Boy, I was coming to realize, was an important man in Christian circles. He sat on various orphanage and Bible college boards and sometimes, when he visited the orphanages, he took me with him. I'm sure the orphans looked at me as a girl with everything, someone they envied. I looked at them and wished I were an orphan. I thought the same when we drove past the Dr. Barnado homes where I always saw kids with happy, laughing faces. I remember thinking that if anyone drove by my house they wouldn't see my happy, laughing face and, if I couldn't be an orphan, I prayed that God would turn me into a Barnado kid. That couldn't happen but hope came from an unexpected source, Boy.

Radios, like just about everything else, were banned by the Plymouth Brethren. However, we owned one because the war had taught Evelyn that the news was important. When the news was on, though, Boy was conspicuously absent. But if a state or international cricket match was being broadcast, Boy had his ear glued to the set.

Things changed when I was about ten. After coming back from the outdoor Sunday school one day, I summoned up my courage and asked Boy if he would teach me to play cricket. He brought out the stumps, a couple of small cricket bats and some balls. He was incredibly patient, explaining the footwork and the different ways of hitting. Then he'd bowl at me for hours.

It was the first time I understood athletic beauty. I had never thought about it before, never thought it was possible. Beauty in poetry? Yes. Cricket? No. But Boy's batting, his sweep to deep square leg, defined elegance. I think if he could have loved books the way I did, and if our lives had consisted of cricket and words, Boy and I might have been a team rather than adversaries.

I loved school, grades four through six anyway. I loved assignments and although I didn't exactly like long division when it came to pounds, shillings and pence, I enjoyed parsing sentences, deriving much pleasure from sorting words into their correct places.

School was the one place I felt free, and I almost skipped my way to Botany Public School every morning. Established in 1849, it was the oldest, continuously operating public school in Australia. It was ironic that it had been built in such a blue-collar suburb as Botany. People living and working there were poor. Even in my day, a good twenty percent of my class came to school, summer or winter, in bare feet. Originally, parents had to contribute to the building's construction and I'd bet most of them paid in labour rather than money.

This history may have been the reason why the school was

blessed with great teachers. I don't know why we had them, but I do know they were superb. Although we often learned by rote–I still remember my multiplication tables all the way to twelve times twelve–the teachers also fired our imagination. In grade 4, for example, the school's audio system was turned over to my class every week for five minutes when we'd present a radio play that I had written. I cannot remember what it was about, or who the characters were, or if it was any good at all, but for the whole year I wrote and my classmates acted. It was great fun and initially I was sorry when I began Grade 5.

W stands for Wonderful, Weird, and the Whatevers.

It also stands for Words.

And words would cause Boy to beat me a second time for heresy.

To this day in New South Wales, schools devote time each week for religious instruction that is usually taught by local people of various denominations and faiths. (Teachers like it because they use the time for marking and other chores.) As a Plymouth Brethren, I was supposed to go into what would be called the "weirdos" room together with a Son of David, a couple of Jehovah Witnesses, and an atheist. There were no outside teachers for us. My friends were Anglican so, after a couple of weeks in the weirdo room, I trailed off to spend the time with them. Religious instruction was exactly like Boy's Sunday school – Jesus stories, Bible bits to memorize, choruses to sing.

Anglican instruction became much more serious in Grade 5 because something called "confirmation" loomed ahead. When the curate asked who remembered being christened, no hands were raised. He then explained that confirmation was an extension of christening and gave out battered copies of the Book of Common Prayer. Everyone groaned.

Thus, I was introduced to formal prayer. In the Plymouth

Brethren prayer was spontaneous and resulted in lots of "ums" and "ers" and that was why I didn't pay attention to the words at first. Soon, though, the musicality of the prayer book's cadences captivated me and the magnificence of the words such as, "the means of grace and the hope of glory" caught my imagination. I stayed after class and asked the curate if he had a "throwaway" copy of the Book of Common Prayer I could have. I knew Evelyn would never buy one and, as she didn't believe in pocket money, I had to rely on the Anglican Church's generosity. To my everlasting gratitude, the curate gave me a very tattered book the following week.

At home, I added it to my prized cache of books hidden behind the toilet and began reading my way through it in private. Theology didn't drive me. I wasn't like some first century Christian with a battered piece of very precious vellum that I'd give my life to preserve. Part of me loved the order of the Anglican services set out in the prayer book. Their services weren't chaotic like those of the Plymouth Brethren where men competed for speaking time and the right to set the tune for the hymns. And, I admired the Anglican practicality. If a person was late for church, they could always read up on what they'd missed. But what kept me reading was the sheer beauty of the prose. I'd sound out some of the words I didn't know, making music out of them, until one day I forgot to be careful.

Three words describe Evelyn's reaction when she found my prayer book – shock, horror, revulsion. She made me follow her outside and watch while she tore pages out of the book and burnt them. Then I was sent to my room to wait for Boy to come home.

He thought he'd beaten heretical thoughts out of me once before. This time he hit harder, as if the bruises on my body could tell my brain to shut down. This time, I didn't mind Boy's beating. Learning about the Book of Common Prayer had been worth the risk. I'd been able to memorize some of the prayers, so I hadn't lost the magic of their words. At church on Sunday, when someone droned on in impromptu prayer with its ahs and ums,

I'd think about ones written in the 1550s by Thomas Cranmer and was thankful for their beauty.

But different words, acceptable ones, soon captivated me.

Mr. Spongberg, my Grade 5 teacher, was the first person I truly loved. Obedience and loyalty dictated my love for family. Mr. Spongberg's own love of learning was infectious. He engaged all of us in his class, even the boy who'd had to wear the dunce's cap in second grade. And, he was kind. The children who had bare feet because their parents couldn't afford shoes always sat near the fire in winter and nobody was jeered.

Before grade 5, words had been an escape. I read hymnbooks in church to avoid boredom, and fiction at home kept me from being lonely. The girls in my books were my only friends, and I still have annual reunions with the ones I loved the most. But Mr. Spongberg taught me that words could be different. He showed me cadence and made me understand its meaning. He used Hillaire Belloc's poem "Tarantella" as an example, explaining how the staccato of lines like "fleas that tease in the high Pyrenees" decelerate into "and the wine that tasted of the tar."

He taught narrative poems — "You know, we French stormed Ratison" by Robert Browning, Homer, and poems to think and think about. For instance, Lord Tennyson's "Ulysses." In this, the hero exhorts his friends to come with him to a better world. He says they may die on the way or never find that world, but it was important that they, "made weak by time and fate, should always strive, seek, find, and never yield." In other words, they should have the temerity of hope.

Mr. Spongberg also believed in making us write. Essays on Monday, revisions on Tuesday, rhyming couplets on Wednesday. He taught us the meaning of blank verse. I'll never feel ingratitude for the hours and hours he made me spend memorizing poems every week. He, more than anyone else, would have understood when later, aged fifteen, I found and fell in love with T.S. Eliot. I have no doubt that Mr. Spongberg knew and loved Mr. Eliot, but maybe he thought twentieth century poets were too mature for us and that's why he didn't teach them.

Evelyn obviously appreciated him as well. It was customary to give presents, things like chocolates or tobacco, to our teachers at the end of the school year. Evelyn was proud of the gift she'd selected for Mr. Spongberg – a thin, leather-bound selection of Lord Tennyson's poems. It looked like a Bible, and I immediately thought it was another of her heavy-handed evangelistic attempts. I felt shame when I handed it over and rushed off. Nobody else gave books to teachers and, as usual, I was the one with the weird gift. But Mr. Spongberg loved it and repeatedly asked me to thank Evelyn. I did, but couldn't understand why. Nobody ever liked Evelyn's presents. It's galling to think back and realize that she might have understood him better than I did.

There was one downside and one more extraordinary discovery in those grade 5 and 6 years. As my reading ability was higher than anyone else in my class, Mr. Spongberg and Mr. Wilding, his grade 6 successor and the headmaster, gave me "great" literature to read. *Great Expectations* terrified me and I didn't like *David Copperfield* or understand *A Midsummer Night's Dream*. I passionately hated a book of stories about Canada's north in which indigenous people flirted with cannibalism and gnawed through frozen skins to alleviate starvation. After shivering my way through *Jane Eyre* and *Wuthering Heights*, I begged, without success, to go back to ordinary reading, knowing that I was just too young to appreciate "good" literature.

The British writer Neil Gaiman recently commented on similar predicaments: "Well-meaning adults can easily destroy a child's love of reading [and] stop them reading what they enjoy... [by giving] them worthy-but-dull books." He also added that the private U.S. penal system predicts the number of prisons it should build by using a statistic revealing the number of ten and eleven year old boys who do not read fiction, or even comic books. There's money to build prisons, but none to buy fiction that might give hope and save kids from becoming future inmates.

The unintended result of my well-meaning adults' best intentions was a life-long antipathy for literary fiction. I need a plot that moves, has clear character delineation and, much to my friends' disgust, a "happy" ending. I want to enjoy fiction and I certainly do not want to be entertained through other people's misery. I had enough of my own and when I hunger for evocative writing, I turn to poetry.

But I do not blame my teachers for that unintended consequence. Great delight soon followed the great lit experiment. Mr. Wilding started a debate team. I had fun. We travelled to nearby schools and learned the elements of verbal thrust and parry. The final debate had the topic: "Should children be told if they were adopted?" For a couple of days, I asked everyone for their opinion, and it was just before I sat down to write my opening statement that I thought to ask Evelyn.

It was one of those times when you know you've asked a golden question. Mouths stop in mid-gape, a needle pauses above the darning, the door stops half ajar.

"What do you want to know for?" she asked.

"The debate at school."

"Well, what you do think?"

The overtone in her question puzzled me. I knew I was fighting for something. But what? I chose a safe answer. "Most people think they shouldn't be told."

Evelyn paused but eventually said, "I agree with them."

Mouths closed, the needle flashed into strands of yarn, and the door slammed shut. I went to the dining table to write my opener, but my mind gave it little attention. What had just happened? I'd hit some kind of family sore spot. Then I started thinking. Who might I know who had been adopted and not told?

I had the answer the next morning. Halfway through breakfast, I stopped eating porridge and looked at Evelyn. "I'm adopted, aren't I?"

Her face held no expression when she looked back at me and said, "Yes."

I scrambled from the table, grabbed my school case and raced out the door. I heard Evelyn call out a couple of times, but I didn't stop. When I came to Botany Road, I saw of couple of friends on the other side, called their names and shouted, "It's true! It's true! I don't belong to them!"

Now, all the taunts like Vera's "gutter-brat" suddenly made sense. So did my feeling of being a cuckoo in a strange nest. That morning, though, I had no time for questions or generalizations. A tremendous glow of happiness surrounded me.

Action. Reaction. I was playing on the bottom schoolyard when a monitor ran up. "You've got to go to the headmaster's office right now," he yelled. Everyone looked at me. I was never in trouble, but this sounded ominous.

I knocked at the headmaster's door with some trepidation and was surprised to see Mr. Spongberg in the office with Mr. Wilding. "Your mother phoned," Mr. Spongberg began, "and we understand you've had quite a shock this morning. We think you might be happier at home."

What had my kind teachers turned into? Sadists? I shook my head violently. "No. No. I want to stay here."

"We think you should see a nurse. You've had quite a shock," Mr. Wilding said.

My mind went as fast as it could. Everyone was taking this a lot more seriously than I was. I couldn't disgrace Evelyn by telling my teachers how happy I felt not to be related to her. On the other hand, it was a cold day and my hands felt like they were frozen. "I've read that a person in shock should drink tea with lots of milk and sugar in it," I ventured.

Mr. Spongberg stood up, a little smile playing around his mouth. "I'll get you some immediately. In the meantime, why don't you phone your mother and reassure her? She's really worried about you."

The rest of the day was negotiated carefully. I was permitted to stay at school with the understanding that I would be able to leave classes if I needed to be by myself. With Evelyn reassured and Mr. Wilding never suspecting that I might be duplicitous, I left his third class and ran down the street to the Anglican church. By happenchance I found the curate and begged for another prayer book from him. He asked what had happened to his earlier gift and, when I told him, he looked worried.

"Are you prepared to go through that again?"

I nodded and the curate, after thinking for a minute or so, said, "May God bless you, young Beverley," and handed over a brand-new copy. I stayed in the church, leafing through my treasure, until it was lunch time back at school. As I ran back, I murmured over and over, "Lighten my darkness, I beseech you, O Lord, and by your great mercy defend me."

CHAPTER 4

C, H AND W

C stands for Chaotic, Calm and Concerto.

It also stands for Change.

When Mr. Wilding announced that I had earned my way into Sydney's most prestigious public school, Sydney Girls' High, I was wildly excited. I was the only one chosen from Botany and I knew my horizons had vastly expanded. The school's graduates frequently became women of renown – famous authors, doctors, lawyers and legislators.

Evelyn beamed with pride. Her joy was palpable. If she'd been capable of it, I think she would have hugged me. But within this euphoria I sensed a kind of relief, as though she'd won a huge gamble. That aside, her happiness expressed itself by providing me with new clothes. She had my new tunics and blazers made by the best tailor. No off the rack for me. At the time, I didn't realize how much these beautifully crafted clothes would make me stand out. There were about one hundred and fifty girls in my year (or grade). Most lived in Sydney's exclusive Eastern Suburbs. I lived opposite a tannery. My bedroom window looked out at tanned cowhides drying in the sun on long clotheslines rather than views of Sydney Harbour. Only a handful of girls had tailored uniforms – the Eastern Suburbs girls, and the nouveau riche like me .

I didn't care. Not much, anyway, because I was still getting over Christmas. If I had believed in Santa Claus, I would have thought he'd emptied his sack of gifts under our Christmas tree. I got everything I'd ever dreamed of, and other presents I'd never thought of hoping for. There was a bicycle, a camera, and every item off Sydney High's optional supply list. There were twenty-seven books and three, ten shilling banknotes for pocket money. I'd never had disposable money before. Evelyn didn't believe in it.

At the time, I simply wondered at my incredible good fortune. I knew Boy was an excellent plumber, but the cornucopia of gifts suggested that he might have won a lottery. The largesse was not limited to me. Vera received a three-bedroom house on a half-acre lot as a wedding present. Everyone was smiling at that time.

Going to Sydney High meant taking a tram to a major intersection and changing onto the right bus. Boy took me a couple of times to make sure I learned my way, but this was independence on a grand scale. The bus stopped in the middle of rows of shops. I could wander around a little and still reach home within the prescribed time barriers.

Life should have been good.

Clichés become clichés because there's truth to be found in them but, sometimes, life does indeed suck. I began to hate school. The transition from being Botany's cherished student to a kid from the wrong side of the social divide was hard. Unlike Mr. Spongberg, my new teachers had degrees after their names and they wore gowns, a la the dons of Oxford and Cambridge, and condescension clung to them. Although they knew their subjects, they never conveyed any love for them, or for their students.

To make matters worse, Boy and Evelyn suddenly announced we

were moving to one of Sydney's wealthiest suburbs on the upper North Shore. Maybe this move was their share in the Christmas largesse because the new house was extraordinary with three stories, four bathrooms—a rarity at the time—and a front room that measured ninety-nine by thirty-three feet. I suppose I remember the latter so clearly because it was pounded into my head by a proud Boy. The grounds had enough bush for me to explore, and a tennis court to go with my Christmas present of a tennis racquet. However, the downside was that nobody had thought about the fact that my commute to school had been extended by more than an hour and a half each way, or that my school day might last eleven or twelve hours.

Evelyn was so proud of me being a Sydney High student that I rarely wore anything but my uniform for a couple of months. She insisted that I wear it to church, to prayer meetings, to missionary prayer meetings, on visits to sick friends in hospital. In short, everywhere. That love for the uniform may explain why it took Evelyn so long to transfer me to another school closer to the new house. Maybe, though, she had wanted to go to Sydney High when she was young, but had been forced to care for her brothers and sisters instead. It seemed she lived vicariously through me.

I became bored and unenthusiastic. Although the long hours and bus and train rides meant that I always had my homework done, they exhausted me. The lessons themselves bored me because I now understood that to please my academically credentialed teachers I had to memorize and regurgitate facts.

I rebelled.

They failed me in English.

I declared war.

The school prided itself on having the highest average IQ per student in the state. When the time came for the yearly testing, our teachers exhorted us daily to do our best. They stopped assigning homework so that our brains could rest, declaring that the honour of the school rested on our scrawny shoulders. If we didn't know a test answer, they advised us not to waste time puzzling it out, but simply press on.

They obviously hadn't seen the first question on the test. It asked for the opposite of the verb "to sow" and offered four possible answers. Among them was "to reap." It was the only conceivable answer but, of course, it was incorrect. The true opposite of sow isn't reaping. Reap is the result of sowing. The opposite really is not to sow. Instead of checking off what I thought was a ridiculous answer, I wrote a minor essay explaining why the question was unanswerable. Before I could really get started on the rest of the questions, the bell rang. When the scores came back, I had an official IQ of zero and our biggest rival, Sydney Boys High, had stolen the state honour from us.

I was shunned. At first I didn't notice and didn't care. I liked having a unique IQ. Then I noticed that whenever menial, horrible tasks were to be done, they always had my name on them. I did the chores and, like Abraham in Romeo and Juliet, I bit my thumb and bided my time. And, I had lots of time to plot revenge in the long commutes between home and school.

July was always a very cold month at school. None of the classrooms was heated and as we shivered and blew on our fingers to warm them, we had consolation in knowing that the teachers in their common room were not much better off. True they had small heaters that they clustered around, but no roaring fire to throw out any welcoming warmth. I knew this because I spent many lunch times washing up their dishes.

In the middle of this misery I made a friend who felt similarly outcast.

Although Griselda had been born in Sydney, her mother had a heavy German accent. This fascinated me. I'd been brought up to hate Germans as the instigators of World War II and had never met the real enemy before. Griselda's mother shocked me with her kindness and love. But there was something different about the family. For example, they went to church on Saturdays.

Now I realize they were probably Jewish refugees. They lived in a very large house in the Eastern Suburbs, a block or so from the harbor. Socially, Griselda should have been one of the movers and shakers in school. But back then; Australia was in the last gasp of a racial policy called "White Australia", and only reluctantly accepted immigrants who didn't have an Anglo-Saxon heritage.

Seldie, as I called her, was tangentially involved in my first battle. Field hockey was the school's premier sport and, half way through the winter we always played a rival team from northern New South Wales. The build-up toward the match consumed everyone as students with spare bedrooms were asked to billet players, and teams were let out of class early to get extra coaching. The Saturday match would be a gala. Old Girls (alumni) would relive their past glories at the school, and it was rumored that the selectors for the New South Wales teams were also coming.

On the Wednesday of match week, Seldie and I were suddenly asked to report to the Sports Mistress's office and Miss Brampton herself delivered the terrible news with a smile. Out of the thousand girls in the school, she had selected us to take charge of the oranges. It sounded so responsible, but I'd had enough school experience by now to realize we'd been awarded one of the worst jobs available.

"I'm sorry, Miss Brampton," Seldie said immediately. "I go to church on Saturdays. If you need a note my mother will be glad to write one, or she could visit the Headmistress."

Momentarily Miss Brampton looked like a child deprived of an ice cream. Then I saw her tobacco-stained teeth as she smiled and looked at me. "Never thought it a two-girl job, myself. Beverley, come in a little earlier. You should finish in time to watch the last two games."

On Saturday? My only free day in the week? This was an age when Gatorade hadn't even been thought of, so players sucked on orange quarters at half time to rehydrate their bodies. I'd have to leave home even earlier than usual just to make it in time to quarter the crates and crates of oranges for the teams.

When I moaned about my horrible fate to Seldie, she said, "Do something about it."

"Like what exactly?"

She giggled. "Make it more interesting. Douse the oranges in brandy or something."

Brandy? I knew nothing about alcohol. "And just how would I get some of that?"

"That's easy. Leave it to me."

On Friday she gave me a square bottle containing a clear liquid. "What's that?" I asked. Whisky should have been brown, according to what I'd read.

"Vodka. Sorry I couldn't get more, but the liquor cabinet was sparse."

I opened the bottle and smelled. "Are you sure this isn't water?"

She laughed. "Positive. Tell me what happens, won't you?"

On Saturday morning, I glumly cut up orange after orange after orange and piled them onto eight huge platters. There were four matches in all – junior B, junior A, senior B and then the only one that counted, the championship game. Miss Brampton claimed the junior B platters almost as soon as I'd finished them. I had planned to douse only the platters destined for the visitors, but after several of our players passed by they pointed at me and giggled, I had a happy thought. Why not make the championship game truly memorable?

And so, I emptied the entire contents of the bottle over the main two platters. I had no idea what would happen, but I trusted Seldie. When Miss Brampton arrived for them, I'd just come back from disposing of the empty bottle. She peeked under the damp cloths I'd covered the platters with to keep the oranges as cool as possible, and gave me a smile of approval. At that point I truly thought of confessing, but the moment passed. Something took her attention and she was off before I'd finished wrestling with my conscience.

When I went outside I realized a huge crowd had gathered for the games – at least a couple of thousand. I liked hockey myself and enjoyed the flow of the game, the skill of both sets of forwards, and the ferocity of the tackles. By the time the referee's whistle sounded for half time, the score was a miserly one-all.

From my vantage point, I watched the teams gobble down their vodka-soaked oranges and wondered if it would work as Seldie promised. But she was vindicated almost as soon as play resumed. Giggling girls missed balls. One player's wild swing made her spin, and for several seconds she kept spinning with a ridiculously wide smile on her face. Fifteen minutes later the opposition's center forward decided to sit on the grass and stare at blades of grass. Our goalie went to sleep. Nothing much was happening anyway, and Miss Brampton almost tore her hair out.

The game was stopped and, before I could leave, one of the prefects rounded me up and escorted me to Miss Brampton's office for an inquisition.

"Beverley, did you have the audacity to bring a bottle of alcohol into this school?"

"No, Miss Brampton," I answered. I hadn't brought the alcohol in so there was the ring of truth in my voice. "After all, remember, I'm Plymouth Brethren and we're not allowed to drink alcohol."

After a couple of easily defended questions, Miss Brampton admitted that the oranges had been fine an hour before the game. She'd been with me when I'd finished up and had, in fact, eaten some. I thought my eyes would bug right out when she said this, but she'd obviously picked up oranges from a senior B tray.

And so I was allowed to go home. On the way, I collected the small package of vodka-soaked oranges I had previously hidden, and during the long commute I smiled and giggled to myself as I ate them because I realized that the Plymouth Brethren were smart. They certainly knew more about alcohol than I'd suspected. It was every bit as potent as they had warned.

Things changed forever after that weekend. The headmistress always seemed to be watching me with an assessing eye. Everyone suspected I'd got away with something. My class smiled when I walked in, as though I'd brought honor to it, and Seldie whispered, "You don't have to tell me about it. Everyone knows."

And everyone included the teachers. One, in particular, carried the battle to a new level. Miss Collins taught French. Even then, I knew the correct pronunciation of je suis wasn't je soo-is. But she was a very much an 'I-must-be-obeyed' teacher, so we dutifully pronounced it her way, just as if it were some weird form of Australian Latin.

That is until Cecilia transferred into class. She was a French diplomat's daughter and why they decided she needed to take beginning French is a question without an answer. Maybe they thought she might be interested in learning how to say je suis. On the morning of her first day with us, things began normally with us singing a rousing rendition of La Marseillaise. Once we'd finished, Cecilia tapped her pencil on the desk and then put her hand up. "The words are correct, Madame, but you have the tune wrong. It should be…" And right there, she launched into song, singing the offending line several times.

Miss Collins was neither amused nor enlightened. She smiled her usual false smile. "We'll sing it my way, I think."

Cecilia stared at her. "Mais non," she began before launching into a spate of rapid French that none of us could follow. After this, she started singing again.

Miss Collins returned the favour in her creaky soprano. And so they sang, turn by turn, while we stood fascinated. Nobody had ever seen or heard anything like this before. However, we all knew it would go down in school lore. Eventually Cecilia shouted something at Miss Collins who blanched and left the room, and such was the obedience level at this school that all of us remained standing. We needed a teacher or prefect's permission to sit down again. Eventually common sense prevailed, but we sat in silence. No one wanted to be the one talking when Miss Collins returned. Her wrath would have been uncontrollable. At long last a prefect arrived, wrote up our assignments on the board and asked Cecilia to accompany her to the office of the headmistress.

Miss Collins became unbearable after that episode. She roamed the hallways like a Baskerville hound, pouncing on anyone travelling faster than a geriatric, or on those unfortunates who had their stocking seams crooked, and on me one time because I had a hole in one of my gloves. The penalty was an hour of detention after school for two weeks.

At this time my school day was almost twelve hours long. Even worse, I had to stand for the fifty minutes it took for the train to go from Central Station to my home station, because in those days my school always stood for our elders. I usually did my homework on the train. But now, I couldn't.

H stands for Helicopter, Halitosis and Horrible.

It also stands for Hughie.

My sense of grievance centered on Miss Collins, and as I swayed in the crowded carriage and the train rumbled its way north, I plotted revenge. At the end of the two weeks, I had an idea and the following Monday afternoon, instead of hopping on the first bus to take me to Central Station and all points north, I went east to Double Bay with Seldie. There, in a fish store, we bought a smallish snapper. Judging by its opaque eyes it had been caught in the past century, making it perfect for what I had in mind.

We called the fish Hughie. I said good-bye to him and caught the next bus towards the city. Seldie carried him to her house for incubation in her family's glass house.

The following Friday morning I got to school at least an hour early and waited and waited for Seldie. Just when I'd given up, I could smell her. The glass house had done its work well. Poor Hughie was more decomposed than I'd expected. Using strips of rags and a small hammer and nails that I'd brought with me, we tacked Hughie onto the bottom corner of the huge table in the teachers' room. It was where Miss Collins always sat, and Hughie's fragrance was our gift to her. When we'd finished, we opened all the windows and ran off as fast as we could.

From a vantage point we watched Miss Collins stalk into the room, take her coat off, shiver, put it back on and close every window. She huddled close to her small heater for several moments, and then she settled down to do some marking. The bell for class rang and when she showed up and taught as usual I thought our trick had failed. The work, the plotting, must have been for naught.

But just before lunch a prefect arrived with the ominous tidings that the headmistress wanted a word with me. The class groaned and rolled their eyes. Seldie looked troubled. For a moment I wondered which one of my sins and transgressions had merited the august attention of the headmistress, but that was only a passing thought.

I knew.

Armageddon had come.

Another prefect stood outside the headmistress's office and when she opened the door and followed me in, there was no smiling welcome. Instead the headmistress looked at me and let the silence stretch on until I thought I'd shrivel up enough to hide under the carpet. When she eventually spoke, each word felt like an icy shard. "Beverley, we have a problem in the staff room. We've had plumbers and drainers in all morning. They cannot find the solution. For some reason, I thought you might do better. Janet and Ida here," she went on, nodding at the two prefects, "will escort you and make sure you have whatever supplies you need to eliminate that smell. You are to make fast work on this. Enough time has been wasted on this matter already."

Putting Hughie, my beautiful little snapper, under the table was infinitely easier than removing him. Decomposition had accelerated to a point I hadn't envisaged. As well, the smell at close range was overpowering. Fighting to control my stomach, I gasped to Janet, "Newspaper. Lots of it." When she left the room, I lost the fight with my stomach and raced for the washroom.

Ida watched with little sympathy. "Hurry up, you little twerp. We're here until you finish. So, work your behind off, will you?"

Hughie had taken about ten minutes to put up. It took more than half an hour to get him down. During that time I made more mad dashes to the washroom, and Janet and Ida rotated themselves outside the room with increasing frequency. After I took Hughie, decently wrapped in fresh newspaper to the incinerator, they presented me with a scrubbing brush and a bowl of disinfectant. Even then I wasn't through. I had to mop the floors before I reported to the headmistress yet again.

I wondered if she'd expel me, and what I'd tell Evelyn if she did. Then I calmed a little and tried to imagine the number of detentions ahead of me. But when the headmistress looked up from her papers, I detected a glimmer of amusement in her eyes. "Well," she began, "I doubt I could give you a greater punishment than the one you've had. So, I expect a written apology to the staff for discombobulating them. Have it on my desk Monday morning and that, I think, should close the matter."

I couldn't believe it. A written apology and it was over? No interview with Evelyn? No apology in front of the whole school at the next assembly? When I turned to thank her, I noticed the amused look again as she continued. "I understand you've also become something of an expert in the matter of oranges. Our last match is next Saturday and you're on orange duty. You're dismissed. That's all."

All?

Beverley, zero.

Game, set and match, school.

But, W stands for Lois Wark.

I counted myself the most fortunate girl alive after my encounter with the headmistress.

I was even more fortunate when I began attending the new church in Waitara. For the first time, I was ordinary because it had a Sunday school that Boy didn't run. Sunday school was held at three o'clock in the afternoon, which completely messed up Sundays, but we didn't do much on Sundays except sleep, or visit Boy and Evelyn's friends for afternoon. My teacher, Mrs. Wark, had four children. The two eldest were older than me and quite brilliant. It might have seemed logical to most people that I should become friends with Helen, the second oldest, and maybe foster this friendship. Mrs. Wark began taking me home with her for a meal before evening church. Evelyn welcomed this as Mrs. Wark's Brethren lineage was impeccable.

But Helen and I had little in common. She played the violin at near concert level and had already decided to become a doctor with a specialty as yet undetermined. Surprisingly, it was her mother that I became friends with. It became natural to talk to Mrs. Wark. Family secrets, of course, were taboo. But one Sunday after Helen had gone off with Lyn, the elder sister, as usual, I told Mrs. Wark about the Hughie prank and grumbled about its outcome: "The worst of it all is that this Saturday was supposed to be my only free day until Christmas."

"What do you mean? You're going to camp at the holidays, aren't you?"

I've only recently realized how fortunate I was in that respect. From the time I was about eight, I always went somewhere every school vacation. Sometimes it was a real holiday with Boy, Evelyn and me staying in a hotel. Most times though I went to a Christian camp, usually one run by the Brethren.

So, yes, Mrs. Wark was right to question me. I would be going to camp. "But you don't understand," I told her and even I could hear the petulance in my voice. "We'll be doing my Bible studies."

"What do you mean? Your Bible Studies?"

I explained that ever since I was eight I'd been driven to an office in central Sydney because I'd been volunteered to become a sort of children's study guide tester. I would not only answer the questions, but I'd try to think through what the study was trying to teach and, if the questions were redundant, what applications, if any, could be drawn. This had to have been the background for my sow-reap critique of the government's IQ test. They should have had me test pilot it.

Mrs. Wark looked at me as though she couldn't believe her ears. She walked into her study and pulled out a booklet. "You mean a bible study like this one?"

I looked and nodded. "Yes, I did that one. Two, maybe three years ago."

"I'm dumbfounded." She put the tea things onto a tray and took them into the living room. "Sit," she told me, pointing to a chair before collapsing into one herself. "Do you get paid?"

I shrugged. "I don't know. I never get any money."

Mrs. Wark looked angrier and angrier. "So, what you're saying is that when you come back from camp, you'll spend the next few months working on Bible studies?"

"Yes. Probably working on the ones for the summer camps. But it's getting worse. Last time I had to do the adult ones and they were much harder. Not the Bible part, but the application stuff. Sometimes I just don't know what they are talking about."

Although she still looked angry, Mrs. Wark stood and looked for her car keys. "Come on. Let's go for a drive. It's too nice a day to be cooped up inside."

And so began a long tradition. Helen, by this time, had graduated to senior youth and naturally spent Sunday afternoons with them. I, as always, was the anomaly. The others in my class were boys. I didn't mind one bit because it gave me lots of time with Mrs. Wark who would become the most influential woman in my life. When she sensed that I needed to talk, or listen, she drove me to Palm Beach after Sunday school. If I were distraught, she'd get herself a cup of tea and watch as I burnt off energy by jumping in the sand dunes. Other times we walked along the beach, and sometimes neither of us would say a word. At the time, I didn't question the situation or ask what was in it for her, and I wasn't yet cynical enough to wonder if Evelyn was paying her to look after me.

At the time, I simply thought Mrs. Wark was a gift from God and this particular Sunday we explored rock pools. As her degree was in biology, I learned a lot. After she drove me home, she got out of the car with me. "I'm coming in."

Looking at her face, I could smell trouble and devoutly wished she'd drive away. But Evelyn greeted her as a long-time friend, and they made polite chitchat while I prepared a class one, grade A high tea. After I put our best porcelain cups and best silver spoons and forks, thinly cut sandwiches and a variety of cakes onto a trolley and wheeled it into our front room, I was excused. Mrs. Wark shut the door.

Of course, I listened at the door. Or tried to anyway. It was as obvious as the nose on Pinocchio's face that they were going to talk about me. But such was the excellence of our new house's draught proofing that I only caught a word or two until the decibel level rose. "She's nothing but a Christian drudge, Evelyn," Mrs. Wark stormed. "She can't go on like this. She spends far too many hours on public transportation, and the first signs of a breakdown are obvious. If you're so attached to the idea of Beverley attending a prestigious school, put her in the boarding school down the street from here. It's very, very good and has a great uniform as well."

I didn't bother listening to the reply. I leant against the door and felt something new in my heart. I could remember only two or three people ever daring to disagree with Evelyn, and none of them had stuck up for me. Something tingled in my heart and my whole nervous system jolted out of kilter.

The argument went on and on. It was the first of the many galvanic rows Evelyn would have with Mrs. Wark, fights that decided my future. But, that afternoon, I felt the first stirrings of commitment and love. I could commit to Mrs. Wark. She would fight for me.

The phrase "Christian drudge" echoed from the room again, and once I realized that things were winding down I opened the door slightly. I used the excuse of taking the trolley away and I heard Mrs. Wark repeat herself. "I'm telling you Evelyn, you're building trouble if you keep doing what you're doing. Beverley's nothing but a Christian drudge."

Evelyn set her cup and saucer on the trolley. "I agree that Beverley's hours are excessive, but not to the point where she's a drudge. She's merely serving the Lord."

I froze, wondering what Mrs. Wark would say. She knew, although we'd never discussed it overtly, that I would never say I served the Lord. I couldn't. I didn't believe in Jesus as my own personal savior as everyone around me seemed to do. But that day, I didn't have to explain anything. When Mrs. Wark remained silent, Evelyn continued with something like a triumphant "I'll trump you" note in her voice. "And Lois," she told Mrs. Wark, "Beverley's going to be baptized in a couple of months."

My goodness. My knees suddenly couldn't support me and I slumped against the door until I was called back into the room. Evelyn broke the news to me and Mrs. Wark got up quietly and left, looking troubled. When I started rolling the trolley into the kitchen, Evelyn put her hand on it.

"Sit down. I've heard that some of your Anglican friends are being confirmed. Is this right?"

I nodded, surprised that she'd asked. Brethren people were supposed to be "separate" from the world and that separation included the "worldly" Anglican church. That's why I knew Boy would have beaten me if he'd found the replaced prayer book. But someone at school had told me that my Anglican friends back in Botany were finishing their catechism classes, and I'd vaguely kept up with them wishing for the old days when I'd liked school.

Evelyn had more pragmatic thoughts in her mind, though. "Well then, there'll be a nice supply of dresses in the shops. I'll buy you a pretty white one for your baptism."

White dress aside, baptism was a big deal in the Plymouth Brethren. It meant I would be admitted to full membership and that, every Sunday from then on, I would take communion or, as they would put it, join in the breaking of bread. If I'd been male, I would have been permitted to give a sermon during the morning service.

Once school holidays were over, Boy drove me to the church very Monday night for questioning by the elders. Of course, I knew all the answers because of the Anglican confirmation classes back in Botany. Surprisingly, the questions were similar.

And so, I was duly baptized together with Helen Wark and three adults. On one level, I expected a bolt of lightning to strike me down for being counterfeit. On a more basic level, I realized that I breathed as naturally underwater while being baptized as I did whilst swimming. But there was one more discovery. White dresses were probably fine for confirmation, but the lacy garment I wore was absolutely not suitable for full immersion baptism.

That night of the baptism was a turning point. I knew it had been wrong, that I should have somehow stopped it, but I was twelve and too frightened of Evelyn. From that point on, I detested communion. To me, Hughie and the oranges had been fun. Wrong, maybe, but not a sin. Taking communion, when I knew I shouldn't, was a sin too profound to contemplate, and I thought

I would be doomed forever to the furthermost reaches of Plymouth Brethren hell.

As the next term wound its way towards the end of the school year, I couldn't see the point of a ten hour school day just to be bored out of my wits. I walked around with hunched shoulders, a sullen smile, and the knowledge of doom.

Mrs. Wark took me out to Palm Beach again. "You've got to do something, Bev," she told me after I lay exhausted after jumping off every sand dune in sight.

"What? Tell me one blasted thing I can do. I don't have money so I can't run away. I can't get myself unbaptized. I can't even stop taking communion without Boy beating me to within an inch of my life. Tell me exactly one thing I can do, will you?"

"Pray, Beverley. God loves you. Pray that he'll help you find a way out of this."

I gave her the teenage shrug I was learning to perfect. "Yeah, prayer. And precisely where has that got me?"

It was Mrs. Wark's turn to shrug. "Don't worry. I'll do the praying. I do have one plan, however, and I can get going on it right away."

She wouldn't tell me anymore; no matter how cunningly I phrased the question, and for that week I had a vestige of hope but a week later, our Sunday school superintendent announced a new policy. Henceforth, anyone who learned a chapter of the Bible would be rewarded with a book of their own choice courtesy of the church. I looked over at Mrs. Wark and one eyelid dropped in a discernible wink.

"That's it?" I demanded later. "Are you kidding? I have to be a different sort of Christian drudge to get reading matter."

"Small steps, Bev. The wording is very precise. If you learn a chapter, any chapter by the way, you can have any book you want. There's no restriction. They don't have to be Christian books."

"Could I get Das Kapital?"

She just looked at me and, for the next few months, people on the trains must have wondered as I stuck my head into a King James version of the Bible and committed chunks to memory. Almost every week I got up in front of the congregation—that was part of the deal—and recited my latest chapter. Slowly I built up a library of books that I wanted to read. Initially, I collected school stories in which the girls had friends and were never bored.

Evelyn could say nothing. The church she had chosen for our family had given me the books. Slowly, Mrs. Wark expanded my leisure reading. First, she introduced me to Sherlock Holmes and then to Agatha Christie. It sounds strange but they, more than Charles Dickens, the collective Brontës, or other literary greats I'd been forced to read, kept me sane, and since that time, for me, the enjoyment factor in a book has far outweighed any possible literary value. I didn't need to read to experience messy, convoluted lives and dark family secrets. Those I had every day.

Although Mrs. Wark kept telling me she was praying, I had quit. But one Sunday at the end of the following year, I went up to her with an astonished look on my face. "You won't believe it. I'm finally switching schools. What's more, I'm going to..."

"Yes, I know. Your new headmistress is a friend, so I helped get you in. Normally you'd have had to wait at least another year."

That was true. I knew. My new school had a waiting list as long as Methuselah's beard that I'd somehow avoided. What was more, wonder of wonders, I was going to be a boarder, and I'd go to Anglican Church on Sunday just like everyone else. Mrs. Wark said she'd pick me up for afternoon Sunday school afterwards, and deliver me back in time for evening chapel.

What on earth had happened?

I can only hope that Mrs. Wark recognized the love in my eyes when I asked, "How did you manage it?"

Later, as we walked along the beach, she told me she'd been giving travel brochures to Evelyn every now and then, firmly implanting the idea of a trip around the world, or a cruise long enough that I'd need to be in boarding school!

I loved my new uniform. Evelyn loved the new clothes she was packing for her cruise. She must have had an extraordinary eye for fashion. She was always beautifully turned out herself. Time flew by. I turned fourteen, and incredibly soon afterwards Mrs. Wark took me down to the wharf to wave Evelyn and Boy off on their ship and then she took me to the new school. She introduced me to the head and, when she said good-bye to me she muttered. "Keep your head down and behave. I know it will be difficult, but try to fit in. And, Bev, don't get your heart set on this being normal. From something Evelyn said I'm certain she's going to change the boarding part, at least, when she gets back. But now you know that prayer works, so promise me that you'll pray every night."

I managed my promise to keep my head down and behave, but I squirmed out on prayer. Soon I became too engrossed in my new school to think of her warning. It was a cricket school and, thanks to Boy's teaching, I fitted in right away. I loved playing for the school and soon started moving up the teams from junior B through to senior B. I got special coaching from the sports teacher and a promise of being in the first eleven the following year.

And, for the second time in my life, I felt carefree.

CHAPTER 5

D AND E

D *stands for Dinosaur, Despair, Diorama.*

It also stands for Disaster.

I should have listened to Mrs. Wark's warning. I should have heeded it. I should have. I should have, because I was caught flatfooted when Evelyn dropped her bombshell. She had done something like it before and would do so again. I should have remembered.

When I was about ten or eleven, the family had been asked to a meal called a fellowship tea before the evening service, featuring Boy and me. There was a gentle question and answer session beforehand and someone asked what I wanted to be when I grew up. The question came out of nowhere. People sat forward and looked interested, and I suspected they thought I would say I wanted to be a missionary. I thought of fibbing, then fumbled with the answer because I didn't know how to say what was on my mind.

"I want to be an arc...key... An..." I said and then stopped. When nobody offered help on pronunciation, I spelled the word out, "a-r-c-h-a-e-o-l-o-g-i-s-t." My written vocabulary was always much larger than my oral one with the resulting problem that, although I might be able to spell a word, I didn't always know how to pronounce it.

"What's she saying? What's the girl saying?" a cross woman asked.

"She wants to be an archaeologist?"

"An archaeologist? Umph. Does she even know what the word means?

"Yes, I do," I interrupted, and Evelyn later told me that I'd been rude. "It's learning what happened by digging up ancient cities and trying to figure out why they didn't last."

There was a lot of humming and hawing. The general consensus was that I was uppity and too big for my boots.

So, about four years later, when Evelyn came back from their trip around the world, she and Boy started looking for country property. I didn't give it much thought and was totally unprepared when she asked me one night, "What do you want to do when you leave school?"

Leave school? I'd only just got there. I knew archaeology was out because my teachers hadn't made mathematics comprehensible. "I love books," I ventured. "Maybe I could teach English."

Evelyn stared at me. "Beverley, you're failing English. What makes you think you could teach it?"

Love, I wanted to say. My English teacher didn't love books. She didn't even love words. But if I taught, I thought my love for them could be infectious. I might have shared this with Mrs. Wark, but Evelyn and I weren't on those kinds of terms.

She broke the silence. "Do you want to be a medical missionary?"

I looked at her, wondering how she could live with me and know so little about me. As far as I was concerned, there were two major strikes against being a medical missionary – math, and believing in Jesus as my own personal savior—but I could explain neither to her. She would say I was being very silly about math because I had a 94% average at the time, and then I'd remind her that my average had been 39% at half term. Even worse, I couldn't talk about Jesus and my doubts. Not with Boy's belt hanging somewhere nearby.

So, I simply said, "No."

She nodded. She had already known my answer, and I wondered why she had bothered to ask. She sat back as though she were a conjuror about to do a trick, and then pulled a piece of paper from a folder and handed it over to me. I looked at it in disbelief. It was an official document giving me permission to leave school even though I was only fourteen. Evelyn's voice had pride in it when she added that I would also sit for a government exam for entry into the state civil service.

In the vernacular, I was gobsmacked.

Being fully preoccupied with sorting out the past, and surviving the present, I hadn't thought much about the future. I thought I'd have another couple of years, at least, before that conversation happened. I had hoped that, like all my friends, I'd go to university. How could Evelyn and I have lived together for fourteen years and still have no idea how the other functioned?

Within a week, Evelyn had sold every last piece of my school uniform and I was selling lipsticks at Woolworths, the Australian equivalent of Wal-Mart. My friends howled with laughter. As a Plymouth Brethren, I wasn't allowed to wear any makeup whatsoever. As a Woolworths employee, I was a disaster. I had no idea what the products were, much less which went with which. Within one week the cosmetics department had the highest return rate in the store. That didn't worry me. But each morning when I went to work, I saw friends and former schoolmates going in the opposite direction, and then I knew how much my life had altered. I tried not to think about it, but I cried myself to sleep each night.

I plucked up courage one day after church and asked why I'd had to leave school. I knew the costs of boarding and the long trip hadn't impoverished the family because of the size of the country properties they were looking at.

"You should be thankful that we gave you time at that fancy school as a kind of present. We could have made you finish up at the local high school," Boy interjected. "Besides, the apostle Paul didn't go to university."

I knew then that nothing I could say would change their minds. There were more shocks to come. When I brought home my first pay packet, I presented it proudly. I had never carried so much cash before. Furthermore, it was mine. It wasn't like a present. I had earned every penny of it. Evelyn, however, ripped the envelope open, pulled out the money, and sorted it into two piles. Then she took the larger one.

I counted the small stack. It was exactly one-third of what I'd earned. I frowned and looked at Evelyn. "Why?"

Evelyn saw the frown and must have thought I might grab the whole lot because she put it into her pocket. "This is payment for your room and food. You're on your own now, Beverley. After you buy your train pass and update your clothes, you should have a little left for other things. You'll soon learn to be canny with your money."

"You didn't appreciate what we gave you. Now it's being taken away," Boy added.

They were serious. They had officially retired from the business of bringing up Beverley. It took me a while to believe that, but I eventually understood that I was now responsible for the rest of my life. If I wanted to go back to school I suppose I could have, but where would the money to pay room and board have come from? The room and board I paid to Evelyn and Boy wasn't a set sum either. It was exactly two-thirds of whatever I would earn.

I hadn't known that a fourteen-year-old body could contain such anger, despair and hopelessness. I had the equivalent of a Grade 9 education. I stumbled upstairs and hid in the back of my closet. I had dreams that were too big for my skull, and my only prospects in life seemed to be one menial job after another. What on earth was I to do? How could I survive?

That was a Friday night. When I arrived at church on Sunday, I accosted Mrs. Wark. "Did you know?"

"Not really. She talked about it once or twice, and I truly thought I'd made her see it as a bad decision."

I looked at her and shook my head. If she couldn't do anything to help me, the world as I knew it was over. I had no one. I was angry with my school, as well. they should have refused to let me leave. I knew I could be a nuisance, but I had paid my dues in detentions. I thought I had more brains than at least half my class, yet I was the only one leaving school. It seemed no one cared if brains went to waste.

During communion that morning, I almost threw up. Where was God in this entire mess? Hadn't I earned a better fate by doing all "salvation features" in evening churches all over Sydney for years? What was my payback?

I staggered upstairs when we got home and refused to come down for lunch or supper. But life went on and, on Monday, I was back behind the cosmetics counter, smiling politely as I sold one disastrous combination after another. On the train home, though, my brain finally began to tick over.

Mrs. Wark was right. I could not afford the feel-sorry-for-Beverley luxury.

The direction of my thoughts startled me and I wondered if I had the courage to implement them. Logic told me that, if I paid room and board, I had a professional rather than familial relationship with Boy and Evelyn. By accepting money, they had changed the rules. The big question remained: did I have enough guts to act on this new idea?

Nothing happened for a few weeks. Life went on and Evelyn must have thought I'd adjusted to my new reality. Then I saw an ad for an office worker in a large insurance company in downtown Sydney. Best thing about the ad? No experience needed. I interviewed, got the job, and then broke the news at home. Evelyn seemed startled that I'd be paid such a relatively high salary and immediately recalculated the room and board. Her reaction to my making this change in my employment was the deciding factor in implementing my new idea.

After I was paid the following Friday, I went to a hair stylist and got my hair cut off—all three feet of it. It was the most public declaration of independence I could make, my equivalent to Martin Luther nailing ninety-five theses to that door in Wittenburg. After work, I sat on a bench in a park, tossing my hair back and forth, feeling the wind and calculating the consequences. Finally, I got my courage together, walked to the train station and as I journeyed homeward I tried to prepare myself for what would be an ordeal.

Boy reacted exactly as I expected. "Heretic," he shouted. "Don't you know that the Bible says that a woman's glory is in her hair?"

"Samson had long hair. Look what happened to him," I replied. I knew I was being illogical, but I also knew that this would throw Boy off the track.

"This is all that woman's influence," he muttered. "I knew we shouldn't have let you go to Sunday school."

He was right, to some extent. Until we switched churches, every Plymouth Brethren woman I met had long, uncut hair. But quite a few women in the new church had short hair, including Mrs. Wark and her three daughters. Obviously, there were other interpretations of the apostle Paul's long hair comment.

Just then, though, Evelyn broke her silence. "Why?"

That was supposed to be my question, but I'd thought my decision through. I told her how difficult my very long hair had become, how much time it required, and exactly how much I hated it. Then, my carefully thought-out speech went right out of my head. "And because," I continued haltingly, "your rules don't apply anymore. Children obey their parents. That's what the apostle Paul said. But since you now take money for my room and board, I've become a boarder, so the rules are different." I pulled my depleted pay packet out of my pocket and counted out the two-thirds share she'd calculated. "There," I continued, "that's yours." I put the remainder into my pocket. "And this is mine, and you can't tell me what to do with it."

Her cheeks flushed with anger but she kept quiet, so I decided I might as well get everything settled. I fiddled with the money in my pocket and said much more quietly, "There's more. I'll go to church and Sunday school, but I won't take communion. It would be blasphemy."

Boy jumped up, his hands already at his belt, but Evelyn held her hand up. "I'm going to think about this. There's nothing we can do about your hair. It's done, and I accept that. But I will think about what you call blasphemy. I understand your point. If you don't believe, you shouldn't take communion."

Gobsmacked again, and I wondered if Evelyn and I might ever be able to talk. For the first time, I had an inkling that, if we could be honest, we might find a lot in common, and that maybe she could help me with some of the questions that plagued me—like, who my parents really were.

More good news awaited me when I reached home the following Monday. My civil service exam results were in. I had the best marks in the state with the result that I had my pick of government offices to work in. I thought hard, did a bit of eenie-meenie, and chose the Housing Commission.

At that time, Australia paid people to immigrate and start a new life in its new world. To make the package even more attractive, the government offered free or assisted housing to the newcomers and the Housing Commission oversaw all of this. Its main office was on historic Macquarie Street in Sydney, and what had been the kicker for me was that the building dated back to 1816 and had been designed by a convict architect – Francis Greenway. It had been a hospital for convicts in the early days of Sydney's inception, then a wing of the state legislature, and then the mint. I loved the simplicity of its Georgian sandstone columns and just roaming around the place was almost better than my bigger and better paycheck.

I was a general clerk. There were eight of us crammed into a rather small office, so we got to know one another rather well. As the youngest, I was sent out on errands and thus learned the ins and outs of the city of Sydney. To some extent, though, I was everyone's little sister. When I was asked out on my first date, the girls lent me makeup and gave me lessons on how to wear it. Clothes were more difficult and soon the office mantra became – "whatever you do, Bev, leave the church clothes at home." The men took great pains to teach me "this is what you do if this happens" tactics, and one borrowed jewelry from his daughter for me to wear.

Although some of us did much the same work, few earned the same money. I was at first delighted with my pay. It was a huge improvement on the shop girl's basic wage. But after I'd worked there for a few months, I learned about pay inequality. There were six pay scales for the work I did, with married men earning the most and unmarried junior women (me) earning the least. What was the most galling was that a junior male could earn almost as much as a woman with children to support. At first, I didn't think about it. But after a lazy, good-for-nothing man transferred in and did nothing, I did begin to care. We did the same job but I worked hard and he did not. He took home more money than me. It didn't make sense, but it was the law and there was nothing I could do about it.

But all wasn't doom and gloom and ranting against the unchangeable. I was an anomaly at church. I wasn't a high school student anymore, so I couldn't go to Sunday school any more. Instead I was slotted into the university group. Some of them were five or six years older than me and had been prefects and house captains in regular school when I'd been a lowly first year.

More than that, they had fought serious battles involving different interpretations of the apostle Paul's writings. Older, and more sophisticated than me, they greatly expanded my horizons. I often think of the 1950s as the greatest and most exciting musical decade because ordinary kids, like me, didn't think anything of going to a symphony concert one Saturday night and a rock concert the next. Or we might go to hear beatnik poetry accompanied by jazz. Sinatra and Bing Crosby still sang hits, but were challenged by Chuck Berry and Elvis Presley. Jazz swung from Louis Armstrong to the coolness of Dave Brubeck. And, the beautiful thing was that we enjoyed it all. It says much for my older friends' influence that the first record I ever bought was Bill Haley's *Rock Around the Clock*, and the second was Camille Saint-Saëns' *Introduction and Rondo Capriccio*.

And, E also stands for Eliot.

By a mere fluke, I made two life-long friends one weekend. My university group combined with some Anglican counterparts for a long weekend retreat, Friday night to Monday afternoon, on the central coast north of Sydney. Wonder of wonders, Boy didn't forbid me to go. I think he had given up ranting against combining with the Anglican youth. Maybe he was intimidated because they were university students, or perhaps I didn't tell him all the details of the weekend. More probably, though, he and Evelyn had meant what they had said. They weren't in the business of bringing up Beverley anymore.

One of the cars arranged to pick me up after work at the Hornsby train station. My only problem was that, shortly after afternoon tea that Friday, I realized I'd have nothing to read but my Bible.

I'd left home that morning with a perfectly good, half-read, Agatha Christie. But I'd read the whole thing on my commute to work, and in assorted ten minute breaks here and there, and during the lunch hour. I'd only had a couple of chapters left to read, and I'd finish those on the train to Hornsby. Somewhat panicked, I asked the boss if I could leave work fifteen minutes early. He agreed, providing I took fifteen minutes off my lunch break one day during the coming week. I was good to go.

I didn't frequent the closest bookstore. Its window display didn't say, "Come on in." But, beggars cannot choose. When I walked in, I asked someone where I'd find books by Agatha Christie. He raised his eyebrows half way up his prodigious forehead and said, "Madame, we don't sell Mrs. Christie."

Whoop-de-doo.

I raced around the store trying to find something that looked appealing and something that I could afford. Besides not stocking Mrs. Christie, the store didn't stock paperbacks either. I finally settled on *Murder in the Cathedral*. The cover said something about the murder of Thomas à Becket. I'd thought Becket's murder was stone-cold fact not a mystery, but what the heck? It beat being without a book for a long weekend. I stuck my new book into my luggage and set off with a happy heart.

The car that waited for me outside the station was jam-packed already. I would be the fifth passenger in a Morris Mini-Minor. Happily, seat belts hadn't been invented yet so I crammed myself in amidst shouts of welcome and laughter. Discomfort was forgotten as I got caught up in conversation that bounced around the world, stopping briefly to examine Britain and the Suez crisis before haring off to debate the merits of ancient Greece's individualism as opposed to the collectivism of early China. Then someone would start singing and one of the guys told about an ear-biting incident in a rugby game he'd played in.

We arrived happy, checked in, got our schedules, and listened perfunctorily to an introductory talk on Paul's letter to the Philippians. Then we drank cocoa and talked some more. When the time came for personal study the next morning, I concealed my new book in the retreat package and found a quiet spot amongst some trees and settled down to read. Once I'd opened the book, I thought of throwing it away. *Murder in the Cathedral* definitely wasn't a murder mystery. It was a play unlike anything I'd ever seen because it was written in poetry and I didn't recognize the poet, T.S. Eliot. Mr. Spongberg hadn't taught him. I wanted to cry. The book had cost more than I could afford and I'd rumpled a page and therefore couldn't take it back. I was stuck with a play written in poetry. Not exactly long weekend reading.

Half an hour later, tears poured from my eyes. I hadn't imagined the wisdom cloaked in the beauty and savagery of Thomas à Becket's soliloquy at the end of Act I: "The last temptation is the greatest treason / To do the right deed for the wrong reason." Or, Thomas's terse summing up of the barons as being men whose "manners matched their fingernails."

Caught up in the world of Becket, I was genuinely startled when a male voice said, "So this is where you are. Didn't you hear us calling for you?"

I held up *Murder in the Cathedral*. "I've just discovered T.S. Eliot. Isn't this beautiful?"

The guy looked and sounded as though I'd asked if he was gay—a crime in those days. "He's a poet," he replied.

"But *what* a poet."

"Had to read him last term. Couldn't see what the fuss was about. Now, hurry up. We've got a cricket game going and you're on my team. I chose you first, seeing we had to have four girls on it."

I walked back with him to the game where my team greeted me joyfully. Thanks to Boy, I could bowl a little, could bat against male bowling and, because of superb reflexes excelled in the slips (a suicide fielding position about six to fifteen feet away from the batter). Afterwards, there were jokes about people who read poetry for fun and when we went for lunch, a rather patrician-looking girl called Moya sat next to me. She'd been the Head Girl at my school and our only previous meetings had involved detentions.

"I hear you've fallen in love with Eliot," she began.

I shrugged. I'd had enough Eliot jokes for the day.

"I absolutely adore him too," my new friend went on. "Have you read the poem about time and men wearing their trousers rolled?" When I shook my head, she recited bits of other poems, and when we left by different cars Monday afternoon, Moya and I had plans to meet the following Saturday for coffee. I don't remember learning anything about Philippians, but these university students and I travelled to and from Sydney at much the same times, and now I knew the commute would be much easier because I had friends to talk with.

That I read poetry became a standing joke in the office. When my boss announced one day that I had to go to the director's office, someone said that maybe he wanted memos written in blank verse.

My boss looked awed though. Nobody in his office had ever been sent for before, and once the people finished with the jokes, they looked apprehensive. I walked slowly towards the director's office and worried what I had done as I climbed the stairs. So what if I occasionally took an extra five minutes to window shop while on office errands? But I knew my boss was pleased with my work and I was relatively happy doing it. What could the director possibly want with me?

Then, it hit me.

A short time before, Aubrey, a guy I liked had asked me out. I was surprised. We were GIs—geographically impossibles. He lived as far south of the city as I lived north. I'd been over the moon with happiness at the prospect of going out with Aubrey. My office friends rallied around, lending scarves, make-up, a box of bath oils, etc.. The daughter of one man was an international model and the day before the date he brought a large bottle of Chanel No. 5 to work. "This is for you. My daughter said to use it sparingly."

Evelyn was in the country, but I could sense her disapproval from afar. Brethren women, if they were brave, like my new friends, occasionally wore a hint of spring-like scent. No girl my age was supposed to wear Parisian perfume.

On that Saturday, I played cricket as usual and then raced home to get myself ready. I luxuriated in the bath, dressed with more care than usual, and then opened the Chanel perfume. I heard a car brake outside and, thinking it was Boy and Evelyn, stood on tiptoes to hide the bottle on top of my wardrobe. But two things happened. I let it go too early, and I hadn't stoppered it properly. Suddenly, Chanel No. 5 showered over me. The sound of the doorbell was anti-climatic.

I scrubbed at my hair and neck, and realized I'd have to shower. The doorbell rang again so, drenched and bedraggled; I ran downstairs and opened the door.

Aubrey uttered the only words possible. "You stink."

I thought of the time and effort everyone had put into making this a glamorous date and I could have cried. Aubrey, bless him, didn't give up and said words that guaranteed him a part of my heart in perpetuity. "I've got my surfing gear in the car. Why don't you take a long shower and I'll change. Then we'll head for the beach and grab some burgers."

Although the top of his MG was down, and the wind whipped through my hair, nothing could eradicate the smell. Chanel No 5 was expensive for a reason. One dab lasted forever. I didn't go to church the following day, and dreaded the moment Boy and Evelyn would get back from their hunt for a country property. When they arrived, I hid in my room. But Evelyn had never learned that a closed door meant "Keep Out." She came looking for me, opened the door, took one breath and stopped dead in her tracks.

"This room smells like a brothel."

I'd read about brothels, but had never imagined their smell. Evelyn's horizons suddenly became much broader and interesting than I'd thought. "How do you know what a brothel smells like?"

She didn't answer. She just stared, as though trying to work out if I was being cheeky or genuinely curious. She must have thought cheeky because her look became a glare. "Leave all the windows open when you go to work tomorrow."

The next day, on the train, it was outrageously easy to get and keep a seat. Nobody wanted to share the odor of Chanel No. 5 which still clung to me even after the trip to the beach. At the office, once everyone heard the story and finished howling with laughter, I was ostracized to the filing dungeon and ordered to make sense of 1940s records. My boss, venturing down with a handkerchief over his nose, said I'd done such a good job; I should work on the '30s as well.

So, that day, climbing the stairs to the Director's office, I wondered if someone had complained about the scent of Chanel No. 5 lingering in the records office.

It was a good job that I had no preconceptions about why I was being called into his office because what he told me made my jaw drop. He congratulated me on my last round of civil service exam results. I had come top, again, and he confided that he and some colleagues had tried to work out where I would best fit. They had decided that I should report to a doctor's office the following week for some tests. In today's terminology, I probably was sent for advanced psycho-educational testing by a psychologist.

It sounded awful. Four days of examination by a Macquarie Street psychologist, but I had great fun. I loved the tests he gave and, it didn't matter how quickly I finished, there were always more questions to answer. Some were written; something like the IQ tests I'd done at school, others involved blocks of wood, and then still more were puzzles. When I'd finished for the day, he took me for my first espresso coffees and we talked. That was probably the most enjoyable part of all.

The results came the following week and I reported once more to the director's office. He looked at me and tapped the papers against his nose. "We sent you there to get clarification. But the esteemed doctor has puzzled us more than before. If only you had finished school," he went on.

That was something I thought about constantly myself, but I couldn't imagine why it interested him. But it did. "If you'd finished, we would offer to send you to university to get an engineering degree. You'd be paid a stipend, and have to work for us for three years after you'd graduated. But, as it is, we're truly puzzled."

As was I. The little bit I knew about engineering was that it entailed mathematical expertise. "Why engineering?" I asked.

He smiled. "Because, it seems, you have a genius IQ for it."

I sat stunned. First, a zero IQ and now I was a genius?

The director handed me a packet of papers. "These are the part of the doctor's findings that are for you. He told us to give it to you and advise you to read it carefully and think about your future more seriously. He hoped it would be of use to you. Let's meet again in three months or so."

I thanked him and went slowly downstairs. I scanned the report quickly and couldn't make much sense of it. But on the train home, I puzzled over the numbers, graphs and tables until I reached the doctor's conclusion. Then, I'm sure my mouth fell open because he'd written, "Beverley can do anything she wants to in life. I suggest her greatest happiness and success will come through a job involving words."

It didn't make sense. In fact, I became blindingly angry. I took the report with me to church the next Sunday and afterwards showed it to Mrs. Wark and asked, "What do you think of this? What does it mean?"

She smiled. "It confirms what I've said all along. You're very bright, young Beverley. This doctor says you can do anything you want to, and have anything you want."

I looked at her as though she was insane. I was fifteen, a full time junior clerk in the civil service. I had no real education. Her daughters were at university studying medicine, yet she said I could have everything I wanted? "Think of what you truly want, Bev. Then, go get it."

"I already know what I truly want."

"What? What do you want?"

"You," I said, trying to keep my anger out of my voice. "I want you to be my mother, but nothing's gonna make that happen."

That was pretty much the last conversation I had with Mrs. Wark for six months or so. The question of mothers consumed me because, by then, I had worked out exactly who my birth mother was.

Only another adopted child can maybe understand the yearning, the burning need to belong. I had nothing in common with Vera and Junior. Only the times spent playing cricket gave me peace with Boy. Evelyn seemed too distant to be a mother. But, someone had to be. On my long commutes, I used to stare at faces, wondering if one of them could be my father or mother. Someone had to look like me.

Therefore, it came as a shock that, when rummaging through a cupboard, I came across a stash of Evelyn's early photos. At first, I didn't recognize her. There was one extraordinary sepia portrait of a young woman in black with the most horrific expression on her face. Just by looking at it I knew that woman's world had ended. I turned it over. There was no identification, only a date and, as I did the math in my head, I realized that it was Evelyn and, even worse, in the photo, she was seven or eight years older than me and only a year or so older than some of my university friends.

I rocked back on my heels as I felt an unwanted gush of love. Not even the sorrow I'd felt when I had to leave school was remotely close to the pain etched on her face. I wanted to go back in time and hug her, or do anything to take that despair from her. Then I looked carefully at the rest of photo and specifically at the two children standing beside her.

One had to be Victor, my favorite relative. But the little girl? I dug through the stash and found other pictures of her. I studied that face and felt my insides harden into a rock the size of Uluru. It was the woman from my kidnapping. It was Girlie. Everything inside me wanted to deny it but I knew the truth. She was my birth mother.

I let my mind reel in disbelief for several weeks. I did not want to belong to my family and, yet it seemed I did. Who could I ask about these photos? Who could tell me about my family? Evelyn, who had given me shelter for fifteen years? Mrs. Wark?

Finally, unable to bear the confusion, I scavenged around and found Girlie's last name and current address in Evelyn's address book. My letter was short, although it took several drafts and many hours to write, and enough tears to make flowers bloom in the Sandy Desert. Was she or was she not my mother?

The reply, sent to the Housing Commission as I'd asked, was immediate. She was overjoyed. She wanted more than anything to have the entire pretense taken away. I should live with her, not with Evelyn, maybe even starting the following week. But I'd been around the block too many times by then and I detected a note of bitterness in her letter far greater than my own. I did not want to grow up in her footsteps. And, in all fairness, I owed Evelyn something for all those years of care. I had to respect that generosity as well as her harshness. She had taught me well. I sent Girlie a thank-you-but-no letter and buried this new secret deep within me to pick over in nights of despair.

Only now, as I'm writing this, have I realized what that letter revealed about Girlie. She only told her husband about me in 2005, but she was already married to him when she asked me to live with her. It seems that she lived through impulses. When they went wrong, she'd doggedly defended them to the end, and didn't care who she might hurt in her need to justify herself.

It was a confusing period for me and I know I hurt Mrs. Wark because I refused to have anything to do with her at this time. Contempt replaced the empathy I'd felt for Evelyn. Why had she settled for the charming, but occasionally brutal, Boy? How could she dish out so much pain when she knew exactly what it felt like? And who had been her first husband?

I finally knew why I had never felt love in her house. She must have been wondering all the time I lived with her and Boy when I'd revert to my roots, become Girlie, and break her heart all over again. I thought back to the Housing Commission's report on me and laughed. Anything I wanted to be? Was happy included in that? Worst of all, I knew that somewhere in Sydney there was a man who didn't want to acknowledge me as his daughter.

We don't talk openly about suicide. Not now, not then. But the thought of it became my best friend. Its truth was unambiguous – "Life has no meaning. If you can't take it anymore, let me end it for you." I began dividing my life into segments. Can I get through the next twenty-four hours? The next seven? The next ten minutes?

And, as I rode the train back and forth to work, I wondered what Evelyn and I had done to be punished with so much misery.

PART II

FINDING THE SKY

CHAPTER 6

E AND C

E *stands for Egotistical, Egregious, Elucidate.*

It also stands for Examinations.

With the end of family-directed religiosity, I gradually rebuilt my life while keeping my church friends as the foundation. I was sixteen. They were older than me, some by six years. Most were highly intelligent, one was brilliant and I was the only one not going to university. We were a chaste bunch, mainly because the birth control pill hadn't been invented. Most of us would have checked off Christian on census or tax forms, but there was one confirmed atheist in our crowd. A few cynics, like me, called ourselves agnostics.

Most of us played competitive sports on Saturdays—cricket, field hockey, rugby, according to sex and season—then met up at a house with a grass tennis court. After a few sets, we'd have a barbecue, and then pile into cars to seek out the night's entertainment. Sometimes, we'd go to the symphony. Other nights we'd frequent seedy jazz clubs in the King's Cross area, ride the Manly ferries, do something "churchy," or just talk, trying for sophisticated banter but ending up, I'm sure, with teenage mocking derision.

All of us read voraciously and, in our discussions, Tolstoy might

find himself sharing the road with Kerouac, Marx or Thomas
More. C.S. Lewis's *Surprised by Joy* was a bit of a struggle but
everyone loved his *Screwtape Letters*. We'd talk and reshape the
universe to our liking.

Unlike everyone else, I lived by myself. Lived, though, might not
be the right word because I only slept and ate breakfast in Boy's
mansion. Only the times spent with my friends, together with
the wide-ranging discussions I had with Max, helped sublimate
my desperate unhappiness. I had too many questions running
through my head and no hope of finding answers. Inevitably,
with Evelyn and Boy now living in the country, I discovered
movies and sometimes lived vicariously through them. After all,
if I wanted someone to rebel with, who better than James Dean?

I closed my eyes to the fact that my attendance at night school
had become sporadic until one night in late August when I faced
the real possibility that I was going to fail one of my exams. The
problem was my Economics course. I loathed the subject, didn't
understand it and, to make matters worse, we had just changed
teachers. When the new one gave the class a mock exam to find
out strengths and weaknesses, I scored twelve percent.

Me? Twelve percent?

There was no smartass reason this time. This was real and so I
did what I'd always done–I took the problem to Mrs. Wark.

She asked to see the test. "Umm," she said, pushing her glasses up
over her forehead. "Your teacher's being generous. I would have
given you five."

I swallowed hard. "What can I do?"

"Let me think about it."

The real problem was that ordinary students did six subjects and
dropped their lowest mark when applying for university entry
or a scholarship. At night school, we only studied five and that

meant we had to do exceptionally well in all of them if we wanted university admission, much less a scholarship.

Mrs. Wark met me a day or so later and rescued me from my depths of despair. She had a plan. "I've read all the rules and regulations. You still have a chance. On Monday, you must declare geography as your science component and pick up a new subject."

I thought her insane. "You're joking. There's only two months before the exams."

"So," she said, "You'll have to do French. You've had three years already. It should be enough. Are you willing to work hard?"

French and I had a chequered background from my days with Miss Collins. "I've forgotten just about everything I ever knew," I blurted out.

She pushed her fingers through her grey, curly hair as she always did when I exasperated her. But she was right. It was my best chance, even though it meant doing the equivalent of two years schooling in two months. No wonder she'd asked if I was willing to work hard.

"Okay," I said after a few moments. "Where do I start?"

She pushed two tattered exercise books and an equally manky textbook across the table. "Start at the beginning and do every exercise. Make notes every time you don't understand something and use my daughters' books to correct yourself. I'll teach you for four hours and go over your work each Saturday. OK?"

"OK. And thanks."

Mrs. Wark wasn't finished. "I have a friend who teaches French diction to the Sydney Opera Company. She will teach you every Thursday at the Conservatorium during your lunch hour. It's on the opposite end of Macquarie Street from the Housing Commission, but you can bus down and back."

I was truly awed. Once again, Mrs. Wark had made the impossible, possible. I had no idea how she knew things or was able to produce rabbits, like the French opera coach, out of her magical hat, but I was grateful and knuckled down to work. In the words of the old hymn, life became real and earnest. I read French, wrote French, thought French, dreamed in French and, if I'd known how, I would have kissed in French.

Eight weeks later, the exams began with the five-hour English marathon. I felt really good afterwards. I'd been able to write sentences for all the vocabulary words to show that I understood them, handled the compulsory essay well, and written decent essays in the lit section. My mood didn't dissipate after modern history because the most important question happened to be about the Weimar Republic and, thanks to my Austrian reporter friend Max, I knew a lot about it. Geography went equally well. I shaded in sections on one map to show the steel producing areas in the United States and the U.K. glass blowing centres on another. I knew the differences between isobars, isotherms and isohyets, the temperature needed for tree growth, and I could predict the time at Y and Z when it was noon at X.

There was a three-day break before the all-important French exam. I tried to study but my brain became damp tissue paper. I memorized vocabulary list after vocabulary list before I went to sleep only to recall nothing in the morning. The part of the exam I dreaded most was the "unseen" where we'd have to translate a random passage. Out of desperation, I'd bought *Le Monde* daily for a couple of weeks. We'd also have to write an essay in French and answer myriad questions in French, of course. Worst of all, I'd go into the exam handicapped by five percent. Night school students were never tested for fluency in oral French, hence the deduction. I grumbled to Mrs. Wark that if anyone deserved five marks I did, but she laughed and told me to worry about vocabulary.

I woke up early on the crucial day—far, far too early. When dawn arrived, I was busy, trying to cram obscure words into my head and hoping I'd remember some of them. When I entered the exam room I felt groggy and, once the "unseen" reached my desk, I felt even groggier. The words blurred in front of me until one stood up and shouted, "Hey, remember me? From this morning?" *Pur sang*. The passage was about thoroughbred horses and so I began. Feeling pleased with myself, I thought I wrote a respectable essay but when I reached the question and answer section all sense deserted me. I showed off. What was my favorite activity? Exercising my *pur sang* horse. Where? There was only one place. *Sur la plage*. What did I receive for my birthday? You guessed it. A thoroughbred horse.

The last exam was my favorite—ancient history. I had seriously neglected it though. So I pulled an all-nighter—sorting out Hannibal and his elephants, getting the Gracchi brothers right and refighting the Peloponnesian war. The exam was a mere half page with only six topics but, as I read them, I began feeling hopeful. We only had to write on four. The Gracchi and their reforms were one and the golden age of Greek literature, another, and I could write sensibly about the evolution of the Roman republic. When I reached the sixth, I smiled. First, we could designate it as our major question worth forty percent of the total mark and, even better, we could make up our own question.

Just like that, my interest in the Minoans and Linear B turned into pure gold. I wrote about Michael Ventris, the academic debate about his theories and gave them a historical setting. Then I wrote the other essays and finished fifteen minutes early.

The euphoria lasted another couple of days. Then I worried that the examiners might never have heard of Ventris? Had I really cracked the unseen in French? Numbed, I went back to work. The newspapers would publish the results in mid-January. Until then, the best I could do was put in time.

It turned out that I was right to worry. Like crowds of other hopefuls, I kept vigil outside one of the newspaper's distribution buildings the night the all-important issue was published. When a shout went up, "They're here," I paid my money and scanned the results. The examiners indeed had heard of Ventris and I'd done well in three others as well, getting the equivalent of an A+ and three As. But French? Sixty-five percent. I'd needed at least seventy for the scholarship.

I'd wasted yet another year going to night school. I circled the result and left the newspaper on the kitchen table for Evelyn whenever she came back. No words were needed. She'd won.

Like an automaton, I kept going to work but, with no purpose in life, I cut myself off from my friends, knowing that jealousy would consume me if I heard them talking blithely about university. I'd thought a lot about suicide since my bout with hepatitis and those thoughts now became my constant companion. Was living until the following day worth anything? Was I worth anything? Would my life benefit anyone in the long run?

I could feel myself being pulled into this abyss of self-misery, but I didn't care enough about anything to fight it. When Mrs. Wark phoned to congratulate me on my results, I hung up on her. She phoned again and again, and each time I refused to talk. After a while, I knew I had to talk because she'd just keep phoning and phoning.

When I finally answered she didn't bother to say hello, she just said, "Come for dinner tomorrow. I need to talk to you."

Great. Another talk. I didn't want to go anywhere near her, particularly with my exam results the only topic of conversation. But I could no more ignore her than I could confide in Evelyn. After I'd dutifully plodded to her house after work the next day, I knew she meant business. Her husband and children were at their beach house. It would be just the two of us, lamb chops and roast potatoes.

Sure enough. Once we'd eaten she began a drag-em-down fight. "You silly girl. Why didn't you have the sense to apply to Teachers College?"

I stopped drying a plate and looked at her. She knew my dreams and why I'd endured night school.

She stared back.

I shrugged and started drying dishes again.

"Beverley. Listen to me." I could tell that she was angry with me by the way her brush pounded on the bottom of the dish she'd roasted the potatoes in. She scrubbed away then sort of threw words at me. "Listen. Unless you want to go to night school for a third year, you have to get it into your head that studying Arts is out of the question."

I just looked at her. What planet did she think I'd been living on? Of course I knew that Arts and the coveted B.A. were out of the question—that is, unless she had access to Evelyn or Daddy Warbucks' deep pockets.

She ignored my look and continued her diatribe. "Now, we both know that you'll have to do something by yourself. You've got to have faith in God. He has a purpose for you and he never closes one door without opening another."

I wanted to smash every bit of crockery in sight. Cliché after cliché. Christian twaddle after more Christian twaddle. "Yeah, like working hard and getting further behind?"

She threw a tea towel at me. "Get over it. Think about Teachers College."

I kept silent for a moment and then said, "Okay. I've thought."

"But you haven't thought of applying, have you?"

I put my hand up to stop her. "Um, let's see. First, I've never really heard about it until tonight. Like, it's not my dream. And, you must be senile if you think Evelyn's going to allow me to quit a fulltime job."

Her sudden smile illuminated the room. "And that's exactly what you'll have. A full time job. With your results, you'll get a large stipend. Not quite as much as you earn now. You'll have to be careful. No more cashmere sweaters. No more buying books. You'll have to use a library. But, dear girl, the end result is that you'll be able to support yourself and still pay your grandmother. Don't forget, her demands for two-thirds means it's a sliding scale. She won't get quite what she's getting now, but it will be a lot more than you gave her when you sold lipsticks."

My jaw dropped a bit and then I grinned. I knew Evelyn never envisaged a lower paying job when she'd set up her room and board requirement. It was almost like legally cheating and I felt like laughing until I remembered something that would botch the whole plan. "What about French?"

"If you apply to teach in the elementary schools, they only look at your top four marks. You'll get the highest money they offer."

I leaned against the counter and stared off into the middle distance. I had no other reaction. I didn't know what to think.

Mrs. Wark put the last of the dishes into the cupboard and wiped down the sink. "Don't worry, Bev. This seems to be the door that God's opening. You apply and leave the getting in part to me. I'll make sure the selectors know that anyone who's worked as hard as you have for an education should get one."

After she'd driven me home, I thought long and hard about her idea. Having never aspired to be a teacher, I didn't know anything about the mechanics of becoming one. But, eventually, the pros outweighed the cons and, without telling Evelyn, I filled out the application that Mrs. Wark had just happened to have and mailed it off.

And then, impossibly, I forgot about it.

On the train the following day, a help-wanted ad in the newspaper had jumped out at me. An American advertising agency, J. Walter Thompson, wanted an apprentice copywriter. I changed gears, interviewed, got the job, and walked upstairs to the Director's office at the Housing Commission to hand in my resignation. He wished me luck and told me I could always come back, but we both knew my time as a junior clerk was over.

When my friends went back to university, I was only the tiniest bit jealous. J. Walter Thompson galvanized me. Just the sheer speed and excitement with which things happened gave my previous life the alacrity of a crippled slug.

My first assignment was overseeing ads in movie theatres. Back then, it meant I had to mail the correct glass slides to operators each week and check they were flashed onto the screens during intermissions. After my probationary period ended, I was allowed to tag along to the notorious three martini client lunches of the 1950s. The first time the waiter asked for my drink order I hemmed and hawed, wondering if this oh-so-elegant restaurant stocked the lemon cordial I was used to as my fancy drink of choice. After the server's hovering turned into impatience, someone waved a hand and ordered me Pimm's No 1. I loved the long glass it came in, and the cucumber and orange slices and, after one long sip, it became my new favorite drink.

Sporadically and unsuccessfully I looked for it in specialty grocery stores. None of my friends had heard of it, so I decided it had to be the drink *du jour* served only in chic restaurants. Then I was assigned to a different account executive who had Coca-Cola as a client and, again, it was love at first sip. My friends had heard of Coke and were envious of me because a crate arrived at my house weekly, courtesy of Coca-Cola. Then I rotated to a third exec and tailed along to yet another client lunch, too new to have familiarized myself with his product. When asked for my drink order, I requested Pimm's.

Silence rose, as thick and enveloping as a San Francisco fog. The person next to me poked my ribs rather hard and whispered, "Idiot. Get some white wine. Our client owns a winery."

"I can't. My family won't let me drink alcohol."

There was a spontaneous burst of laughter. Finally, my new supervisor wiped his eyes. "Beverley, just what do you think Pimm's is?"

"Italian lemonade?"

Another burst of laughter. Not of the malicious kind, but of the kind that let me know that the story would be told and retold. "Keep thinking it's Italian lemonade," my executive said gently, "but, right now, enjoy the wine."

On the way home, I thought about the matter. I had, apparently, been drinking alcohol for months. Yet, no demon had struck me down. No Plymouth Brethren ghost had haunted me, and the fact that I was legally underage bothered no one. But I'd learned one thing—if I had to choose between Pimm's and Coca-Cola, it was Pimm's in a landslide.

Government mills grind slowly. They always have and perhaps it's a definition of government that they always will. The 1950s Department of Education was no exception. Unlike North American school boards that govern relatively small areas, the New South Wales Department of Education controlled every part of the state education. Its power was such that a teacher could be transferred from the southern-most school to one on the northern border and aspiring teachers might be sent to any of the several teaching colleges throughout the state.

Months after my application went in, I received a response. I'd been selected for an interview.

I'd grown quite contented with my lot in life. My new job had enough variety to keep my interest and, providing everyone remained ignorant about what it would call the "worldly" aspects of my job, I was safe. Not even my wild imagination could conjure up a scenario in which Boy would storm the office, his belt unbuckled.

When I hinted to Mrs. Wark that I might not keep the appointment, she was so seriously displeased that I would have preferred Evelyn's stare. "Why did you bother to go to night school? To make up advertisements with half-truths in them? To learn how to make people buy things they don't need?" she asked, glaring at me over the top of her glasses.

"Everyone has to get a refrigerator, eventually. We just try to make sure that they ask for a Kelvinator. There's nothing wrong in that."

"Humph," she grumped and, being a purist, "and, of course, the money Kelvinator pays your agency isn't added to the final cost? Is that moral? But leave all that alone for a moment and just explain why you've given up on your dream. Is the advertising world so glamorous?"

I've always had a nodding acquaintance with "glamour" but only as a word in a dictionary. No one has ever used it to define me and it looks like no one ever will. Yes, I met so-called stars as they passed through J. Walter Thompson, but I wasn't impressed. The one exception was Katharine Hepburn. I'd seen her play Kate in the *Taming of the Shrew* with the Old Vic Company and when she showed up in the office a couple of days later, I worshipped from afar.

The real answer to Mrs. Wark's question was that I hadn't finished exploring the advertising world. I enjoyed my job and my performance reflected it, and now my supervisors, like their counterparts in the Housing Commission, had the same dilemma. They saw potential in me but didn't know how to unlock it. They decided the best person to give me advice would be the owner of a modelling agency.

After the first hour, I wished I were back at work. She'd never heard of Michael Ventris, and I'd never heard of Yves St. Laurent, the twenty-one-year old Dior sensation. She'd begun wearing lipstick when she was twelve; I'd yet to buy my first tube. She tried to change to way I walked. I worked on her thoughts. Years later I realized that Marilyn Monroe was her ideal woman. However, as soon as she figured out that I was hopeless in terms of fashion, we walked along a city beach while she reminisced about show biz in World War II. That was fun.

When her report arrived, it echoed the Housing Commission's psychologist's: "If Beverley could keep her nose out of books, pay attention to her appearance and to this world rather than the next, she'd do exceptionally well." I sighed.

There'd be no rapid promotion to New York.

One aspect puzzled me. I had no idea that I'd talked about God with her. And while I worked on this puzzle, Mrs. Wark struck again, nabbing me on my way home after teaching Sunday school. "Jump in," she ordered and as we drove towards Palm Beach she asked, "Why didn't you go to your Teachers College interview?"

I'd long since stopped trying to work out how Mrs. Wark knew everything, but her omniscience was disconcerting. "I've managed to get another time for you," she went on. "Promise me that you'll go, even if it's only to find out what they're offering you."

With visions of her arriving at J. Walter Thompson on the date and then walking me hand in hand to the Department of

Education, I hastily promised. When the day came, I dutifully spruced myself up using some of the fashion tips from my modelling friend and a tube of newly bought lipstick.

In the 1950s, the Department of Education occupied a block long Victorian edifice on Bridge Street in downtown Sydney. The exterior showed many years of industrial pollution and typical government décor exemplified its interior. Together with fifteen others, I waited in an anteroom painted in dung-inspired brown and, as the minutes ticked by, I thought of the vibrancy of my office and tried to work out how many minutes I'd waste before going back to work.

The cheerful interviewer surprised me. He had the knack of making me, and presumably everyone else, feel like I was the person he'd waited for. He asked why I wanted to teach and, instead of shrugging him off, I talked about my Sunday school class. By now I'd been teaching it for two years. I'd had a chance to see the children grow and I felt pride in having had some influence on their maturity.

He listened indulgently, and then suggested I go to a room two doors away for my singing test. Too astonished to question—after all, I'd never had to sing for a job before—I went down the hall, guided by a voice manfully attempting melodic thirds and telling myself I didn't have to sing to be a school teacher. But yes, I did. Music was part of the curriculum, the technician told me, and if I were posted to a school on the far reaches of the state's boundaries, out of radio range, how would I teach songs to my pupils? Feeling extremely silly, I sang scales, a folk song and the melodic thirds. After that I was given sheets of paperwork to fill out and they told me they'd be in touch.

Fine. I didn't care either way. But a few days later a letter arrived that blasted every vestige of teenage blasé away. I'd been selected to join an additional intake and classes would begin at the college on the grounds of the University of Sydney almost immediately. All fees were waived, books and incidentals were covered, and the stipend was incredibly close to my current wage. I'd have spending money and Evelyn would receive only a little less for room and board.

There were two problems. I had to sign to contract that committed me to work for the department for three years after graduation and, as I was under the age of contractual consent, I needed my parent or guardian's witnessed signature on the enclosed document.

Hell.

Bells.

Quells and knells.

C stands for Conviction, Coercion, Capitulation.

It also stands for Courage.

How would Evelyn react? Would she automatically say no, in spite of the fact that I'd met her financial criteria? Would she be so angry that she'd tear the contract up? I had no idea. Nobody else in the family questioned, much less challenged, her authority. I was truly in terra incognita. Worse, I would not know her reaction for two weeks. She was in the country and refused to come down to handle one of my problems.

Two weeks was fourteen days. The contract became void in ten. I phoned the department, told them my predicament and got an extension. That still left me on pins and needles for two entire weeks. I called in sick a couple of days and walked the university campus, had lunch with my friends, and tried to sort out priorities. I really liked my advertising job and was good at it, but I also trusted Mrs. Wark. With Evelyn's refusal to make an early return to the city, deadlines became impossibly tight. I couldn't give my notice until I knew what I wanted, or how Evelyn would react. One thing I had learned at J. Walter Thompson, though, was the importance of initial impressions, so I polished the silver and persuaded the housekeeper to work extra hours. The house would shine and gleam. On the actual day, I had a roast in the oven surrounded by potatoes, fresh peas from the garden in a pot and a table set for royalty. When the car arrived, I willingly carried in the luggage.

Wrong, wrong, wrong.

Evelyn's eyes widened when she saw the meal preparations and her mouth pursed. "Something's up. You want something. Well, what is it?"

I pushed the contract towards her. She scanned the pages, and then reread it more carefully. Without a word, she handed it across to Boy.

"What's this?" he asked with a frown.

"Beverley thinks she's found a way to get to university."

"It won't cost you anything," I blurted out, knowing that I'd have to fight for something that was only a small part of my dream.

Evelyn sniffed. "Tell me one thing. Since when have you wanted to be a teacher?"

She'd asked the unanswerable. How could I admit to a two-week ambition? Evelyn and Boy seemed to host the entire Brethren community of Sydney—with one exception. The Warks. How did I explain without exposing Mrs. Wark?

Instead I explained about my Sunday school class and how I'd learned to love teaching through them. It said a lot about how little they knew about me that they were surprised that I still taught the class. Equally obvious, though, was their mistrust.

They had never expected me to honour the bargain we'd made. But if I expected good works to count for something, I was swiftly disillusioned. Evelyn would not sign the contract and she would not allow Boy, even if he wanted to, to sign either, and that was that. Oh, except that she thanked me for dinner.

I was truly astonished. There was zero risk for her. I'd prepared for a hard argument, not an implacable "no" at the beginning. "Why?" I asked.

"It's not proper."

Proper? Did proper suddenly have a definition I'd never heard of? She thought the advertising world with its three martini lunches and topless photo shoots more proper than learning how to teach?

"I'd have a guaranteed job at the end," I began arguing, trying to appeal to her love of pounds, shillings and pence.

"No."

I tried again. "If I went back to night school, studied again and got a scholarship to med school, would you let me go?"

"You wouldn't need a scholarship. We'd pay for it, but only if you signed a contract that you'd become a medical missionary after you got your degree."

Her smugness almost goaded me into going back to night school and specializing in the sciences, but we both knew I'd never do it. Her obsession with the medical missionary thing was incomprehensible and I couldn't let it rest. "I don't understand. Why is medicine permissible but not teaching?"

"Luke, the gospel writer, was a doctor."

Luke? What had happened to the apostle Paul? "Okay. Luke was a doctor. But doesn't Paul say that teaching is a gift and shouldn't be thwarted? Shouldn't that count?"

What teaching counted for that night was Boy's temper. He called me a heretic and ordered me to my room where I tried to understand Evelyn's stubbornness about university and me. I didn't know what plan she'd had for me. By making me leave school at fourteen, she'd virtually scuttled the medical school thing anyway. Maybe she thought I'd marry a good brethren male. I sensed her underlying conviction that I'd screw up somehow. The family predicted at every opportunity that I'd follow in Girlie's footsteps and become a sex trade worker. The evidence that nobody knew if Girlie had become a prostitute seemed irrelevant to that belief.

Evelyn's intransigence backfired. I now wanted to become a teacher in the worst way. I phoned Mrs. Wark the next day and told her what had happened. "I'll meet you at the station after work," she promised. "Just trust and give in your notice."

I may have been numbed by Evelyn, but I wasn't dumb. Turning in my notice seemed stupid beyond belief. "Why? You know the department won't take me without that signed contract."

As soon as I reached her car the next day she asked, "Have you got the contract with you?"

"Of course. I didn't want Boy finding it and ripping it up." I handed her the now somewhat crumpled document.

Her smile was impossible to describe—a mixture of determination, feral-like cunning and a whole lot of enjoyment mixed together. "Fine, listen, Bev. No matter what she says, don't argue with Evelyn. If she brings the subject up, go outside or to your bedroom. Just stay out of her way."

On Sunday, after Sunday school, I caught a train into the city and went to a movie, then walked around, filling in time, doing anything to avoid facing Evelyn. When I got home, Boy waited for me at the door, his tanned face an ugly red. Angry sunset red. "That woman's been here."

No need to ask which woman.

As I tried to walk to the stairs, Evelyn entered the fray. "Don't you dare walk away. Say something." I tried to keep silent but she grabbed me. She never touched me. Now, she held my arm tightly.

I snapped. "What can I possibly say that won't make you angrier? I never do anything you approve of."

"That's because you never do anything right. If you're not careful, you'll end up in a gutter like Girlie."

I wanted to yell "Like Girlie, my mother" to her, but that would have been our equivalent of the atomic bomb on Nagasaki. Instead I said, just barely able to control my voice, "You keep saying she'd ended in a gutter. What gutter? Give me the address. Take me there. The truth is that she never was there and I won't be there either. Why can't you accept that?"

Evelyn sighed and played her weary warrior card. "I'm just trying to ensure your eternal salvation."

"Funny way you've got of showing it."

Of course, that was stupid. Mrs. Wark had pleaded with me, telling me not to argue, but there I was, up to my armpits in a slanging match. To make everything worse, this confrontation had been a long time coming. All my life, in fact, and it went in its inevitable direction. When Evelyn started attacking Mrs. Wark for her pernicious influence on me, I lost my temper for the first time in my life.

"Why say those things about her?" I stormed. "What has she ever been but kind? You think I'm the worst sinner you've ever seen. I never please you. You've never told me that I've done well, or that you're proud of me. You've never said you love me. Mrs. Wark does. She loves me, she listens, and she tries to help. Don't you understand why I love her back?"

Immediately, I knew I'd said way too much. I didn't wait for the axe to fall, or for Boy's hand to go to his belt. Without another word, I ran from the house, down the street and I just kept running. By the time I stopped, I was miles from home and dead tired. I'd left my purse on the table, but I had my train pass and some money in a pocket. I thought about taking a train home, but I was still too raw to face Evelyn again.

I was dead cold. It was August, the middle of winter. I knew there was a park with a grandstand close by and my immediate thought was to sleep on the benches. Then I noticed the door to the men's changing room was slightly ajar. This was the 1950s and my age of innocence. I'd been on trains and walked home between nine and eleven p.m. for a couple of years and hadn't had a problem (except for one man masturbating quietly in a backseat). I wasn't afraid of the dark, so I pushed the door further open.

I found the light switch, shut the door, and then dragged the heavy equipment box against it. (Not quite so innocent after all, apparently.) Then I turned the hot water on and showered until I could feel my toes again. After I dressed, I explored more thoroughly. The urinals puzzled me. I couldn't figure how men made them work but, to my great relief, the regular toilets functioned just fine. Eventually I made a bed out of a pile of dirty uniforms I found in the laundry basket and drifted into an exhausted sleep. Another shower in the morning revived me and, before heading off to work, I left five shillings behind. Evelyn's teaching about room and board ran deep.

When I walked into the offices of J. Walter Thompson, the receptionist beckoned me over. "What the hell is going on? The phone's been ringing for you ever since I got here and it's not even nine yet." Then she ran an experienced eye over my crumpled clothes. I watched as the fact that I was wearing yesterday's wardrobe register on her face and her smile become knowing. "Yo, everyone. Young Beverley's found herself a boyfriend."

Evelyn was the first to phone. In retrospect, I can see it must have seemed like a hideous echo of the time Girlie had run away. Maybe she'd even told herself: like mother, like daughter. I'll never know. As I've said, we weren't on those kinds of speaking terms. That morning, however, she told me she'd been worried and I believed her. I told her what I'd done, but I don't think she believed me.

Mrs. Wark phoned next, and then almost every one of my friends called to check that I was okay. Boy had apparently pounded on everyone's door till they woke up. By noon, the constant trilling of my phone and the whispering in the office made it clear that everyone thought I'd spent the night with a nonexistent boyfriend.

It all made giving notice ridiculously easy.

I dawdled my way home that night, and by the time I got there the house was empty. Boy and Evelyn had left without leaving a note. To all intents and purposes, the fight might never have happened. I holed up in the house and didn't budge when people knocked on the door or phoned. My funk was extreme. I'd given up a job I loved. The Department of Education contract expired at noon the next day. I was between the proverbial rock and hard place. Finally, I decided that I could confide in my boss and ask for my job back.

I should have trusted Mrs. Wark a little more. She rang and rang the bell until I reluctantly opened the door. Stalking into the house, she demanded an explanation for my behaviour. Dry-eyed I told her about the disastrous fight and how well and truly I'd destroyed any hope I had of obtaining Evelyn's signature. Even though Mrs. Wark raised her eyebrows several times during my accounting of myself, she seemed curiously unconcerned. After

I wound down, she reached into her purse and produced the contract opened to the last page.

There, in the space for the parent's signature, was Evelyn's name. Equally incredibly was the name of the witness, the senior elder of our church. I looked at it, then at Mrs. Wark, then back to the page again.

"You forged her signature!"

My bowels went weak. Both of us were well and truly in the suds. "What will we do?" I asked and felt embarrassed because my voice quavered. "She'll raise holy hell."

"She certainly will if she hears language like that," Mrs. Wark responded, but her voice had a smile in it. "We're good, Bev. I told you to trust me, and you should have. After your adventure, Evelyn and I had a heart to heart talk. When she said she'd never allow you to become a full time student, I made her open her Bible and we read the parable of the talents in Matthew. You know it, don't you?"

As if I'd ever forget it. I'd had to do several Bible studies on it and it still made no sense to me. That afternoon, though, I couldn't muster a debate on Christian logic. Once I nodded, Mrs. Wark continued, "So I asked Evelyn to show me where Jesus commended people who stopped others from developing their talents. While we were talking about it, Boy came in and said, quite out of the blue, 'Spare the road and spoil the child' and I knew there was no point in talking further."

Her hands clenched as she seemed to recollect the encounter. "Go on," I said. "Don't stop now. What else happened?"

She stared into the distance, then from side to side. Anywhere, it seemed, rather than at me. "Bev," she went on, "I owe you an apology. A huge one. When you've spoken about your family, I haven't always been sympathetic. Your stories sounded so unbelievable, I thought you were making them up. But I got a small taste of what it must be like to be you this weekend." She finally looked at me with a sort of twisted smile.

I didn't know how to respond, or what to think. I'd never considered that Mrs. Wark wouldn't believe me. It had never crossed my mind that she'd distrust me and I wondered what she'd think if I had told her everything. I could see in this moment that Mrs. Wark finally accepted that the extraordinary had become normal for me.

She must have sensed my hurt and withdrawal for she continued rapidly. "Up to that point, to the moment before Boy came in, things had been relatively civil. But, after he began talking and showed no indication of listening, I pushed my teacup aside, pulled out the contract, and signed it right in front of them. Then I told Evelyn that she was welcome to charge me with forgery, and that I'd love to see her in court."

Now I was really scared. I hadn't thought of legal ramifications and I knew, far better than anyone except Evelyn and Girlie, just how mean Boy could be. "Do you really think they'll go to the police?"

"No. It's a done deal. You can stay living here, but you will still have to pay them though."

For decades, Mrs. Wark was the only person on earth that I loved completely. She cherished me, fought for me, pushed me upwards and enabled me to hope. I never did, and never can, thank her enough. I will never forget her courage.

CHAPTER 7

B AND H

B *stands Beverley, bombastic, braxy and beautiful.*

It also stands for Boring

After the initial excitement wore off, Teachers College became both leisurely and boring. Leisurely because I soon realized exactly how few classes were needed to keep my stipend in good standing. Boring because I had just done two years of high school in one year and two years of French in two months. I had become used to learning in voracious gulps, not genteel nibbles.

The students in the special intake were a varied lot. A few were my own age, but most were mature people who wanted a complete change in life, or servicemen who had fought in either World War II or the Korean War. The professors varied from a couple of brilliant men who engaged and kept our attention to a few flat-out awful ones. For a brief time, I learned to love English lit thanks to a prof, Dr. Couper, who resembled my beloved Mr. Spongberg. Math became fun as most of our assignments bordered on the zany—such as wandering the university's campus and measuring towers using ancient mathematical systems like those, for example, in pharaonic Egypt.

For the first time in years, I had free time. Saturdays became hedonistic bliss. I'd rent a boat and explore the waterways of Bobbin Head or ride the various harbor ferries. A smallish restaurant in Watson's Bay became an idyll after a server brought me a glass of wine as I ate fish and chips while wriggling my toes in the bay's gentle waves. I could not have imagined such a world in the past couple of years.

But the fact that I had free time did not go unnoticed. The first approach came from leaders of various Christian camps. Would I help? I'd never forgotten the world of camps and exactly how much I'd loved them, so the answer was an immediate yes. The Department of Education also came knocking, offering me work at their camps. Better yet, they'd pay. Then came the total surprise. One Sunday, the elders of my church waited for me after Sunday school.

Nobody wanted to go to their youth group, one explained, not even his own daughter. However, she had been at a recent camp, been in my cabin, had totally loved what we'd done and how I taught. Their proposition was simple—would I take over the leadership of the girls in the youth group.

I recognized a familiar tactic that they must have learned from Mrs. Wark. I knew, if I waffled or said no, they'd come back every day until they got what they wanted. I felt like one of Max's wobblers. I knew my Bible, could teach, kids liked me, and I was probably the best person for the job. And so, very reluctantly, I agreed.

My free time was soon occupied with another activity—field hockey. The director of one of Sydney's biggest sports clubs, and the father of a girl I met at another camp, asked me to try out for one of their field hockey teams. Julie had been in my cabin and I remembered her because she'd coerced me into playing goalie as she practiced her field hockey shots. She'd never talked about her father or what club she played for. It had just been something we'd done in free time. My reaction to her father's offer was astonishment. I'd never hoped to play for such a prestigious club, never thought of being a goalie. I went to the try-out with much trepidation.

For the afternoon, I blocked and cleared shots. Julie's father and a couple of other men stood behind, sometimes yelling advice, telling me "Well done" a couple of times, but mostly they scribbled notes. After ninety minutes, I was exhausted.

When Julie came over with a cup of cocoa I was relieved. "How much longer?"

"Longer?" she laughed. "That was the warm-up."

The whistle went and furious play commenced. By the end of the game, I had only let in three or four goals and Julie's dad beamed when he handed me the A team's uniform. "Best investment I ever made, sending Julie to that camp. Goalkeepers are born, not made. I hope you'll try out for our cricket team as wicket keeper when hockey finishes. I coach that and I'll make sure I remind you."

And there went all my free time!

My two years at Teachers College sped by almost without me noticing. When it came to filling out a form indicating preferences for my job assignment, I was surprised that my training was coming to an end. This was unexpected. My life was on the most even keel it had ever been. I thought hard about where I wanted to start my teaching career and eliminated the cities right away. Everyone else was applying for them, including teachers from far out places in the country who wanted to transfer back into an urban situation. Eventually, I decided on the Moss Vale-Bowral area, the Riverina district, and the coastal far north.

It was hard to think about leaving the stability I'd had for the past two years at home, church and with my friends. But already my group of friends was getting smaller. Most were saving for a year or two in England, and a few were dating with the prospect of marriage in mind. I consoled myself with the thought that if I taught in the country, I could start again with a clean record.

And, in the country, I might find out if I really was a Christian.

Like every other student, I waited for the job assignments to be posted; consoling myself with the fun my new anonymity would give me. But when the results were thumbtacked to the board, I stared at them in bitter disbelief. I would not be going to the Moss Vale-Bowral area, the Riverina, or to the beaches in the far north. God had confirmed, yet again, that he had a wry sense of humour.

Of all the students in college, I was the *only* one assigned to a school in Sydney.

Admittedly, it was Sydney-West, an area with a high crime rate. A few weeks later, I took three trains to get to my new school, hoping to arrive early enough to meet the headmistress and my new colleagues. When I arrived, though, there were only a couple of other early birds and once I introduced myself, they offered commiserating smiles.

"Come along," one finally said. "There's no use putting it off. You'll have to meet *HER* some time."

My knees lost some of their solidity immediately. *HER* had to be the headmistress and things did not sound promising. Once we arrived outside the office, the teacher sped away and when the door opened, I understood why.

Miss Hyatt stood a little over six feet. If she'd played rugby, she would have been part of the pack. Her hair was pulled back into an unforgiving bun worthy of a Brethren woman. Dense lisle stockings cloaked the small amount of leg she displayed, and her feet were shod in the black lace-ups favoured by British constables patrolling their beats.

The most memorable item was her dress. It never varied during the entire time I was in her school. Her entire wardrobe consisted of shapeless tents of maroon cotton, with beige cuffs and collars. Eight buttons, about an inch and a half wide, marched down the dress and I had to assume a man's help with their unbuttoning would never be required. I thought of Medusa immediately and when she boomed, "Come in, gel," I walked towards her with disappearing idealism.

"I suppose you think you know everything," she began and I think my silence reconciled her the tiniest bit towards me because she began ranting about the know-it-alls that came into the system and how different it had been in *her* day. I nodded dutifully while wondering if Methuselah had been one of her classmates.

Eventually she began telling me about my class. "I've given you the smallest class in the school. Only thirty or so. Sixth grade. A little older than usual. Should be a snap."

As she grated out each phrase, I felt a sense of pulverizing terror. What did "a little older" mean? I told myself that life hadn't always been easy, so why had I expected this to be any different? Then I wondered if Miss Hyatt always spoke in sentence fragments. I had unspoken questions when she thrust the official class registers, lesson planners and her own ten-page list of expectations at me.

When I got back to the staff room, it was full of teachers and everyone looked at me through a blue nicotine cloud. "Come on, tell us what she gave you," someone called out.

"Three to one she got 6H," another shouted and, in the background, I heard serious discussions about odds. Apparently, there were two new teachers and two unassigned classes. The other newbie was a transferee from the country. Logically, she, with her experience, should have been given the more senior of the vacancies but, Miss Hyatt was unpredictable.

"6H," I said. Instantly the room erupted with hooting and laughter and I saw a lot of money change hands.

A smallish woman detached herself from the crowd. "Want a cup of tea?" When I shook my head, she laughed. "Wise girl. I swear they just reheat yesterday's leftover brew. Now, let's find your classroom so you can settle in before the monsters come."

The school had three buildings and 6H was in a portable. "Here we go," my guide said. "I'm in 3A, right next to you. As you'll find out, we have a distinct advantage. We're as far away from the office as you can get, so we get less of her majesty's attention."

If a classroom could have been said to be battle-scarred, 6H was it. Projectiles fashioned from pen nibs hung from the ceiling and red smudges, remnants of messages originally written in lipstick, covered the walls. There were no maps or books on the shelves. The room contained a solitary chalkboard, and a bare light bulb dangled from the ceiling.

Fortunately, I'd come prepared. I assembled a mobile and then pinned pictures and maps to the walls. When my colleague next door stuck her head in to take me over for Assembly, she admired my efforts. "Good stuff. Too bad it won't last till lunch time."

When I met the thirty-two girls in my class, I wondered if I, much less the pictures, would make it to recess. Miss Hyatt had said they were older, but I'd naively assumed that they were in school because they wanted to learn something. The girls standing in front of me, waiting for my permission to sit down, were just filling in time until they turned fifteen and legally able to leave school.

They oohed and aahed at the pictures. I let them sit. They laughed and began their interrogation. "How old are you?"

"Nineteen," I said and, after I saw the looks in their eyes, some remnant of Brethren morality kicked in and I added, "Well, almost."

"She's a baby. They're given us a baby," someone announced, disgust evident in her voice.

"Why not? They've tried everything else."

I stood in total shock as the debate waged. Just as I was about to assert myself, someone altered the topic. "Anyone want to bet she's not a virgin?"

Teachers College had warned us that we must get control of our classes as quickly as possible, but had offered no ideas for interrupting a discussion of our sex lives. As the class bantered ideas back and forth, I heard some new words for the first time in my life. The free-for-all might have gone forever if not for an authoritative knock on the door.

The girls stood facing the door, looking so pious that I wondered if a priest might be outside with his communion case. But no. Miss Hyatt marched in and boomed, "Good morning."

After the girls chorused "Good Morning, Miss Hyatt" she turned to me. "Any problems with these gels so far?"

"Not a single one," I said with all honesty and caught a look of respect on a couple of faces.

"You have to show them you're boss. Send them to me immediately at the first sign of trouble. Don't wait till you can't handle it. Understand?" She didn't waste time waiting for my answer but stalked over to examine the picture display. "Pity you've taken so much trouble with this bunch. These," she went on, flicking a finger towards a print of Utrillo, "will be in the garbage by lunch. You'll see. Waste of energy to pretty up this room."

I wanted to ask if she'd like to wager a bet on that, because I'd sensed a shift in the room. Sure, I was a baby, but I was *their* baby. I don't know if Miss Hyatt realized that the easiest way to get 6H's cooperation was to disparage me in front of them, or if she was simply impossibly arrogant. The pictures stayed on the wall for another week until I put up another set. I designated another area for the girls' own pictures, and gradually James Dean, Elvis and their Australian counterparts covered the lipstick-stained walls.

Miss Hyatt remained terrifying and difficult. She stalked the hallways and found her way into crevices intended only for mice. An advocate of corporal punishment, she wielded the cane as well as any Victorian headmaster. My class firmly believed that she used it on teachers as well as students, and they banded together to protect me. Her movements about the school were impossible to predict and she had an annoying habit of walking into a classroom and commandeering entire sets of workbooks. One Friday afternoon, she walked into 6H and demanded the girls' English books.

When she walked back into the room at 9:35 Monday morning, everyone could see she was livid. Her cheeks were red and, I swear, flecks of foam flew into the air when she stomped over to me, pushed her finger into my chest, and shouted, "What do you think of this, young missy?"

Her huge bulk dominated me and I felt as if I had walked into the valley of the shadow of death. When I looked to where she pointed in one of the girls' books, it took a gargantuan effort of will not to faint. To show that she'd examined each book, she had stamped it and her signature read, "L. Hyatt, Mistress." The cause for her ire, that particular day, was that one of my students had added "Of who?"

"Well? What do you have to say?"

I tried to balance conflicting paths for survival. If I didn't stick up for my students, I could kiss away any chance I had with 6H. On the other hand, if I did, I could expect retribution from the grim reaper standing in front of me.

I took a deep breath and said as politely as possible, "I'm sorry, Miss Hyatt. Sorry that I've taught English so poorly. It should be "of whom" shouldn't it?"

The class and I were entirely silent as we waited for the hand of doom to fall. Miss Hyatt looked stunned. Then, she stood even straighter and said, "You deserve each other. All of you will stay for extra English classes after school for three days." With that, she left the room.

Every single one of us breathed a sigh of relief. Extra English seemed a small price to pay. Safe in the knowledge that Miss Hyatt wouldn't return, the girls danced for joy. If the song "I Will Survive" had been written, it would have rocked the classroom.

After that, a strange sort of bond developed between the girls and me. They took down the projectiles from the ceiling with as much enjoyment as I imagined they'd had putting them up. They raced through lessons because they believed they had a pact with me. If there was time at the end of a lesson, it could be used for question time.

No gold stars for guessing who'd be questioned.

My life fascinated them and slowly they drew bits of it out to the point where they knew more about me than some of my friends. The fact that I had left school when I was younger than they were fascinated them. They couldn't understand why anyone who had escaped the grind of school would willingly go back. Night school made no sense to them.

Several said that I'd probably met their mothers when I worked at the Housing Commission, finding this a hilarious coincidence. "My mum says you used to work for the Housing Commission and that it's steady work. She says you even get benefits. So, why did you leave?"

I tried to explain that I wanted to learn. They understood the need to rebel and to fight, but learning for its own sake was a new idea and they kept coming back to it time after time. One afternoon they managed to rock the serene bubble I lived in. This time the interrogation began with a simple declaration. "My dad says learning is rubbish. He says life is simple. You get born, you go to school, you get a job, you get married, you have kids, you die."

"That's her dad who spends all his time drinking his and her mum's money down at the pub," someone jeered.

They all knew the exact amount of time their parents spent in various drinking establishments to the minute, who gambled how much on horses, who went and how many times to sex trade workers and they managed to make me feel juvenile without this breadth of knowledge. This afternoon they gossiped for a while and then segued back to me, until one girl put her hand up. "You know what, miss? You're just like us, only a little richer and you've got more schooling. But, you're the same, because you've given up too, haven't you?"

It took a while to understand what she meant. Usually they looked at me as some kind of modern St. George always off slaying the many dragons that stood between me and the sacred goal of learning. Not this day though.

"You're here today, aren't you? You're teaching us because no one else would take the job. It seems to me you've had to settle for second, maybe third best. We're really the same, even if we don't live on the north shore and come here," she broke off and waved a disparaging hand at the classroom's wall, then continued, "instead of a posh school."

I knew I had to say something to counter her arguments but I couldn't. Despite everything, the freckled, gap-toothed kid was right. I had settled for second best, albeit a very comfortable second best. I'd been seduced by its ease and I had put my hopes aside. My dreams had disappeared. Suddenly, that weekend and many more that followed were filled with discontent.

My class was more sanguine than I was. They knew they had little choice but to follow in their parents' footsteps. They'd have a couple of kids by the time they reached my age and be grandmothers sixteen or seventeen years later.

But what to do? Going back to night school wouldn't help as I was bonded to teach for almost three more years. Worse, I couldn't use Mrs. Wark's shoulder to cry on.

When I'd done my final practicum, that is, taking over a class under a teacher's supervision, I received an assessment. Astonished and overjoyed by it, I raced home to show Mrs. Wark. When I reached her house and saw that she had visitors I didn't bother knocking, but went in via the back door. As I sat around the kitchen table, snippets of conversation drifted through and only when I heard my name did I bother to listen.

"I don't know why you let that Beverley girl monopolize so much of your time," an unknown voice complained.

There was a muffled explanation from Mrs. Wark and a couple of other interchanges then the visitor's voice rose again, "What's more, if you only knew the run around that girl has given poor Evelyn. She doesn't do what she's supposed to do, she says the most outrageous things, and...." Here, the visitor paused and when she continued her voice had a dramatic emphasis in it, "I don't think she serves the Lord."

"She'll be a jewel in my crown, Mary. You wait and see," Mrs. Wark answered.

Another burst of muffled conversation followed this outburst before the visitor's voice became clear again. "Oh, now I understand. Jesus will certainly give you a jewel for your crown for the time you've spent on that renegade. Given her attitude, I'm sure it will be the finest diamond he has."

I didn't wait for anything else but crept from the kitchen, my dignity in tatters. I knew what the visitor was talking about. The Brethren preached that good deeds resulted in jewels in a heavenly crown. To think that I had only been a means to that end made me feel wretched. I'd loved and trusted Mrs. Wark like no other human being and this seeming betrayal flung me back into the worst of my despondencies. Except, that this was worse. This time I had no one to pull a rabbit out of a hat, or give me handkerchiefs to dry my tears.

I never discussed this episode with Mrs. Wark and it remained an unscarred sore deep within me until this last decade when I've been thinking seriously about my life. My common sense now tells me to look at Mrs. Wark through the lens of her actions. Did the woman who fought so hard for me do it so that she'd get a jewel in her crown?

The worst thing of all is that I searched for the exact Biblical reference when I was writing about this and there is none. It appears the "jewel in the crown" story is a concoction of Brethren theology and an old wives' tale. I am ashamed that I never told Mrs. Wark why she'd lost my confidence, and that I lacked the courage to open my bruised being to her and sort everything out. The lesson Evelyn taught me after the kidnapping in 1945—bottle everything up inside—had been well learned.

Without a confidante anymore, I was left with the questions raised by 6H swirling around my mind, day in and day out. What was wrong with a comfortable second best in life? And with being a hypocrite? Most people were.

The Saturdays I had spent in the University of Sydney's library seemed so long ago. Nothing in my present life gave me the thrill I'd experienced when discovering the ancient Minoans and I doubted that I had the energy to track down Michael Ventris anymore.

What had happened? Had I finally grown up? If I kept on my present path would I transform into Evelyn? Mrs. Wark had once told me that God never tested people above their tolerance level. Now, I wondered if he'd found mine and had moved away to torment some other hapless soul. Mrs. Wark was also convinced that I'd have a great career in teaching and that it was the "door" God had opened for me. Somehow, I couldn't believe that God was happy with complacent wobblers. Was the key to a happy life dependent on a vault inside me where I locked away all my harsh memories and disbeliefs and pretended they didn't exist?

Oblivious to this internal debate, life went on. I bought a vintage English car from Vera's husband—actually, several vintages that he'd cobbled together. It had three gears, a three-foot long gearshift to change them, no turn signals or other conveniences that we take for granted today. But it ran beautifully, was well within my price range, had a radio, and gave me tremendous independence.

Until the car, I hadn't realized how much time I spent travelling. Now, I had chunks of free time again. I was a regular at Bobbin Head in Ku-ring-gai Chase, either swimming after school or pottering around in boats and, on Sundays, I prowled around the historic towns of Richmond and Windsor to the west of Sydney. Designed by Francis Greenway, the convict-architect who had also drawn up the plans for the Old Mint Building that the Housing Commission's offices were in, they tapped into my deep love of history—the only abiding love I seemed to have.

I also found myself driving to the Eastern Suburbs more and more. One reason was Doyle's. I felt so sophisticated sitting on the sand outside the restaurant, eating fish and chips and drinking white wine while wavelets washed my feet. It was the most hedonistic thing in my life and, of course, would have been totally impossible today. For one thing, I was wildly underage and secondly, Doyle's today is so upscale that such relaxed dining wouldn't be tolerated. But the 1950s was a gentler age when so many more things were possible.

Doyle's aside, there was a much darker reason for driving to Watson's Bay. Above it is part of the coastline known as The Gap. I'd stand on the cliffs and look out at the Pacific, the wind racing through my hair while waves smashed incessantly against jagged rocks below. Hundreds of ships had foundered on those rocks and it was a place to think about mortality. What was life's purpose? Was one life important? Did I matter?

H stands for Hagiology, Halitosis. Heretic and Hula.

It also stands for Hubris and Humiliation.

Sometimes, something happens in our lives that pushes boundaries and takes us to a place we never thought existed. It can happen after a long build-up or can come out of the proverbial blue. In my case, I answered a phone call.

I'd developed a friendship with a guy that had escalated into dating. I would have been hard pressed to explain my feelings about him at the time. Unreal, might have been the primary word I'd have used. Will was very different from the rest of my friends—more urbane, a little more cultured but less thoughtful. He was the most handsome guy around, looking good in any type of clothes and his self-assurance rivalled Evelyn's stubbornness. I don't know how he managed it, but Will made me feel like a woman, not quite up to Marilyn Monroe's standards, but someone he wanted to be with.

At first, I was simply grateful. Overnight, it seemed, I'd become wildly attractive. His interest somehow validated my femininity and other men, who had previously avoided me like the Brethren plague, now phoned regularly. But, as weeks progressed into months, I stopped analyzing everything, relaxed and enjoyed the new experiences. He didn't read as much as my friends, so our personal *quid pro quo* was that he bought books and I upgraded my wardrobe.

When his mother phoned and asked me to lunch, I was puzzled. It was a school holiday, so Will would be at work in his father's law office. I dressed with care and presented myself at the front door at the requested time. When a uniformed maid took my overcoat and gloves, I raised my eyebrows. While some of the homes I visited looked equally luxurious, none had maids or butlers.

Will's mother wore the upper-class uniform featured in the English magazines of the day—a tailored silk dress adorned by pearls. After polite chitchat, she showed me into the day room and luncheon was served. The meal was simple yet elegant: a clear soup, salad, and a mushroom omelette. Once a poached pear with ice cream and the tea service were brought to the table, she dismissed the maid and turned to me.

"It's been nice meeting you," she began, the blue veins in her hand protruding as she lifted the silver teapot. "And, I must say, it is reassuring to know that Will hasn't totally lost his mind or been seduced by a voluptuous body."

I swallowed and carefully placed my teacup back on its saucer. Suddenly I saw the woman's elegance as a mere *façade* and the jungle as her *milieu*. Nobody in their right mind would have ever described my body as voluptuous and I now recognized her cloak of friendliness as the veneer of etiquette. I said nothing, just looked at her and waited.

She seemed eager to take the metaphorical gloves off. With no more pretence, she let me know the real purpose behind the luncheon. "My husband and I," she began, "have invested heavily in Will's future. So far, it's been twelve years at Sydney Grammar, holidays abroad and, oh, yes, university. You've never been, have you?"

I didn't deign to answer. But, then, she didn't expect me to.

"You must realize that's a lot of money," she steamrollered on, so outwardly gentle, yet so relentless. "And, I'll tell you this Beverley, it's far too much for us to stand by and see him waste himself on a bastard like you. We've told him not to see you again."

I'd heard about blows to the solar plexus but never expected to feel one. I never imagined that the circumstances of my birth were so widely known. I bit back a gasp and, in a strange metamorphosis, became Evelyn. I shifted my glance from the linen tablecloth to her beautiful dress, and concentrated on one breast, implying that the tuck there was too tight, destroying the line of the dress she'd probably paid three months of my wages for. Then I asked that the maid show me out.

I drove home in state of shock.

I wanted to do something. Like a rape victim, I wanted to stand in a shower and scrub myself for hours on end. Anything, really, to scrape off her filth. I'd shaved my legs that morning. Now, I felt each tiny piece of stubble pushing against my nylons, protesting my humiliation. I wanted to cry, great noisy, disgustingly loud sobs to expel my mortification. I wanted to run to Mrs. Wark, but I had no one to confide in. Will's courtship had been intensely private. I hadn't told anyone about him, hadn't boasted about having a drop-dead gorgeous man. Maybe, I never expected it to last.

T.S. Eliot's Thomas à Becket had bested barons whose "manners matched their fingernails." I'd slunk away from a woman whose elocution matched her manicured claws. Eventually I learned to live with the pain and it was the only time my illegitimacy was publicly held against me. I've buried the episode for close to sixty years, never wanting to relive it, never able to understand Will's mother and her dispassionate cruelty.

It would be a long time before I could trust a man again. The immediate effect, though, was a kick in the pants. Her bile gave me an incentive. I needed a place where no one had ever heard of me or my dubious parentage.

I had to get out of Australia.

CHAPTER 8

D AND X

D stands for Drone, Dap, and Dungaree.
It also stands for Despair.

Decisions made through despair are not necessarily desirable.

Once I decided to leave Australia, I faced two insurmountable obstacles. I had contracted to teach for three years and completed only one full year. I suppose I could have broken the bond by revealing that Mrs. Wark had forged Evelyn's signature, but I never thought of it. I could only break it by paying the amount of salary owed—in my case, what I'd earn during twenty some months. The other mountainous problem was the necessity for Boy or Evelyn's signature on a passport application.

The combination of 6H and Will's mother irrevocably altered my life. Added to this was the diminishment of my circle of friends. Two of my closest announced their engagement, and thus dated almost exclusively. Others sailed off for "home" as we used to call England. Casual intellectual chats at the jazz clubs on Saturdays nights became fewer as people settled into their grown-up lives.

White wine at Doyle's aside, I was doing my best to be an exemplary Christian as defined by the Brethren. But that didn't mean I was succeeding as a model for the girls in my youth group and, while being virtuous gained me some acceptance, I always worried if another Will's mother would pop up and shatter everything?

Did I want acceptance from those I'd once sneered at, though? When I read Thomas à Becket's soliloquy from *Murder in the Cathedral* now, I cried. Doing the right deed for the wrong reason, he'd declared, was the greatest treason. My professed goodness wasn't bringing me closer to God, but it was well and truly on its way into making me the nice, bland hypocrite I'd once decried.

Part of the problem, I realize now, was that Mrs. Wark remained the only person I knew who was both happy and joyous in her Christianity and, at one of our now rare lunches, she told me off. I was a successful teacher. Why would I not accept this? Why would I want re-open the scars of my past? I knew, but couldn't tell her, that they weren't scars but scabs. She, like everyone else, seemed to think I'd grow out of my discontent if I married. I, however, could only see disasters in that scenario. I did not want to become another Evelyn with a husband I called Boy.

So, I spent many lonely nights, defying the wind on the Watson's Bay cliffs and the siren call of the waves below while trying to decide if life was the ultimate folly. The world, as I knew it, had no place for a young woman who dared challenge accepted wisdom. What would I lose if I succumbed to the seductive waves and jumped into them?

One day, and I have no idea when or how, I heard something that galvanized and set me upon a totally different course. Again, it appeared, I might have my cake and eat it too. The United States of America, according to rumour, had universities that offered courses in the Bible. These courses were not the polite liberal theology of the mid-1950s that turned Jesus into such a bland moral philosopher that it was impossible to imagine anyone working up sufficient anger to crucify Him. Nor did they upgrade Biblical precepts to fit the twentieth century. Instead, these American universities and colleges offered plain, straightforward (in Brethren terms), evangelical exposition. In such places, I convinced myself, I would be able to both learn and have my doubts about God destroyed.

I began haunting the U.S. Information Services office in Sydney, paging through catalogues of myriad universities and colleges. The rumour, I quickly found out, was true. The problem would be choice and from what I could understand, my relatively low French mark would not be a deterrent if I could score well on the required scholastic aptitude exams or SATs. They had multiple-choice questions though, something new to me. But, the Information Office had samples and they didn't seem difficult. Again, I began to hope, that is, until I totalled the costs of tuition, books, and room and board. It was impossible.

But that was exactly what my life had been about to that point – impossibles.

Therefore, I refused to see money as an obstacle and convinced myself that Evelyn and Boy would be so delighted that I wanted to study the Bible, they would subsidize part of the costs. Talk about optimism. However, I drove up to their house to tell them my news in person and see whether I could shake a little spare change loose. As I talked about my plans, Evelyn listened intently. At first, I thought she was pleased.

Then she frowned. "What about your bond? Have you forgotten that little detail?"

"If I teach for another year and save, I'll have more than enough money to pay the bond off," I assured her. The thought of leaving Australia without repaying it never occurred to me. If it had, however, making Evelyn and Boy responsible for my debt might have been the ultimate temptation.

"And then what?"

She knew what I wanted, but she seemed determined to make me beg. We sat in silence. I stewed, wondering how else I might plead my case, while she seemed unconcerned. As well she might. She held all the cards. When I eventually summoned up enough courage to answer, the butterflies in my stomach were in deep fall and my throat seemed incredibly tight as I mumbled, "I was hoping you might help me."

"Us? Help you?"

Unfortunately, Boy had chosen this moment to arrive and he entered the fray with a vengeance. I was the most ungrateful, deceitful, scheming child any parents had the misfortune to bring up. Not only was I a disgrace to the family, but to the Lord as well.

"Then help me get the faith you have," I begged.

"There are Bible colleges here in Australia," he answered. "And you don't even have to go outside the Brethren to find one."

I knew some of the men who taught at the college he referred to and I respected them. However, they could not answer the major theological question that bugged me—that is, if God is omniscient, why was humanity created or "allowed" to evolve? God would have known from the beginning that we would not measure up, that we'd succumb to temptations and thus earn a one-way ticket to hell. Jesus was almost an irrelevancy to me. God had screwed up when he'd given humanity free well and Jesus was the solution. I could understand that though I didn't understand God's need for us. Could not he have loved us better by not creating us at all?

Boy didn't understand the question either and would never see why the search for an answer might drive me overseas. So, instead of saying something that I knew it would enrage him, I appealed to his better instincts. "You know how long I've wanted to go to university. This way I can learn and the devil can't corrupt me because I'll be studying the Bible as well."

That was the high point of the afternoon. Eventually Boy

reminded me that when I had gone to Teachers College against their wishes, they'd washed their hands of me and would not give me another penny.

"Or a signature," Evelyn added. "The passport people are much more stringent about signatures than the Department of Education."

Disappointed, I drove home. I had not expected them to subsidize my education, but some sort of gesture, even the necessary signature, would have been nice. Back in Sydney, I sat down and began working out numbers. Now that I knew I would be solely responsible for supporting myself in the United States, I began adding up certain and projected costs.

Paying off the government contract might be the easy part. Putting together the money for my tuition, books, room, food, airfare and an emergency fund would be far more difficult. For a while I thought of following the footprints of several friends and simply go to England for a year or so. It was the grand Australian rite of passage and there I would be allowed to get any job I could find. I might see several places I dreamed about and maybe acquire a little culture but I couldn't expect any answers to the spiritual and other questions that bedevilled me. I seemed at a crossroads. Again.

While I pondered options and desperately wondered how I could make things happen, suddenly, and totally out of the blue, one of the family decided to help. Vera, who had obviously been told about my plan to go to America, kindly, offered me a room in her house. The amount she expected for room and board was far less than the amount I was currently paying and without her generosity, I might never have reached North America.

I remembered some advice Mrs. Wark had given me earlier about God's supervision of our lives. That he never closed a door until another opened. With this incentive, I narrowed my choice of universities down to five; reread their catalogues from cover to cover, then finally sent letters across the Pacific asking for application forms.

With that, I began looking for extra jobs and, overnight, I was back into my old swimming regime, getting up at 5:30 and heading down to a pool to teach basic swimming under the supervision of an Olympic coach. Next, I found an office that needed an evening receptionist and I worked there after I'd finished my teaching day. Not only was it good money, but also it allowed me to develop speed with my hunt and peck method of typing. I'd need more speed to compete against ten-fingered technicians for other secretarial jobs.

Saturday mornings I worked in a bank, filing. At the Housing Commission, I'd hated that job. Now, every time I finished a stack of papers I told myself I was that much closer to America and felt satisfied. There were no more voluntary jobs at camps. I taught swimming for the Department of Education at an extremely good wage during school holidays and also worked for a firm specializing in providing temporary help to offices. On Sundays I kept up my church responsibilities. The only luxuries I really had in that period were cricket or hockey on Saturday afternoons, and going out with my friends afterwards.

One by one the obstacles fell away as my savings mounted. The scholastic aptitude tests were dead easy – although they were the first objective tests I'd ever taken. When my results arrived, I found my verbal score was almost perfect. I'd got one answer wrong. I'd somehow expected that, but my score in the non-verbal section astounded me. I had not studied mathematics since I was fourteen. That I ranked in the 94th percentile was truly amazing and had been made possible only by working out answers by sheer logic rather than mathematical formulae.

Those tests opened a lot of doors. Wheaton College in Illinois not only accepted me but also offered a partial scholarship. As well, a letter explained that it was willing to grant me senior standing in English (because of my near-perfect verbal SAT), Bible and American history.

The latter was particularly unnerving because the only American history I knew had been garnered through reading *Time* magazine. A little of the excitement about going to an American university evaporated once that letter arrived. None of Australia's universities would have given me advanced standing. Were American standards so low? Furthermore, part of my reason in going to America was to study the Bible – not validate it. Still, I figured they knew what they were doing, so I kept working and saving.

X stands for Xanthians, Xenopus, Xerox.

It also stands for Exit.

In a way, those were magical months. My money multiplied and gradually I allowed myself to become excited. I'd turned twenty-one and thus didn't need parental signatures. Providing I could save the money, nothing could stop me. I read everything I could find about the United States and its culture, but truly didn't understand much. Hollywood offered such a mixed picture as, for example, the contrast between Paul Newman, Rock Hudson and James Dean.

Terminology was puzzling as well. Wall Street had bears and bulls running around and the political arena was dotted with G.O.Ps, elephants and donkeys. I knew there were two political parties, but where the Whigs fitted in I could never figure out. The laces on football pants seemed as sexy as some of Elvis's gyrations and much more alluring to the virginal me than the shorts Australian men wore to play rugby. But the fact that American footballers needed padding negated any fantasies I might have had. Typically Australian, I thought they had to be sissies.

The blue and the grey uniforms of the Civil War confused me as much as the differing blues of Oxford and Cambridge. When I talked with various Americans, they sometimes seemed as confused as I was, particularly over the status of African-Americans. One Christian called them "niggas" who needed to be retaught their place in God's universe, unapologetically describing them as an inferior race that had not been made in God's own image. Seeing how important colour was to them, I cynically wondered what colour skin they thought Jesus had.

When the time came to apply for a visa to study in the United States, I found the racial question was indeed huge. In fact, the application asked that I declare my own race. I thought of writing the hundred yards sprint but something in the stern visage of the immigration officer warned me that flippancy would not be tolerated. I asked if I might take the form away and was granted permission.

My friends didn't know what race we were either and had some rather ribald suggestions. "Mongrel," one declared immediately.

"Mixed," another advised. "Put down you're a mixture of English, Scottish and Australian."

"She can't do that," a more sensible friend answered before suggesting that I simply write "Australian."

But I didn't think I could do that either because my passport said I was a British subject and an Australian citizen. So that meant there had to be some other answer for race. Eventually, I drove to Mrs. Wark's house. After showing her the form I asked, "What do I put here?"

She thought for a while, went to an encyclopaedia and came back answering, "Caucasian, you're a Caucasian."

"What on earth's that?"

After a longish lecture involving history, ethnology and linguistics, I dutifully filled in the racial blank. The next day I returned to the U.S. immigration office and handed over my form and visa money. The official glanced through it only to stop at the Caucasian answer. "You Australians," he said. "Always have to joke about something." Then he crossed it out and substituted "white". When I told the story to my friends there was a burst of laughter.

"He should have put tanned white," joked one, looking at my skin.

Those last months in Australia passed in a blur. I was working and spending every spare moment I could tracking down things I might need in Chicago. I sent a trunk across by cargo boat, but I still searched for cold weather clothes. Eventually, I found something called a parka, which, I was assured, would keep me warm. It was thigh-length, lightly padded; yet it seemed enormously bulky. Since I'd be arriving in the middle of the American winter I knew I'd need it. In December, I began soaking up my last impressions of my country and friends. Christmas, 1961, was especially poignant.

All too soon, the months had become weeks, and then the weeks turned into days. There was an unending round of dinners and parties that my friends held for me. Their parents would slip me gifts of money that they knew I'd need, and my church friends hosted a particularly bitter-sweet party at Mrs. Wark's swanky new house in Wahroonga. They rented my favourite movie, *Genevieve*, set up an outdoor theatre and presented me with smallish items to take on the plane – a travelling chess set, and a beautifully engraved travel clock. When we said good-bye, I doubted more than ever if I was truly doing the right thing.

Those doubts stayed with me until I reached Mascot airport. It felt ironic that I'd leave Australia almost exactly from the field where Boy had run his outdoor Sunday school. Once I'd felt at home in those environs. Now, I'd begin a glamorous journey away from them. Glamorous, because my Boeing 707 would touch down in some exotic locations: Fiji, Hawaii and San Francisco.

Today's passengers cannot imagine the farewell scene at Sydney airport. About sixty of my friends, and many of their parents came to see me off. Everyone gave me a bon voyage card with a small amount of money inside, the equivalent of a good luck charm I guess. Evelyn and Boy were conspicuous by their absence, but Vera and her husband were among the crowd. Most of us knew we might never see each other again. The fastest turnaround for letters was five weeks. So, amidst the wild excitement and party atmosphere, there were tears.

When the time came to walk out onto the tarmac most of my friends came with me to watch from about twenty feet away as I climbed the stairs into the Boeing 707. Jet propulsion engines were still newish and some of my friends had never seen them before. They themselves would leave Australia in a year or two, but they would sail to London. Flying to America was a very, very new mode of travel for ordinary people.

It's impossible to describe that afternoon. It was a farewell in the truest sense of the word. I never saw or spoke to most of those people there again. International phone calls were prohibitively expensive. There was no Skype, no email, no international texts, no social media. There was no way of remaining in constant touch.

Once I stepped aboard that Qantas plane, I changed my life irrevocably. I'd experience incredible, heart-breaking sorrow, greater than I'd ever endured. I'd explore incredible highways and by-ways.

And, I would come to know the meaning of joy.

PART III

THE TEMERITY OF HOPE

CHAPTER 9

N

N stands for *Nether, Newt, Next.*

It also stands for New.

The long flight to Chicago was a bridge in so many ways. Of course, from the known to the unknown but, it felt like I was tearing myself in half. At the time, I had no way of knowing that my love for Sydney was deep and so profound that I would never stop missing it. I hadn't realized how Australian-centred I am. When it snows here in Vancouver at Christmas, I long for warm water, golden sand and blue skies.

Looking back on that day in January 1962 I realize that my journey also reflected a dying world. Once I found my seat and put my seat belt on, the attendant gave me a blanket, a champagne cocktail and once we reached cruising altitude she came back with a refill and the menu for me to study. It was beautifully produced with a painting of Sydney in the 1830s on the cover and a choice of foods that passengers in tourist class only dream about nowadays.

For starters, I had a choice between a cream and clear soup. Then I would choose between two hot dishes – roast sirloin or lobster Newburg, then make more choices between Mandarin cheesecake and ice cream cake. After this, came a cheese tray, a fruit basket, Irish coffee and dinner mints. The sommelier came by with complementary wines for each course. We ate off china plates with silver knives and forks. Meals of equal excellence were served on the flights between Fiji and Honolulu, and then Honolulu to San Francisco.

Such luxury. Such decadence. And an incredible overload of my senses.

When the cotton-batten clouds wafted away, I stared down at the Pacific, enchanted. I could see right down to the ocean's floor, especially in the water around Fiji. Nadi, the Fijian airport, delighted with its scent of frangipani everywhere; Honolulu, however, reeked of gasoline and commercial coconut oil.

Expectations based on movies are destined for disillusionment. The reality of the San Francisco airport gave the first clue that I might be in trouble. I had a long layover and when I first started walking around, I thought I must be in the middle of a Mormon conference. Sydney had recently become a Mormon mission field and pairs of men in skinny ties, longish, tight jackets and very short hair knocked on doors everywhere. It took a while for me to realize that the hundreds of men wandering the airport were not latter-day saints and were probably not saints at all—just Americans in everyday business suits.

Similarly, the prevalence of uniformed men was another shock, because I wondered if World War III had broken out while I was in flight. I knew what American sailors looked like because Sydney was a port of call for the U.S. Navy. In the San Francisco airport, the navy uniforms were among the brown of the army, and the blue of the air force. I know now that there are always personnel going back and forth on leave, but in 1962 their sheer numbers disoriented me.

To settle myself, I found a bookstore. It had sold out of Harper Lee's *To Kill A Mockingbird* in paperback, so I bought the hardcover version. Then my stomach rumbled, and I remembered the Qantas flight attendant telling me to eat before I got on my plane to Chicago. Most eating establishments seemed attached to bars, but I finally found a quiet place. There was a line-up outside, so I thought luck must be with me when a table for one quickly became available.

I studied with menu with great intensity and, as its prices were higher than I'd expected, I pulled out my American cash, counted it and then ordered the cheapest meal. When the bill came, I stared at it in horror. It was higher than the price on the menu. I recounted my money but I hadn't made a mistake. I didn't have enough to pay my bill. Slowly, I walked towards the cashier, wondering if I'd have to wash dishes or something equally dreadful. I tried arguing with the cashier but she pointed to one notation that I hadn't deciphered.

Sales tax. In Australia, it was always added into the price so that what you saw was exactly what you paid. In the United States, it was an extra. As a line-up grew behind him, I pulled my money out and the cashier shook her head. Then, a man pushed his way forward.

"How much is she short?"

He laughed when he found out how little the fuss was about and gave the cashier a five-dollar American bill. "That should cover it and her tip." He turned to me. "I don't suppose you left a tip, did you?" My new friend then walked me to a place where I exchanged my Australian dollars for American ones. I thanked him and attempted to repay the five dollars but he laughed as he waved goodbye.

The veneer of world traveler sophistication had thoroughly slipped away and I felt rattled. I'd gained wisdom but made myself look like an idiot in public. Adrift in shame, I never realized that the restaurant experience was a harbinger.

The next morning Chicago seemed, not just half a world away

from Australia, but a totally different universe. The brilliance of the sun made the snow glisten, and I wondered why everyone had warned me about Chicago being cold. When I'd left Sydney, one of the airport gauges showed the temperature at thirty. That was in Celsius because, in a couple more years, Australia would switch over to the decimal system. It seemed so funny – to leave at thirty and arrive into thirty. The sun shone equally brightly, but in Sydney it contained warmth. Thirty degrees in Sydney meant a dangerous sunburn. In Chicago thirty degrees couldn't even melt snow.

Bemused, I collected my luggage and retrieved a wallet with traveler's cheques that I'd buried deep inside one bag. My next steps seemed simple: find the Travelers Aid people, cash a cheque, get directions to the train station. Suddenly, though, I heard my name being paged on the airport's loudspeaker. Inexplicably, Travelers Aid, the very place I was trying to find, requested my presence.

I wondered what I'd done wrong. I hadn't spent any money since the restaurant incident, so it couldn't be the tax people after me, and my passport and student visa had been thoroughly checked in Honolulu. What had I done? Visions of deportation slowed my steps as I trudged towards the Travelers Aid booth.

I'd barely reached the desk when a young woman jumped up from a chair. "Beverley?"

"Yes," I answered, not knowing whether to trust her smile or not.

"Hi! Welcome to America! I'm Ann. Your brother sent me."

My brother? Then I remembered that Victor worked for International Harvester, a company whose headquarters were in Illinois. My smile became as bright as the sun outside. "Vic? Vic sent you?"

He had written to me before I left, giving his blessing and a small donation to the cause, and telling me how sorry he and his wife Gene were not to be able to wave good-bye in person. Now, Ann told me, he'd worried about me landing in Chicago, not knowing a soul. He'd talked to his boss in Melbourne, who had wired his equal in Illinois asking if someone could meet me. Ann's father had read the telegram, understood the need and volunteered her services. It was that simple and, I had my first lessons in the smallness of the world, and the generosity of individual Americans. It seemed little short of a miracle that someone halfway round the globe would go out of their way to ease Vic's worry. I started to thank Ann, but she held up her hand.

"Thank me after our shopping spree, and when your wallet's a couple of hundred dollars lighter."

My smile faded. "I'll thank you now. I don't need to go shopping."

"Beverley, we have to go shopping. Look at your shoes."

I looked. I was kind of proud of my shoes. They were made from beautiful navy calf leather. The heels were three-inch Italian state of the art craft. I thought, with any luck, they'd last me through my American sojourn. "Are the heels too high?"

I'd worried about the height of my heels. We'd recently gone through a phase where five-inch heels were *de rigeur*, so I'd chosen that I'd thought was a compromise.

But Ann wasn't through. "It's not just your shoes. It's your clothes. You'll freeze outside."

I thought my clothes were fine, although I'd noticed some curious looks that I'd put down to my deep tan. I knew my skirt was a little crumpled from the various flights and I was a little chunky on top because, just before we landed, I'd put on a long-sleeved undershirt under my prized Viyella wool blouse. On top of these I'd added a chunky Aran sweater that I'd knitted especially for the American winter. I was so hot I could feel perspiration pooling under my armpits and I carried my Australian version of a parka rather than wearing it.

So, it was with deep scepticism that I looked at Ann and scoffed, "Freeze? I'm boiling."

"In here," she countered. "But outside? You don't just need clothes, you need boots as well."

Boots, or Wellingtons as we called them, were something children wore when splashing around in puddles. I tried to explain this to Ann, but she'd already made up her mind. She pointed out my luggage to a hovering red-capped porter, gave him some money and stalked off, saying over her shoulder, "Put your jacket on and let's go. It's the only way you'll understand."

And understand I did. We'd barely left the protection of the building when I went ass over teakettle. Ann giggled as she helped me up. "Sorry. I forgot to warn you. Look out for the ice."

I took another step with exactly the same result. She helped me up again and, this time, held onto me as I made baby steps towards the bus station while seething with frustration. I can't remember how many undignified tumbles she saved me from, or how long it took to walk the short distance. All I know is by the end of it I was willing to buy whatever shoes or boots she recommended. Skis, snow-shoes, whatever. Anything that would prevent the indignity of being unable to walk three consecutive steps without help.

The detour to Marshall Fields, a huge department store, wiped out most of my contingency fund even though Ann hunted for bargains as diligently as if the money was her own. Finally, we finished with sodas. I had dreamed of having one after seeing them in the *Saturday Evening Post* and I felt euphoric as I watched the kid behind the counter pour the flavouring into a long glass, add ice cream, soda water and whipped cream. By the time he added a cherry on top, I was a salivating mess.

Satiated, and about five hours after I'd landed, we sat in a train heading for Wheaton. I'd last slept sometime between Fiji and

Honolulu, so I smiled and listened while Ann talked. She, herself, went to college on the east coast and she'd be travelling there the next day. But, did I like music? The Four Lads were in concert at her old high school. She'd bought tickets and her dad had promised the car if I'd like to go.

At the Wheaton station, she insisted on taking a taxi to my dormitory and made the bed while I had a bath, changed clothes, and she then took me home for "supper," a new term to me and one I learned meant dinner. After the concert, she introduced me to friends who promptly promised to take me tobogganing the next day. Ann's mother heard the offer and insisted I stay over. She also made me phone my dorm for permission. I felt like I was fourteen again. All in all, though, it was probably the most fun weekend I had during my time at Wheaton.

When reality intrudes, all the beautiful dreams built on watching girls in bikinis on Californian beaches explode. The grind of staying alive kicks in and life becomes real and very earnest. And, that's how it was with me at Wheaton College and living in the United States of America. In retrospect, I can understand why my college experience was so disastrous but, at the time, as I tried to make it work, it seemed a mountain I could never climb.

The reasons why are easily categorized: clothes, language, food, academics, and faith.

Clothes preoccupied me for the first few months. In my naivety, I'd thought that my Australian winter clothes would suffice. But, I faced an annoying problem. My clothes were too warm for American interiors with central heating, and too flimsy for outdoors. My beautiful woollen skirts and sweaters were useless and had to be packed away. Replacing them ate up anything left in my contingency fund, and swallowed up my spending money as well. I don't think I ever recovered from clothes-shock.

Winston Churchill once remarked that England and America were two nations divided by a common language. He should have factored in Australia because I made all the now-classic gaffes like asking a male student if he would knock me up. I'd never heard the word eraser so I asked another student for a rubber. Of course, the language unfamiliarity went both ways. My jaw dropped when rooting first came up in mixed company as it meant fornication in some circles in Australia.

Sexual innuendo aside, verbal difficulties reached everywhere. I had to call my jumpers by their American name, sweaters. I went happily to a function that promised free sloppy joes, expecting a sweatshirt, not a messy hamburger bun.

I never quite knew where I was with food. In Sydney, I'd eaten steaks, roasts, lamb chops and meat pies. I'd never heard of pizza, fruit in jelly (now called jello), cottage cheese, and yoghurt. I had to wrap my head around pies as deserts, especially those made from pumpkins. To celebrate the mid-point of my first semester, the cafeteria promised steak and for the first time I looked forward to the Friday night meal. When it was served, I looked at my plate in dismay. All around me, everyone else was happily eating. I'd expected something along the lines of a broiled New York steak. Definitely not chuck steak. When we'd lived in Botany, one of the few chores I had was picking up chuck steak and a free bone for the dog. Now, years and thousands of dollars later, I was in a place where people cheered because they'd been served dog food.

However, needs must. By the end of my time at Wheaton, I'd learned to love pizza and to tolerate cottage cheese. I pined for Vegemite but happily ate peanut butter and jam. French toast took some getting used to and while I never liked pumpkin pie, I ate it politely whenever it was served as I did with servings of chicken and turkey. Hamburgers and fries replaced meat pies and salad sandwiches as my snack food.

I have no way of evaluating Wheaton food. Cafeteria food is cafeteria food. It was probably good and I should not have been critical, but the culture shock was too great.

Sometimes the clash of cultures worked in my favour. Used to the non-stop action of rugby, I found football with its many stoppages tedious but I loved the excitement of basketball, even though the men played in short satin shorts. When spring finally came, I tried out for the softball team. Because I sprained my thumb every time I used a glove, I fielded barehanded as I had done in cricket. Not only did it feel more natural, it gave me a better range because I catch equally well with right and left hands.

The sport I eventually came to enjoy most, though, was tennis. I'd never played it competitively in Australia, so I happily settled for being the forehand half of Wheaton's doubles team. I enjoyed and respected my partner as a person and gradually became less prickly and more approachable. With more friends, I felt more at home. When the time came for our dorm banquet, I even felt confident enough to invite one of these new friends to be my date. He eventually became the Speaker of the U.S. House of Representatives and was held in high esteem until disgraced by a sexual scandal. So much for my judgment.

Thanks to friends, I played tennis at the Merion Cricket Club in Haverford, Pennsylvania and explored a mining museum near Yuma, Colorado. Visiting my friends' homes allowed me to see the almost unimaginable prosperity of the American middle class and the riches enjoyed by a privileged few. Those times made me understand the extraordinary wealth of the United States and helped me later gain a better understanding of why I had never fitted into it.

But the basic fact was that I was too old. Since my Botany days I'd never had friends of my own age. Usually they were four to six years older. I knew going to Wheaton that I would be a couple of years older than my classmates but didn't see it as a problem. What I hadn't factored in were my seven-plus years of being responsible for myself. Ninety-nine percent of my classmates had their education paid for by their parents – at least to varying amounts. I, on the other hand, had worked four or even five jobs at a time to get the money for my fare, to pay off my Department of Education bond, to save a contingency fund and earn enough money to pay for textbooks and all the extras that Wheaton's scholarship didn't cover.

Therefore, I had little sympathy when my roommate complained that Daddy had given her last year's model car for her birthday. But the differences between me and my fellow students were vast and not easily summarized. For them, going to college was a rite of passage. The women expected to graduate not only with a mortarboard on their heads but a ring on their fingers. For the men, it was a time of networking, and their degree put their feet onto the first step of their vocational future.

Precious few students looked at Wheaton as a time to learn. In a way, the system itself discouraged it. Learning at Wheaton was largely measured through tests and pop quizzes. I'd grown up in a system where we showed mastery of a subject through writing about it. I found multiple choice questions irritating and trivial. In history, for example, when and who were more important than why.

After a while I gave up. I had no idea what my professors would consider sufficiently significant to test me on and although I read the textbooks, I didn't study. Nothing ignited my imagination and I almost failed my history final. I only understood the consequences a week later when I was asked to see the Dean of Students and warned that I was on academic probation. That meant, shape up or lose the scholarship.

Before the mid-term, the history prof had been talking Fulbright Scholarship for me. Now I was just an underperforming student under threat of losing her Wheaton scholarship. Woe was me.

CHAPTER 10

D AND H

D *stands for Dabchick, Dementia, Decession.*

D also stands Desolation.

Angry and scared about my academic standing, I got ready for a lucrative baby-sitting job near Evanston, Illinois. The parents were attending a function in the southern part of the state and had warned they might not be back until five or six the following morning.

With the children already in bed, they showed me where everything was, gave me some contact numbers, and then the father took me to their bedroom—a designer's fantasy of blues and creams in a style I would later know as Laura Ashley. While I looked around, he strode across the carpets to a French provincial nightstand and pulled a revolver from its drawer. "I keep this for emergencies," he announced matter-of-factly. "Do you know how to fire a gun?"

One of Evelyn's cousins had taught me to shoot a .303, supposedly to help him kill rabbits that were overrunning his farm. When I told my employer this, he laughed and said it was a start. Then, more soberly, he explained the huge difference between firing at cans on fences and shooting at intruders in a house. Then, for the next ten minutes, he concentrated on teaching me how to load and fire the gun from the approved shooting position.

I tried to listen but most of my mind rebelled. The disjunction between the ultra-feminine bedroom and the succinct explanation of what parts of an intruder's body I should aim at made everything unreal. When he finally showed me the guest bedroom and detailed the remainder of my duties, I was extremely relieved.

Babysitting was an easy job. Usually I appreciated someone giving me money to read or study. This employer, however, had offered a small ransom to protect his children to the point of killing anyone who intruded. It was unsettling, to say the least. Chicago had a notorious reputation, but I'd never expected to be part of Elliott Ness's clean-up crew.

After he and his wife left, I checked on the children and then settled down to study for my last exam in creative writing. Shattered by my history mark, I began calculating what I'd need to keep my A+ in the course. The answer was zero. The professor didn't believe creating writing could be measured by exams. She'd already marked and handed back my final assignment and the exam was worth only two percent of the final grade. The decision was easy. I'd go early, explain my thinking, and, if she agreed, I'd skip the final.

With nothing but a long night ahead, I pulled the disastrous history exam from my bag and carefully reread my professor's copious comments. He disagreed with the slant I'd taken when writing the mini-essay at the end and thought that I'd shown arrogance by not trusting his role as teacher and mine as student. That so-called lack of respect was both my sin and the reason for the harshness of my punishment. I read and reread his justification until I decided that maybe he was right after all. I should have trusted his system. If he wanted to test knowledge of arcane dates and people, I should have said okay and not worried about the why. Finally, I put the exam down, picked up the gun and stared at it.

In that moment, it represented America as well as my confusion and despair. Since reading the professor's comments, the knowledge that my time in the United States was extremely limited had seeped into my bones. I hadn't received an education. Nor had I discovered a faith in God. In fact, he seemed further away from ever. Rather than finding his essence, I'd found an excess of hypocrisy.

After all these years, I can say with certainty that the only person at Wheaton whom I thought knew God was the Dean of the Graduate School, Merrill C. Tenney. I was his part-time secretary, and he was as fine a Christian scholar and gentleman as one could hope to meet. The way he talked made me hunger for such a relationship, but he was the only one amidst thousands.

The famous pledge that forbade everything, except sex, was legally flouted by guys holding poker parties using Rook cards instead of the usual ones. Chapel attendance was mandatory, but the guy who sat next to me made it easier for himself by reading *Playboy* throughout the thirty minutes.

My years of compulsory church going had taught me what lip-service adherence to Christianity looked like whether it was given in an Australian accent or an American one. Of course, students were convinced that they were Christians but, when they spoke, Christianity sounded very, very similar to their views about the Republican Party, except that their fervency for their nation sounded louder than that for their Christian Lord.

I'd read enough Bible to yearn for it to be true. I wanted what Mrs. Wark and Merrill Tenney had and, in the stillness of that night in Evanston, I was angry that I couldn't find it. I missed my Australian friends unbearably and now I realized that I'd burnt my boats when I'd left Australia. Going back to rebuild would never satisfy me. But what could I do, where would I go?

I could see no future in America for myself, and none in Australia. The God I'd chased seemed more like a will-o-the-wisp than ever, always dancing beyond my reach. As the hours passed, darkness became absolute. Literally and spiritually. Far away from anyone who gave a damn, tinker's or otherwise, I could see nowhere to go, no one to turn to and I lacked the will to face the following day.

Looking back and thinking about that night, it's hard to believe that I reached the point where I had zero hope. It's even harder to describe my mixed emotions. Anger. Bitter anger. But I had a tremendous feeling of yearning. Exactly what for, I cannot remember. There was sorrow as well, because once more I had failed and there was no Mrs. Wark in Illinois to bully me forward. But at the same time, I also felt a monumental relief. My struggle to survive was over. I'd worked as hard as I could, soared as high as possible to chase my hopes and, in the end, my years of denial were worthless.

I'd more than paid any debts I owed society. Finally, the time had come when I could indulge myself and end my struggles. I remember being remarkably clear-headed once that decision was reached, even to the point of thinking about the aftermath of my suicide.

I did not want to traumatize the sleeping children. I also wanted to leave as minimal a mess as possible and so I walked into my employer's office. It was off-limits to the children and, if the master bedroom epitomized femininity, this office exuded masculinity. The leather chair would have been found acceptable in any English Edwardian country mansion. Ornate brass handles gleamed on the drawers of a desk that looked like something in the Oval Office. Paintings of dogs with sad eyes and dead ducks drooping from their mouths stared reproachfully from three walls. Diplomas and photos of the owner with famous people jostled for position on the fourth. I felt out of place as they watched me sit at the desk and write letters of explanation and apology. When I'd finished, I dragged myself out into the snow and thumbtacked the notes to the garage and front doors.

I started crying as I walked. I had only two more things to do. I returned to the office and, not knowing or caring if it was legal, wrote a holographic will. Lastly, I wrote a letter to Mrs. Wark and asked her to explain things to Evelyn and Boy. Then I sat back and looked at the sad-eyed dogs.

I'm sure that my eyes matched theirs because I no longer felt certain about my decision. Of course, I didn't want to kill myself. On the other hand, I couldn't see any reason to live. I was such a poor excuse for a human being and it was rather ironic that I'd failed so badly in the land of "life, liberty and the pursuit of happiness".

I thought about my birth. How much different would the world have been if Girlie had aborted me? Would anything have changed if I hadn't been conceived? Maybe Girlie's life would have been better and her personal cloud of bitterness would never have engulfed her. Of course, I know I indulged in grade A, number 1, self-pity, blaming everyone but myself for my misery, but back in that room, I didn't care. So, chiding myself for cowardice, I picked up the revolver, released the safety, and stared at it for a few seconds before putting it underneath my chin. Time slowed, and it seemed to take forever just to raise it. My hand shook uncontrollably and I cursed while I tried to steady it.

H stands for Heresiography, Hippocras, Hogwash.

H also stands for Hope.

What happened next turned extraordinary into unbelievability. Even now, I don't know how to describe it. Something happened that was impossible. Someone touched my back.

I jerked in shock. Luckily the revolver didn't go off. When I turned around to face the intruder, no one was in the room. The door was shut. There was nobody there but myself.

The touch was real—so real that I wondered afterwards if I'd have a bruise. I felt censured about my right to end the life I'd been given. There were other, more important overtones, though. I'd seen fathers rumple their children's hair in love and exasperation. Now, I knew what that felt like. I had no doubts about who touched me. I might not have had an earthly father who loved me but from that moment, I knew, with absolute certainty, there not only was a god, but that he loved me.

The bluish steel of the gun gleamed dully as I slowly absorbed the knowledge that God, the God I'd heard about and yearned for all my life, had intervened directly in it.

This was not supposed to happen. I wasn't Moses, or even the apostle Paul. Nobody I knew had experienced anything similar happen to them, yet there could be no other explanation. I had felt the touch on my back and the accompanying sense of love had vanquished the previous bleakness of despair. Furthermore, I've never once doubted that it happened.

Did it mean I was a Christian? No. At the very least, I was certain God existed and that he was interested in me. Jesus had spoken about his father's eye being on sparrows and now I felt like one myself.

The concept of a loving father had always seemed far-fetched. Boy had never loved me. My birth father had done his best to ignore my being. Jesus, I thought, would have told me that his father's love had sent him into human existence to save me. And, while I accepted that something had just saved my life, I would have argued with Jesus. The god I'd been brought up with didn't seem a loving or caring god. But, if it wasn't the Christian God I'd experienced, what had happened?

All I knew for sure was that the easy door to non-existence had just slammed shut and that I'd have to stumble on in hope.

One morning, the following week, Sharon, one of my friends, rushed into the cafeteria. "Bev, what are you doing this summer?"

"Getting a job."

"You haven't got one yet?"

When I shook my head, she smiled. "Becky's just got engaged and is going to Maine. She and I had this job in a grocery store. Fourteen hours a day and six days a week. Big money."

If I lost my scholarship, I'd need big money. "Where?"

Then Sharon said the magic word. "California. We'd have to leave in four days."

If I had prayed for a job in the summer, this would have been at the top of the list. Finally, I might get to be a bikini beach babe. How good was that?

We left a couple of days later. Five of us crammed into a VW, driving out on the storied Route 66, stopping at cheap motels, rating the various fast food places and singing continuously. Our mood was so upbeat that it forced me to rethink some things. I was amongst a group of American college kids having one of the best times of my life as I anticipated the sand and surf of California's beaches.

After crossing the Nevada-California border, we detoured to Lake Tahoe to drop off one of my new friends and, next morning, calamity struck.

It turned out to be another small thing that changed the course of my life. We had talked about the latest dance, the twist, in the car and I'd earned kudos because I knew how to do it. Just before we set off again the next morning, they challenged me to show them. None of us realized that the surface we stood on was loose flagstone. Halfway through my demonstration, a stone shifted and I flipped over. As I sat on the ground, moaning, I held my right ankle, knowing it was broken.

I stayed there, gritting my teeth, as everyone tried to work out the next step. Hospital was out of the question. My medical coverage had ceased once I'd left Illinois and wouldn't recommence until I began work. Finally, one of my friends remembered an orthopedic surgeon-uncle just north of San Francisco, so we piled into the car without further ado.

I soon discovered the meaning of working through pain. My friends did what they could. One spent hours teaching me card tricks. We told each other jokes and confided stories about first dates while I gobbled aspirin. Eventually the pain subsided into numbness and we reached the doctor's hospital. I was even able to laugh and joke while the x-rays were done, but the results wiped every vestige of a smile from my face. I'd fractured my calcaneus. It's one of the rarest fractures and so serious that I couldn't have a walking cast. As the doctor proceeded to encase my ankle in about thirty pounds of cement, he told me that I was to be completely immobile for two weeks, moving only when absolutely necessary. The grey ceiling seemed to swallow up my dreams of earning big money. Supporting myself that summer would take all the money I had in the bank.

By the time we reached our boarding house in Capitola, outside of Santa Cruz, I gave the appearance of being resigned to my fate, but as I struggled upstairs to my bed overlooking the beach, I was bitter. Below, mothers watched as their children flirted with waves and the beach looked like one I'd like to explore. But I knew I'd be room-bound for weeks.

Checking out groceries for nine and a half hours a day didn't sound glamorous, but the money would have given me choices at summer's end. Now, it seemed, I had none because going back to Wheaton meant money. I couldn't work in the United States unless I was a student. After my cast came off, I wouldn't have enough money to even leave the U.S.

Being deported from America wasn't a future I'd envisioned.

Sharon and my landlady, however, were not enamoured by my self-pity. Before I knew it, I was enrolled in night classes at the nearby Cabrillo College in Aptos studying philosophy and psychology. They found textbooks for me and my fellow students arranged a transportation roster to get me to class. I'd never received such altruistic kindness from complete strangers such as these secular Americans and I blossomed, becoming far more extroverted than I'd ever been. The classes were great and, during my free time, I doggedly explored the area on a bike, using my good foot for both the up and down pressure on the pedal. All in all, had things been different, financially and otherwise, I would have happily transferred and finished my degree in that area.

By the end of summer, I knew beyond a doubt, that a transfer was an impossibility. Once I had a walking cast, I began working, saving enough money to get me back to Illinois to get my possessions, but leaving me with a paltry sum for emergencies. To further decrease my opportunities, I'd received a letter from the dean warning me that an alumnus in the area had reported me for breaking the pledge. Truth to tell, I had smoked two cigarettes, cut cards with Sharon to see who would do the dishes and, because the students at Cabrillo had thrown a farewell party for me, I'd consumed two glasses of champagne.

By Wheaton's standards, I'd gambled, drunk alcohol and smoked. All three were major no-nos. I felt angry about being reported but not apologetic. When Sharon flew south to visit relatives, I began the long bus trip back to Illinois, planning to explain everything and see what happened.

The drinking, smoking, and gambling had cancelled my scholarship, I found out. It might be reinstated if I confessed my sins and repented during the next chapel. But, how could I? I didn't believe I had sinned, so how could I repent? I had learned two magical words during my time in California. One began with f, the other with y and that's what I said.

I feel no satisfaction in how my American adventure ended. I'd been arrogant and self-righteous again. But I couldn't stomach more hypocrisy. I'd seen more altruism in California than Christian love at Wheaton. My education, room and board there hadn't come tied with strings attached.

I know Wheaton felt that I was ungrateful and, like most divorces, mine from the United States was bitter.

I'll always miss some of my American life. The summer in California, Wheaton basketball games, the generosity of individual people, and playing doubles with my partner and her great backhand. One prof taught me about Søren Kierkegaard, another introduced me to John Donne and George Herbert and it was interesting to learn modern history through an American lens. Those were great experiences and so was another.

I'd fallen in love that summer in California which is why I'll always remember it as golden. Jack was the epitome of dreams – tall, blonde, good-looking and a beach boy. Under his tutelage I learned about the thrills of wooden roller coasters, particularly the one in Santa Cruz, and the joy of long, slow kisses in the moonlight. A cliché now, but something new for me and much to his regret, I managed to preserve my virginity.

Once the decision to leave the United States was final, my optimism reasserted itself because I realized that, while the American experience had led to delusion and much despair, there were other byways in the world to explore. Thanks to the help given by Wheaton's Dean of Women, I knew that one such byway was the true north of Canada. As a British subject, I would be able to work there and make new dreams while I earned money.

And so, with very mixed feelings I boarded a train for the Pacific Northwest. Destination, Vancouver. There were two reasons for this. One, Jack flew for the U.S. Navy and, clever clogs that he was, managed to get himself posted to Whidbey Island in Washington State, about one hundred kilometers south of Vancouver; second, Vancouver was closer to Australia than any other part of Canada.

Jack arranged to meet me at the train station in Everett, Washington and we spent three days (not nights) together. When he showed me Seattle and we toured other parts of Washington, our closeness returned and it was a huge wrench when we said good-bye as I boarded my train bound for the Canadian province of British Columbia. I arrived at the White Rock train station with a little more than $50 and a Leica camera.

At the time, I felt saddened by leaving Jack, yet again, and the unrelenting greyness of the sky

and sand depressed me. I could not imagine spending more time in this northern bastion of the British Commonwealth than I had to. Looking at the grey placid water, I longed for Sydney's golden sand, its rambunctious water, and home.

Everything was still grey when we reached Vancouver an hour later. A taxi driver knew of a good pawnshop where I'd get a good price for my camera and, when I registered at the inexpensive hotel he suggested and told my story, the receptionist pulled out a newspaper and circled several jobs she thought worth applying for. Again, I was struck by the random kindness of strangers.

To my astonished delight, teachers were in short supply. Even in the middle of October, I had my pick of many jobs in rural areas. I had no idea where Nanaimo, Nakusp or Nanoose Bay were, but the receptionist pulled out a map and together we circled all the towns in the ads. Some looked too far away to reach with my limited budget and I didn't want to go too far north. Two winters in Chicago had given me a healthy distaste for frozen water. When she pointed to Campbell River, I knew we'd struck gold. Situated on the eastern side of Vancouver Island, it was renowned for its salmon fishing and I'd always wanted to taste fresh salmon.

I pawned my camera for $100 and phoned the superintendent of schools in Campbell River. He immediately offered me a job teaching a composite grade 2 and 3 class at a school about fifteen kilometers south of the town. All I had to do was go to Victoria, on the southern tip of Vancouver Island, present myself at the Department of Education and apply for a letter giving me permission to teach until my Australian credentials and references arrived. Once I'd done that, he'd wire an advance of $100, and not only organize a bus ticket, but arrange for someone to meet me in Campbell River. He had also rented a waterfront cabin within walking distance of the school and he had my luggage sent up from Vancouver.

This cosseting of a grade 2 and 3 teacher sounds unthinkable nowadays, but in 1963 the teacher shortage was so desperate that good candidates for jobs were treated royally. Struck by his generosity, I willingly accepted the offer. My starting salary was a shocker though — $3000 per annum. It wasn't a princely sum, then or now, and strangely enough it was about the same as I had paid almost three years earlier for my Sydney to Chicago one-way fare.

That year in Maple Bay was marvellous. The school was small with a teaching staff of ten split between seven grades. The principal was British. Nobody had been born in British Columbia so we were all outsiders. The children were eager to learn and their parents were supportive. I knew nothing about Canada then, and for an entire year made lots of mistakes, particularly when teaching geography. For nine months my class dutifully coloured in their maps of Canada, labelling the provinces from west to east as British Columbia, Alberta, Manitoba, Saskatchewan, etc. It was genuine ignorance on my part and never corrected by a colleague or parent. I still see those wrongly identified maps in my nightmares.

As the superintendent promised, the small cabin I rented was about ten meters from the water's edge. Many times I came home from school and walked along the beach, dreaming of Australia, wondering when and if I'd go back. When I finished my walk, I'd frequently pry oysters from the rocks and cook them on the huge wood stove that heated the cabin. The parents frequently took me fishing and once, in the spring, I caught a thirty-four pound salmon.

In many ways, Campbell River was a veritable paradise, but when I was handed a permanent contract in May, I vacillated for days about signing it. Part of me wanted to stay there. I was having a great time and surrounded by friendly people. For almost the first time in my life, I had forgotten about the annoying problem of Christianity and hadn't gone to church for almost a year. However, I craved a large library and intellectual companionship. Gradually, and sadly, I accepted that Campbell River, for all its charms, was nothing more than a stopgap. I resigned and applied to attend summer school, taking English lit and ancient history, at the University of British Columbia. After that, I'd figure out the next step.

When summer school ended, I still hadn't worked things out. While I ached for Australia, I didn't want to go home yet and I began to think about teaching another year in Canada if I could get a job in the Vancouver area. It didn't help my chances that I made this decision on the Friday before the school year commenced. But I'd learned a lesson that previous October and, so, I bought a newspaper, opened it to the teachers wanted section, thinking to have my pick of jobs. To my dismay, very few city jobs were available. The most promising was a grade five position with a specialty in music offered by the Surrey School

District, a large community south of Vancouver and between the Fraser River and the U.S. border.

I was given an immediate interview with the Surrey superintendent. By now, my Australian credentials had arrived; I had my B.C. teaching certificate and glowing references from Campbell River. All I had to worry about was the music aspect of the job, but luck was with me. All it really necessitated was teaching music to a grade seven class for a couple of hours a week. "Oh, I can do that," I assured the superintendent, Earl Marriott. He handed me a contract which I signed immediately, neither of us suspecting that I would be employed by Surrey for more than the next thirty-five years.

At the time, I looked forward to exploring another part of the world. I knew no one in Surrey, or even the larger Vancouver area but, by now, I was a veteran of going into the unknown and surviving.

CHAPTER 11

M AND S

M stands for Masticate, Malapropism and Metamorphosis.

It also stands for Music.

Grosvenor Road Elementary in the Whalley area of the 1960s would be classified today as an inner-city school. Too many students looked forward to low-income jobs, crime, or welfare. The school itself had some comically sexist aspects that reflected the past rather than the mid and late sixties because only men taught grades 6 and 7, and they taught on the upper floor of the main building. Everyone else was in the original building or the ground floor of the new one.

My grade 5 class was on that level but directly across from the library—a blessing in disguise, as it turned out. I wandered in almost immediately and began reading my way through Canada, particularly its history and literature. After a while, Catherine, the librarian greeted me with her selection of books I should read, and she always had another stack waiting for me the next day. We'd talk, and those wide-ranging discussions satisfied a deep need in me. Finally, I'd met a North American who was not afraid of her thoughts, and had questioned her Christian background to almost to same extent as me.

Of course, as I settled more into the school, various teachers kept warning, "Don't get too comfortable. IT hasn't started yet." They referred to the principal's pet project, the segregation by sex of the grade sixes and sevens for P.E. That it involved a complicated blocking of time and much teacher swapping seemed irrelevant. In my case, it meant that while I taught music to the grade sevens, someone else taught art to my class.

But, when I met the grade sevens for the first time, I understood why the job had been vacant until the day before the school year began. I well remember the wariness with which I approached the Grade 7 classroom. I had low expectations and, after ten minutes with the class of forty-three adolescent boys, I had zero.

I was challenged almost immediately by a rough voice from the back. "I'm not gonna sing and you can't make me."

"Yeah," another chorused, "not even if old Fester straps both hands."

Old Fester was the vice principal and the only person in the school who actually seemed to enjoy strapping the students. Most of the boys had survived Fester's punishments many times and didn't fear him. So, "You can't make me" became a constant refrain during the first couple of classes. I felt as if I were in an old-west movie. Something like *Gunfight at the O.K. Corral* with the class waiting to see if I'd blink.

Unfortunately, the principal, Mr. Reimer, blinked first. One day, after another unproductive class, he asked to see me at lunchtime. "Oooh," the class jeered in mock horror. Mr. Reimer had firm ideas about my handling of the boys. "You're too nice," he pronounced with administrative loftiness. "You have to show them who's boss."

That wasn't the problem, I thought. They already knew who was boss—themselves, and not me nor anyone else in the school. They waited for three o'clock with ill-disguised urgency. Then, most escaped to their various nefarious enterprises. But Mr.

Reimer seemed not to understand this and called in the district music specialist who handed out black Bakelite recorders to the class.

Since I'd first seen him, Joe, the leader of the class who always sat in the back row, had terrified me. His black leather jacket caused constant speculation in the staff room with the majority of teachers suspecting that he'd stolen it. Naturally, he'd been the first to shave and proudly showed off new razor-nicks each day. He was everyone's personification of the person they least wanted to meet in a dark alley on a rainy night.

He stared at his recorder as though it was a pile of dung. "I'm not playing this and you can't make me."

The specialist just smiled and started playing "Greensleeves". Joe stared. Few people ignored him. He got out of his desk slowly and walked to the front desk. "I'm not gonna play this," he repeated as he put the recorder onto the desk.

The specialist kept playing and, grinning hugely, some of the boys tried to harmonize with him and, for several long seconds the keening of banshees filled the room.

It was so horrible that I felt nothing but relief when Joe snapped his fingers and ended all thoughts of musical cooperation. "We're not playing," he announced as he raised his hands and smashed his recorder against the desk. Immediately, as if they were choreographed, the forty-two other boys stood and copied him, right down to his sneer. Particles of black Bakelite spewed throughout the room while some of the smaller boys kept smashing away, not quite strong enough to break their recorders with one blow.

I don't know how much money those instruments represented. Obviously it was enough to make the specialist blanch. He looked at me but I was of no help whatsoever. I'd always wanted to smash plastic recorders into bits because I hated their sound. Finally, with something resembling a howl, he fled the room.

The principal burst through with the punishment record book and the strap with him. He didn't bother to ascertain facts or even ask me what had happened. He simply took off his jacket, rolled up his sleeves and asked, "Now then, who shall I start with?"

Joe had guts. "Me," he answered immediately, walking to the front. He snapped his fingers and his cohorts began lining up behind him. Mr. Reimer strapped him six times on each hand, dutifully recorded the fact in the punishment book and asked me to sign as the witness. Stomach-roiling, I obeyed but Joe winked me as he walked by. "Don't worry, miss," he whispered. "His arm will give out after Billy. He can only do five or six at a time and then he's had enough. Now, old Fester, he'd finish the lot of us."

Joe was right. Suddenly after strapping the sixth boy, Mr. Reimer beckoned me over. "I've just remembered an appointment at the board office. You carry on here and we'll talk about this after school." Then he faced the boys who were now snickering again. "Behave yourself. This class has detention every day for the next three weeks and if that doesn't teach you a lesson I'll make it for three months."

I angrily watched him scuttle away. I knew full well who'd be supervising the detentions. Me. I felt put upon. I'd hadn't asked for a specialist to teach recorder playing. Shell-shocked and fuming, I wondered what to do with the bits of recorders that still littered the room but Joe had some surprises up his sleeves. He walked to the piano, flexed his fingers and sat down and, for the first time in my life, I understood raw power.

Joe had me and that class totally in his control. He grinned while he played an appalling bad version of "Chopsticks." His friends laughed and pounded their desks. But he quietened them and made me sit with surprise when he segued into a medley of Fred

Astaire and Ginger Rogers songs from the thirties. Finally, he began playing the current Beatle hit, "Can't Buy Me Love" and his friends sang along. There was an infectious joy in his music. Everyone responded to it – the class with smiles and me with awe, for he had more musical ability in his little fingers than I had in my entire body.

"He's good, eh," one of the boys closest to me commented, though "good" didn't begin to describe Joe's ability.

"He plays at the pub, Monday through Thursday. They get a real band for Fridays and Saturdays," another told me.

Joe scowled. I couldn't tell whether he was annoyed by the fact that his illegal employment was being talked about, or if his scowl was directed towards the pub's management who hired "real" musicians for the weekend, money-making crowds. But he continued playing and while my feet began tapping I realised a couple of things. First, and most important in this context, I had just solved my problem of what to do with the grade seven class. All I had to do was convince Joe to teach it.

The second was more fundamental. I'd known that few students, if any, hoped to go to university. By now that seemed a lost cause for me and somewhat irrelevant. Nobody seemed to understand my love of learning.

Hope that had brought me this far. Joe obviously had his own hopes. I'd been privileged to see one of them and I'd long since learned that dreams come in all shapes and sizes. Joe's passion for music shone through his depressing environment and the stereotype he'd been fitted into. He looked like a grade seven hoodlum and was treated as such while I personified a prissy, elementary teacher. Our dreams, though, made us greater than those images.

Suddenly, I had a mission. I wanted to unlock the hopes of every student in that school to show them that life did not have to be prescribed. I wanted them to know that no matter how difficult their economic circumstances might be that, if they dreamed, they could do anything.

For the remainder of that term, I stayed late at school, marking, working on the next day's lessons and fulfilling a series of *quid pro quos* I owed Joe. After much negotiation, he had condescended to help with the music classes but there were big "ifs." I had to play goalie for his rag-tag soccer team two afternoons a week. It said a lot for his influence that nothing was said about having a girl in goal – much less a teacher one at that.

As the days became impossibly short and the rainy season arrived, the field became a gravelly quagmire. The fact that I was female and a teacher didn't seem to matter much to the boys for I was shown no quarter. I learned to give none, frequently going home bruised, muddy and bloody. At the onset of winter, we moved the game indoors, played with a deflated ball and a set of made-up rules.

Another *quid pro quo* involved me learning "honky-tonk" from Joe. In return the class listened, with varying degrees of disinterest to some of the greater pieces of classical music. I felt we were finally getting our act together when Joe suddenly disappeared from the school. It took a couple of decades before I found out why, but that's a story for another day.

Although everyone missed him, my credentials were too firmly established by this time for the class to regress and eventually we did some outrageous things. Outrageous enough that a choir formed from those same boys came second at the Vancouver Kiwanis Eisteddfod's school competition, and they sang at some local churches' evening services with wide grins on their faces.

S stands for Sagacious, Serendipity and Stoic.

It also stands for Sports.

The years at that school, and they became years as thoughts of going home became increasingly rare, were different from anything else I had ever experienced. I made good money at only one job and, for almost the first time in my life, had lots of spare time. Too much really. I continued to stay late at school, developing my friendship with Catherine, talking with students and playing goal for them a couple of afternoons every week.

Soon I realised there were real differences in terms of prospects facing male and female athletes in Whalley. The local high schools usually fielded one team per sport per gender, meaning that very few students ever played for their school. Boys were fortunate in that they could play competitively outside the school environment on soccer and hockey teams. There was nothing equivalent for girls.

As I slowly assimilated this, I began thinking that I could start a kind of club programme along the lines of those I'd grown up with. But what could they compete in? There was no pool in the area so my swimming experience was useless. Basketball, my North American love, was not played in elementary schools. Somewhat reluctantly, I eventually concluded that volleyball offered the best chance of success.

There were several reasons for this. I had athletes with nothing but time on their hands and access to an empty gym. The school had all the necessary equipment as well as boxes of unused uniforms. There was only one problem, and it was huge. Since I'd never played the game, I knew next to nothing about it. There were plenty of rulebooks, however, and, once I'd broached the idea to the girls, tremendous enthusiasm. I attended some clinics where I learnt the basics and began a volleyball club in which coach and players were almost equally ignorant.

If I had known how this grand idea would end, I like to think I would have gone ahead anyway. I still had no idea of my own limits, much less what kind of person I was. Volleyball would give some answers – but at a tremendous cost.

At first, everything about the volleyball club seemed futile. Some girls quit. The remaining ones worked diligently and soon had classic, basic skills. But, we lost every game. The reasons weren't complex. Surrey schools, at the time, used a badminton court for their volleyball games and teams consisted of nine players. It was a confusing bastardization of the game.

Rotations bordered on the whimsical with new patterns created weekly and the host school setting its own rules. The resulting maze of players did not prevent the ball landing on the floor with alarming frequency. As well, most players preferred to throw the ball at opponents, or even each other, rather than use acceptable methods. As our skill level rose, frustration set in. What was the use of learning techniques when the unskilled teams regularly beat us?

We decided to ignore Surrey's rules and began practising on regulation courts and playing against clubs and high school teams. Soon we became unbeatable, but success led to different frustrations. Fewer and fewer local teams would play us and our excellence was deeply loathed. Mercifully the season came to an end. One day, as I was pondering whether to dissolve the club or not, one of the girls rushed into my classroom.

"My dad's found a softball league we can play in," she announced, waving a flyer.

Softball? That was a game I knew. Its rules weren't a mystery and I remembered coaching techniques from my playing days at Wheaton. Enthusiastically I scanned the flyer, phoned the contact number and went to an information meeting. It was daunting. Everyone knew everybody else and when I asked if my school could join the league there was much discussion.

Most thought we wouldn't be good enough. Others objected to

our lack of a home field. We wouldn't be able to host any games at the school because its grounds were gravel. Only after I'd promised to find some place with grass for home games were we accepted. When the meeting broke up I could see the other coaches, the ones who had all-stars on their teams, salivating at the thought of automatic wins when they played this team of rookie players and rookie coach.

I called a parents' meeting and outlined the situation. I could beg used bases and bats from the school and I'd unearthed a set of flannel baseball uniforms in its basement. But, they would have to provide regulation socks and, of course, gloves. The parents didn't bat an eye. Thrilled by their girls' eagerness to play, they went on their own expeditions and when I called the first practice the gloves were a pictorial history of the game.

A few players had brand new gloves and some had inherited their brothers' hand-me downs. One belonged to a grandmother who had played professional baseball during World War II and others should have been in a softball museum. My first job was teaching the girls how to catch with this array of gloves. Unexpectedly, one father came to practices after work and coached throwing drills, and, to my great delight, unearthed two natural pitchers in the group. One was extremely fast but wild and untrained; the other was slower but deadly accurate.

When our first game started, we were extremely nervous. As fate or a malicious scheduler decreed, we opened against the previous year's champion. They, of course, were dressed in the latest uniforms while we wore our discards from goodness knows when. The results were predictable and, of course, a Hollywood scenario. Our pitchers were wild; no one could catch and throws either ended up in the stratosphere or in the stands. After much snickering, the umpire called the game as soon as she could, invoking the mercy rule.

I thought the girls would be downcast when we met for practice the following day. But they had learned one important fact from volleyball that transferred to softball. They believed they would win if they worked hard, and knew they had lost the game because of their jitters. So, with a mixture of determination and grit, we began practising again and our situation unfolded like a script that no director would have bought. We won our next game in the first inning, outscoring our opponents by fifteen runs. After our fifth game, the league knew it had made a mistake when it had admitted us. Although none of the girls had played softball before, they were the fittest athletes in the league. More than that, except for the first game, their belief in their ability to win was palpable.

The league and my coaching colleagues thought the situation untenable. They called a special meeting to discuss their perceived problem. I was not invited. The following day we had no sooner started practice than the president arrived. She called the girls in to announce that she'd like to award them a trophy.

The first place award, no less. The other coaches had solved their problem by forfeiting all future games to us. Although we had won first place, the league also declared us ineligible for play-off games. The girls who had worked so hard were devastated. Their parents rallied round, however, and for the remainder of the season we played exhibition games against other leagues in the Vancouver area until summer came and the team disbanded.

There are many prices for excellence. The one that is talked about least is isolation, because most people today only see the glory that excellence usually brings. These young girls in grades four through six, though, had just learned one of life's harder lessons, courtesy of that softball league.

When school began the following fall, so did the volleyball club. It and teaching dominated my life. I had been bitterly hurt by the league's decision, for I'd never associated with people who took athletic success so seriously, not even in Australia.

Sport, to this point, had been enjoyable. As a player, I had been knocked around, dirtied and physically hurt in various games. That I accepted and bore no ill will. I enjoyed playing and I loved watching athletes with extraordinary elegance and grace in any sport. The decision to kick a team of young girls out of a league smacked of meanness and I couldn't understand it. Where had sportsmanship gone? Whatever the reason for that league's decision, it soiled our achievements. But, if that was to be the price demanded for excellence in Canada, so be it. Without discussion, we reached consensus: we would become the absolute best and never apologize for it.

With half the team small enough to walk under a volleyball net, we were too small to implement any real offence. We could inflict damage only through deep jump volleys. On the other hand, our defence was immaculate and with the ability to always put the ball back into play, teams had to work very hard to beat us. Soon, we began winning senior B tournaments and travelling throughout the Pacific Northwest.

As word of our successes spread throughout the North American volleyball world, clubs throughout British Columbia and the three Pacific states began inviting us to give clinics. During one extraordinary period, I was flown to Los Angeles, with a few of the team, for thirteen consecutive weekends and I knew that being part of the volleyball club had radically changed the girls. Having tasted success and seen a wider world, they looked to a future where they would be participants. Loitering on street corners afternoons and weekends was forever out of the question for them.

My ideas about the future changed as well. I quickly grew used to acclaim and I loved our international successes. I'd always hoped to be able to wear a green blazer with the Australian cost of arms emblazoned on its top pocket. Now, I represented Canada, not my own native land. It felt strange to stand on podiums as the maple leaf climbed flagpoles and "O Canada" was respectfully played. But I also felt tremendous pride. Pride, both in the club's accomplishments, and in the country I was slowly learning to love.

CHAPTER 12

V AND P

V stands for *Vacuous, Vainglorious and Vie.*

It also stands for Volleyball.

Pride goes before falls. Mine certainly came a cropper one night in Los Angeles.

I learnt a lot about love and sex during my many visits to Los Angeles. On one level, it was everywhere in a city notorious for the words "casting couch." Aspiring actors still believed that scouts frequented bars and restaurants and dressed accordingly. Perhaps it was inevitable that I should meet Pietro in that city.

Pietro was a man who loved women, all women. He didn't care about their age, shape or size. I have only ever met another man like Pietro and I didn't succumb to the temptation to share Eddie's bed either. I can't claim that I made those decisions on the basis of virtue. Fear drove my refusals for I'd suddenly understood something C.S. Lewis had written. His attempts to define "joy" had puzzled me because he doubted that "anyone who has tasted it would ever ... exchange it for all the pleasures in the world." Somehow, I knew that a night with Pietro or Eddie would be so exquisite that I'd spend the rest of my life trying to find it again and pining for more. In either case, sex would enslave me.

Neither of them were handsome, overtly sexy or even great clotheshorses. They had none of the facile charm that is usually associated with the world's great lovers and Hollywood would never have cast either as a leading man. Their attraction came from intangibles – from their worship of all women; fat, middle-aged, old-aged, young, nubile, whatever. Sex wasn't necessarily the culmination of their worship. Obviously, they preferred it, but conversation also made them happy and, of course, they made every female feel infinitely desirable.

It was perhaps fated that one of the more farcical episodes of my love life should happen there as well months later.

Our club had been invited to represent Canada at a major tournament in California and we were allowed one "ringer," that is, a star player from another team. With her coach's blessing, I selected a girl who would go on to represent Canada for years. A previous commitment prevented her from travelling with us and we promised to meet her scheduled flight, never suspecting a problem. Her flight arrived, but no player. I panicked, and then noticed that another plane from Vancouver was scheduled to arrive at a different gate within minutes. Thinking she must have changed flights, I ran through the airport to meet that arrival. Again, I waited. Again, no player. Desperate now, I phoned Vancouver only to find that her coach had indeed checked her onto the original flight. Thoughts of kidnapping surfaced immediately. I wondered though how a teenage girl could be abducted from a plane in flight and where should I go for help.

At that time, my team and I were being recruited by an organization that believed in spreading Christianity through athletes. Why we qualified I never knew, but given our finances I was always willing to consider potential sponsors. Consequently, on our previous visit to Los Angeles, I had willingly been wined and dined by a tremendously attractive man. He was wealthy and the owner of an expanding technology business with NASA as a client. I remembered him and thought he'd have contacts or, at least, know what to do. I pulled his card from my wallet and phoned.

He was delighted to hear from me. Yes, he knew I was coming to Los Angeles and had hoped to take me out the following night. And yes, he did have contacts he could use. He'd phone them immediately, change his clothes, and be at the airport within the half hour. I waited in agony, thoughts of having to explain the girl's disappearance to her parents making my stomach roll. But Jerry arrived with good news. She had left her original flight in Seattle because she'd been having a good time with a young sailor. The Seattle police had found her, and put her on a plane that was arriving momentarily. Once I saw her walk through the gate I almost collapsed with relief. Jerry drove us to her billets' home then turned to me with a grin, "Let's eat."

The restaurant he chose was intimate, our table overlooked the Pacific and the food was delicious. Jerry was a brilliant conversationalist and by the time we finished dessert I'd relaxed. "Let's go back to my place," he suggested. "I've something to show you."

I suppose every woman has heard variations on the old "Let me show you my etchings" theme and I don't know why I didn't clue in. Maybe I was just too relieved to suspect anything. In any case, I willingly let him drive me to his home and accepted a liqueur before I asked what he had wanted me to see. "Later," he replied enigmatically.

Later turned out to be sooner because when I went to answer nature's call, I used his bathroom rather than the guest one. As I washed my hands, his bath caught my eye. It was humungous, easily the first Olympic size bath that I'd ever seen in a private house. I'm sure it could have accommodated four or five at the same time. Well, almost. But, that wasn't the real shock. There had been a cloying aroma in the bathroom, which I hadn't bothered to identify. Now, looking at the bath, I realised it was two-thirds full of gardenias.

"Why is your bathtub full of flowers?" I asked casually, walking back to Jerry.

"They're for you."

I stared at him. "For me? What am I supposed to do with them?"

He laughed. "Nothing. I'll do all the work, I promise. I always make love the first time on a bed on gardenias."

Nausea warred with amusement. For a while. Then I laughed. "Haven't you seen my leg?" In emphasis, I pushed my right leg forward. I'd broken it at practice a couple of nights earlier and the cast was still pristine white. "I'd smash those flowers and you into smithereens in seconds. Come on, Jerry, don't give me a hard time. Just take me home."

His atmosphere ruined, he sullenly drove me to my hotel. I have no idea how much money he'd spent on those flowers, or even if he'd ever get their scent out of his bathroom. But then, he was probably addicted to it. Needless to say, we received no funding from the Christian athletes' association. In fact, I never heard from it or Jerry again. Every since that night, though, I've never looked at a gardenia without smirking or wondering exactly how it would feel to make love in a bath tub full of gardenias.

P stands for Portentous, Polarize, Pusillanimous.

It also stands for Possibilities.

Those incidents aside, the latter part of the 1960s was a magical time in my life. I'd seen how volleyball changed the lives of the girls in the club. Now I began thinking that if I could inspire my classes to dream as well, the results would be incalculable. I had never felt this elixir of imagination, creativity, and wonder before and, until quite recently, since. Outside the volleyball arena, my mind swirled with questions about the process of learning.

I taught my classes with an anachronistic amalgam of Australian and Canadian methodology. It was effective beyond doubt. The district insisted on standardized testing in each grade and my classes' scores not only improved year by year, but skyrocketed. The reasons puzzled me until I realized how much time I spent trying to make my students think logically rather than teaching them set skills.

If children at age five or six could be taught to write sentences and poems in French, an alien tongue, was it possible to teach musical notation in the same way? What would happen if we had immersion classes for five and six year-olds in music? Would we produce competent composers and the occasional child with Mozart-like magic?

My supervisor was fascinated by some of my ideas and methods and, after a while, regularly took me for a cup of coffee on Monday afternoons. Sometimes she brought Earl Marriott, Surrey's superintendent of schools, along with her and we'd debate educational theories and ideas.

Today, we have walled our superintendents and supervisors behind the crenellated battlements of paper and assistants for all kinds of interaction. New teachers with imaginations and curiosity have no chance of casual interaction or brainstorming with Mr. Marriott's counterparts and I wonder if education is the better for it. In the late 1960s, though, it was just fun to have thrilling conversations.

Maybe, it was because of these discussions, and certainly because of the volleyball experiences, that my dreams became larger and more extravagant. If I could show my classes the world, would their dreams also expand?

One day I had a truly shocking idea. Each class, at the time, was allowed one field trip a year. Most teachers took their classes to the Hudson's Bay fort in Langley or the fish canneries in Steveston. Some saved their trip for a visit to the beaches during the last week of school. I thought, why not make my one trip memorable? Why not take my entire class to California so that it could interact with a different people and values? Imagine how much interest the class would then have in geography and U.S. history?

I broached the idea with Mr. Marriott who neither approved nor disapproved. In retrospect, I think this was because he doubted that I would implement such a project. Maybe, as well, he didn't want to dampen my creativity. As usual, I took non-reaction for encouragement and began seriously thinking about the trip, breaking it down into components.

The first, and most vital item on the long list was somehow wrangling an invitation from a Californian school for a week-long visit. I used every volleyball contact I had and sent off wonderful letters outlining the educational benefits for both potential sponsors and us. Shortly after the letters went out, I received an enthusiastic response from a grade five teacher in Walnut Creek, east of San Francisco. She had spoken with both her principal and superintendent of the Mt. Diablo school district. Her class and school would be pleased to sponsor us for a week in late April.

When I announced my news to Mr. Marriott on a coffee Monday, he seemed numb. As did the parents, because they had never believed in the probability of the trip. At a hurriedly called meeting, the questions flew thick and fast. How could they afford it? How could they know the billeting families weren't criminals? I offered reassurance on the latter question by showing colour photographs of the school and the homes in the area. Some mothers volunteered to come along as chaperones and this helped allay legitimate parental concerns. Support also came from Gail O'Hern, the father of two girls in the volleyball club.

He was tall, tough, and brooked no nonsense. In his deep voice, he told the meeting of his skepticism when his daughters had mentioned they'd been asked to teach volleyball in Los Angeles, and that their trip would cost hardly anything at all. His protective sense had gone into overdrive. His life had proved that something too good to be true usually wasn't. But, he told the crowd, his daughters had now been to Los Angeles several times, been treated to Disneyland and regularly played in less distant cities such as Seattle and Portland. Each time he'd wondered how he could afford such trips and each time they'd been free or subsidised by host clubs.

"Added to that," he summed up in a voice that was about two octaves below middle C, "Miss Boissery has always donated her honorariums to help keep the costs down and if my kids came home one night and said they'd been invited to Australia, I'd start getting them passports and get myself a second job the next day. That's how much faith I have. I say we'd better start saving now. If Miss Boissery says she can make this trip happen, she will."

The now-eager parents voted their approval and the hard work began immediately – setting up schedules, dividing tasks, doing the necessary paperwork that the trip required. I phoned Greyhound and asked the price of a child's return fare to San Francisco. It was about fifty dollars, a manageable amount even for the poorest student, when subsidies from fundraisers were factored in. Added to that would be the cost of a gift for the billeting family and medical and other insurance.

We set up a bank account and designated Mondays as the deposit day. The class chose two students as treasurers (without signing authority) and almost everyone started saving. Math now had a real purpose as the class kept track of its money and learnt about interest. In January, just as we finalized most of the official paperwork, the transportation committee reported a huge problem. It could not see a way of getting the class and chaperones to San Francisco by chartered bus within my cost estimate. After contacting every possible transportation company, including Greyhound, it suggested we double the proposed price. Even Greyhound's quotation had come in at almost twice its scheduled fare. Profoundly disturbed, I called a meeting for the parents to discuss the situation.

I spent that week in needless worry for when the committee read its report to the parents, Gail O'Hern jumped to his feet. He'd heard about the problem and had taken a day off work. He'd spent it at the Greyhound bus stop, counting the numbers of passengers on San Francisco-bound buses. As each bus had left with only a handful of passengers, his solution was simple. Everyone should just show up at the main station. The worst that could happen was that a small group might have to travel on a different bus. If half the chaperones went with that group, though, he couldn't see a problem.

And that, essentially, was what we did. The school in Walnut Creek assured us it would look after any transportation needs once we reached the San Francisco Bay area, even to the point of picking us up in Oakland. Armed with that assurance, Gail spoke to Greyhound. Faced with the threat of a busload of thirty-five chattering, excited students disturbing its regular passengers on a long trip, it bit the bullet and scheduled an extra bus that would even deliver us to the elementary school in Walnut Creek.

It's hard to evaluate the end results of that trip. My most vivid memory is the day we went to San Francisco. I don't think I'll ever forget the faces of my students riding cable cars and shrieking delight. I can also remember how solemn they became when the Mt. Diablo school bus drove into the Haight-Ashbury intersection and how they stared at the young flower people with various degrees of fascination. Newspapers had suddenly come to life.

But they also learned about reality. Most of the flower children we saw were dirty. Some slept on sidewalks and few smiled, much less danced with joy.

Some students later broke out of the low-income syndrome which had so depressed me, going to university and becoming professionals. I don't know if they would have done it otherwise, or what they really received in benefits from that field trip beside fun, wonder and a more comprehensive outlook on the world. And if that's all there was, it wasn't a bad return on my ideas and the work of all the adults involved to bring the trip about.

CHAPTER 13

J AND D

J stands for *Jabberwocky, Jacarandas and Jeans.*

It also stands for Japan.

In 1969 Joe Namath guaranteed that the New York Jets would win the Super Bowl. When he made good on this promise, I won $500 on a $10 bet. I wasn't being extraordinarily prescient. Just the previous night my volleyball team of elementary players had won the University of British Columbia tournament competing against senior clubs and university teams from Canada and the U.S. When one of the American coaches offered fifty to one odds against the Jets, I thought if we could win, surely Broadway Joe could as well.

By this time, we were accustomed to beating teams of older women. We won because we frustrated our opposition. When we lined up before the game, every team felt superior when they saw fourth-grader Kelly O'Hern, for example, still well under five feet tall. Her sister Sherri, our tallest player at five feet seven, inevitably played against a six-foot woman. We started every game with the ultimate advantage – being underestimated. Within a game's first five minutes, opponents began to realise that we would make few mistakes and soon they came to believe that we would retrieve almost every spike or hard serve. Few coaches improvise in championships. They use the stratagems that have proved successful. Time after time, teams continued to set blocks for non-existent hits, and that opened up the court for easy jump volleys. We soon noticed that once a team let its guard down after seeing us line up, it rarely regained its edge and with the imminent possibility of being beaten by an elementary school team looming, played with a ferocious wildness.

That UBC tournament win had tremendous implications for us. If we'd been news before, we now became big news. Columnists, such as Vancouver's respected Jim Taylor, wrote about us and we even received mention in that athletic bible of America, *Sports Illustrated*. By March 1969, we were virtually unbeatable and had become widely known in volleyball circles throughout the province and the Pacific states. It should not have been surprising then that when we met for practice in the fall of 1969 everything changed. For the first time, players from various areas of the greater Vancouver area clamoured to join the club.

No longer would it be just the girls I taught and worked with. While the level of athletes became higher, the problems expanded exponentially as we went from one to three teams. Factions appeared and arguments fractured our small community. Soon, everything split apart. The nucleus of the original group and I walked away and formed a new club. With our ambitions in mind, we called it the British Columbia Olympics – BCO for short. The split bothered me. I hadn't planned on acrimony when I'd worked the long hours, but I hoped that the new club would work out.

I decided we had to face better competition within the age group of the girls. The question was where to find it. We were the cutting edge in North America. In our games against American high schools and clubs, we suffered precious few losses, so potential competition had to come from somewhere else. Cuba and Japan were the leading powers in women's volleyball. It made sense that the sooner we played their top juniors, the more we'd develop. I tried to inveigle a Cuban or Japanese club into entering an exchange programme with us in 1970 and, without

any type of commitment from either country, called a parents'
meeting and told them to start saving and fundraising.

It really was a grandiose plan and denounced immediately by
some as being exactly that. But, I really couldn't see this dream
not eventuating. Some parents made a list of the top companies
in Canada and began soliciting donations. We banked all
honoraria in a special travelling fund but, after a few months, it
seemed hopeless.

I had no idea of international volleyball protocol, much less
politics, and quickly ran afoul of both. Eventually, the Canadian
Volleyball Association decided to sanction any visit we might
arrange and with that hurdle overcome, its Japanese counterpart
made a truly magnificent offer—a newspaper chain would
sponsor a six-week tour of the island of Honshu. We would play
against all-star squads from various prefectures as well as a team
representing Tokyo.

This galvanized us. We had bottle drives every week and sold
zillions upon zillions of chocolate boxes. The more businesslike
parents regrouped and approached companies again –
promoting the club, our long-range plans and, of course, the
trip to Japan. Anything that would help raise funds for the girls'
airfare was welcome. Through a ruthless use of acquaintances, I
attempted to wring blood out of dry stones, or more accurately,
money from politicians. The ambitious mayor of Surrey, William
VanderZalm was polite, promised much, delivered $500 and
provided entry into the murky world of provincial politics.

Soon I was invited to various cocktail parties and given chances
to make low-key pitches for money over martinis. I could have
slept my way to a couple of thousand dollars but I decided the
club wasn't that desperate. Eventually, through the auspices of
a marvellous cabinet member, the Hon. Grace McCarthy, the
province gave a donation. After the 1968 Olympic Gold medalist,
Nancy Greene recommended us, BC Tel became our biggest

sponsor and, seeing the money begin to trickle in, mothers selected bolts of cloth for dresses and uniforms.

As the days and weeks went by, more and more information crossed the Pacific. For example, I had to send a sample diet for the team. Finally, with only ten days to go, a letter arrived informing us that we'd be playing with a smaller ball, and a net four and a half inches lower than North American ones. The lower net meant that my team needed to spike and block – skills that couldn't be taught in days. But the ball? Nobody I asked had seen one so I tried to revamp the offence as best I could. Even with the lower net, though, some girls still were too small to be effective offensively.

With that nagging worry we left Canada. Preoccupied with the intense fundraising, the new offence, getting my own clothes and money together, I hadn't paid much attention to the details of the trip. Only after we reached Tokyo, did I begin to understand its importance to the Japanese.

We were met at the airport by a plethora of officials, reporters and photographers, driven in an air-conditioned bus to our first-class hotel and given an itinerary for the next day. We met the interpreter who would stay with us for most of the trip, and our first opponents, a Tokyo all-star team. We were too excited to take it all in and I dearly wish, in retrospect, that I'd been older and more experienced. But then, in all probability, I would never have had the temerity to hope for the trip to happen.

I see those six weeks now as being bittersweet, something similar to my Wheaton experience, because even when something seemed familiar there was always the unpredictable. Like our first breakfast. When I'd sent our meal plans across, I'd thought in North American terms and suggested eggs for breakfast. I didn't expect that they'd be scrambled or fried the night before, then served ice-cold the following morning.

The following day we travelled to Tatsuno City for our first match against a Tokyo all-star team. At a luncheon hosted by the local Rotary Club we listened to many interpreted speeches, cheering up once the food began arriving.

The first course, a cold corn soup, raised some eyebrows because we'd never seen such but, we were so damned hungry, it didn't matter. A hearty pasta dish followed and we began to feel well and truly sated. Then, came fresh trout that few managed to eat. There was a short interval and finger bowls were passed around. We began thinking of the game we'd play, nervously wondering whether our skills would hold up and if we'd be able to handle the small ball. Then the servers entered the room again, this time with the main course. Steak. I remember that we were looked at each other with incredulity and horror, reacting as one, not coach and team. No matter our age, whether nine, twelve, fourteen or thirty, we had the same question. How on earth would we manage to eat it? We knew steak was a luxury. We also knew that we'd have to give every appearance of savouring it.

The girls looked to me, mute appeals in their eyes. I didn't know what to do. I'd barely managed to eat a quarter of my trout. Suddenly, and in the hope that our digestive systems could work overtime to create space in our stomachs, I stood and gave an impromptu speech, thanking our hosts, our sponsors, ourselves, our country. When I looked around the room, I saw girls slipping morsels of meat into their handkerchiefs but saw no sign of our interpreter. She must have slipped out and, as no one else had spoken a word of English to us, I realised no one other than the team would have any idea of what I said. So, with a quick breath, I began reciting the long narrative poem "John Gilpin" in an impromptu filibuster until I literally ran out of verbiage. By that time someone had managed to locate the interpreter and having missed this bravura performance she looked to me for guidance.

"Just tell them how very thankful we are," I suggested and sat down gracefully as the team giggled. Still, most of the steak had disappeared and by the time someone responded to the interpreted thanks, our plates were respectably empty.

An hour later, we warmed up desultorily – too full to do much else. When we won the first game, by twelve points, we looked at each other. Some of the team were elated, but the experienced players knew it had been too easy. We'd played with an unfamiliar ball, the low net and over-full stomachs. Where was the fierce opposition we'd expected? We went on to win the match easily. Much too easily. We'd surprised everyone. The Japanese officials had expected too little from us and they'd not make the same mistake again. Our last match, five weeks later, would also be against a team calling itself the Tokyo All-Stars. Not one player from the Tatsuno City group was on it.

Overall, the tour was extraordinary. We had a reception at the Canadian embassy, were honoured guests at Expo '70, and visited cities from one end of the island to the other. We rode in the bullet train past Mount Fujiyama, bought frozen oranges as snacks and were weaned gradually from North American food. Our lodging varied from first class hotels, to luxury houses, factory dorms and rural hostels. Gyms everywhere were crowded, even for our practice sessions. A large group of reporters and photographers travelled with us. The girls became celebrities, with two or three receiving offers of marriage. Organizations and individuals showered gifts on us. At the end of every match, there was a line-up of people seeking autographs. Our biggest audience was more than ten million when we played in the Tokyo Olympic stadium on Japanese national television.

Even that, though, was bittersweet. The night beforehand, at the inevitable reception, one of Japan's top shoe manufacturers presented both teams with new shoes especially for the match. Back in the hotel, the girls tried them on. Nobody had seen such beautiful shoes, so we decided to wear them the next day.

As soon as we began warming up, we had trouble. The shoes simply would not grip the floor. Every time a player ran, she slipped. Our opponents, wearing identical-looking shoes, did not have the same problems and as I watched them, I rationalized that ours would be solved as soon as we became used to the floor. Once the match started, everything would be fine. However, as soon as we began playing in that packed stadium and before the millions on TV, matters worsened. Without traction, the girls could not set their feet or run confidently. Within seconds, the Tokyo team had a huge lead. I called a time out.

Some girls, knowing they were under-achieving, were in tears and, as much to take their minds from their mistakes as to deal with the footwear problem, I ordered them to take off the shoes.

"But we've left our others at the hotel," they protested.

"Doesn't matter. If you're slipping, go barefoot."

Hurriedly, they stripped off their socks and shoes and went back on court. The opposing coach was incensed, screaming that we were breaking some rule until the referee told him we were legal. His tantrum gave us sufficient time to regroup and once play recommenced we fought for every point with a ferocity the Japanese hadn't seen from us.

After we'd lost the first game, the shoe manufacturer's representative suddenly appeared with different shoes. We stood, bowed our thanks and the players looked to me for guidance. "Try them," I shrugged. "You can always them off if they don't work." After a few moments, it was obvious to everyone that the shoe problem had been solved. We still lost the match but that first game apart, we'd given a good account of ourselves and made no excuses for the loss.

I've thought about that incident for years. Was it an innocent mistake or a ploy for the opposition to win? No Japanese official could have imagined that I'd order my team to play in bare feet on national television. Such a scenario seems so far-fetched, even ludicrous, to anyone who hasn't been in a similar situation, but I never forgot the softball incident that taught me the lengths some will go in order to win.

We faced another ultra-competitive situation towards the end of the tour—an all-star squad representing one of the larger prefectures close to Tokyo. We were told beforehand that we would lose and I shrugged at the time.

Why not? We were overtired, the players were getting homesick and we needed to get not just our second wind, but our ninth or tenth. There was the usual reception beforehand and more speeches before the game. I remember feeling exceptionally onion-eyed when the anthems were played.

For some obscure reason, maybe a reaction to being told that we'd lose, I changed our rotation just before the first game. The game started quickly with neither team getting an advantage. Strangely enough, my stratagem didn't work. The opposition "broke" Sherri, my best player's serve time after time and eventually won that game with relative ease. Embarrassed, we fought back and just as easily captured the second. In the changeover, I thought that the third, deciding game might be sheer hell. We were playing on the fumes of pride; our more rested opponents faced derision if they lost. I think it took maybe ten or fifteen minutes before the first point was even scored because, in those days, points were only scored when you won on your serve. When Sherri rotated to the service position, she looked at me.

"Number seven," I signalled.

Sherri obeyed. Five serves, five mishits by number seven. Not surprisingly the opposing coach called a time-out. I had nothing to say and so we sat, looking while he screamed, ranted and bellowed. We saw number seven raise her hand, then the coach hit her in the face as hard as he could, like a karate expert breaking bricks.

"What should I do?" Sherri asked in the appalled silence.

"What do you think? Keep doing what you're doing," I replied.

After the teams returned to the floor, she took the ball and resumed pounding it at number seven. Again, she scored five quick points and again the coach called a time-out. This time we watched, shuddering, when we saw number seven raise her hand, expecting the karate chop to her face. Instead, he made her stand apart and then kicked her in the stomach several times.

My team turned its attention back to me when Sherri said, "I don't want to serve to her any more."

I shook my head. "No, I wouldn't expect you to."

"What should I do?"

"Who's their best player?" There was some discussion but everyone soon agreed on one person. "Then, let's serve to her. Let's see what he does with that."

Sherri's serve was beautifully returned by that player and her team won the point and, only after a monumental dogfight did we win the match. Afterwards, I noticed that number seven's head hung low and that her team left her conspicuously alone.

I felt good about our decisions and particularly good about winning that match. That is until a reception about three nights later when I had dinner with the most senior volleyball officials in Japan. In a small ceremony, they presented me with a string of pearls, a certificate and a patch. I was now entitled to call myself a national coach of volleyball in Japan. It was an unprecedented honour. Then, in an even rarer move because, as a woman, I was usually sent to bed with my team, they took me out drinking. I thought I'd made headway and that I was being accepted as a person. I soon discovered their objective was more subtle. They felt their message would be more easily delivered if I were sozzled.

They came to the point gradually after I'd had at least three shots of Scotch. They praised my accomplishments, complimented me on the team's play and decorum, and then finally got down to the dirty by asking, "What did I expect after Japan? Where did I see my limits?"

"The 1980 Olympics," I answered.

That was true and I'd said it for a couple of years. It was part and parcel of the club's aim – to produce Olympic-level players. I'd also believed that I'd make that team as a coach. So, that became the hope for both my players and me.

The most senior official took another sip of his Scotch and, after praising me again for several moments, declared that I'd never reach the top levels of coaching in Canada.

"Why?" I asked aghast. As they had just told me, I was not only the first woman coach to tour Japan, but also the first North American coach to post a fifty-fifty record against their best. They had just initiated me into the highest level of coaching, toasted my originality and the discipline I'd instilled in my team. Small wonder that I felt incredulous.

The president did not wait for the interpreter. He spoke directly to me, leaning across the table. "You're too soft. No killer instinct. In that last match a Japanese coach would never stop serving to number seven. Punishment? No matter. Serve, serve, serve to number seven. You stop. You feel sorry. See? Now, you understand? No killer instinct."

What could I say? If that was how he defined a killer instinct, he was right. I didn't have it. I protested, of course, feeling they were underestimating me.

He leaned across the table again. "We have idea for you. Go home, settle everything. Come back next year. We make you assistant to our Olympic coach. You sleep Japanese style, you learn Japanese style, you win Japanese style, and then go home.

In 1980 Olympics we still win, but you get second. Silver. Good idea?"

D stands for Davening, Diaspora, Diptych.

It also stands for Dreams.

It took many years before I understood the generosity of those men and the magnitude of what they offered. They also had given me the best gift I received in Japan – the truth. Unfortunately, I didn't know it at the time.

The Japanese were tremendous; showering us with gifts and doing everything they could to please us. The press contingent that travelled with us was necessary – we were sponsored by a newspaper chain, after all. But one or more would appear at frequent intervals and never seemed to understand the concept of privacy. The most embarrassing moment, for me, was the time I had dropped a sandal into the hole that served as a toilet and was trying, extremely delicately, to fish it out when my picture was taken.

Other incidents that made me uncomfortable at the time are hilarious in retrospect. My team had no concept of unisex washrooms when we left Canada. One night I walked into a Tokyo washroom and saw that several of my girls had climbed onto the porcelain urinals because they didn't know what else to do. They'd never imagined having to pee into a hole in the floor. So, there they sat, about five or six of them, in their red and white Canadian dresses, astride the urinals, hiding their faces from the men in the room. Of course, the men in the room could not believe their eyes. Some turned away politely, others pointed to the girls. Most, I'm sure, thought they were American-looking aliens from outer space, particularly when one hygienic soul got a wet towel and washed the urinal down after she'd finished as I struggled to repress hysterical laughter.

During the weeks in Japan, I was constantly off-balance. Only the games kept me grounded. 1970 belonged to a less sophisticated age and to a much less sophisticated me. I wondered, for example, why the interpreter who usually roomed with me, was always dressed when I awoke. I never saw her undress and for a while surmised she might sleep in her clothes. But one morning I woke first and lay in bed contentedly, thinking about the coming day and trying to anticipate problems. When the interpreter's bed moved, I kept as still as possible. Finally, I thought, I'd discover the mystery.

She raised her nightgown over her head and it took every ounce of self-discipline I had not to react to what I saw. Her back was an obscene mess of scarred flesh. I could not imagine the pain she must have endured. As I looked lower, I saw that the terrible burns extended as far as her heels. I let her dress silently and turned towards the wall, crying and trying to recover from what I'd seen.

One night after everyone else was asleep she told her story. It was simple and something, maybe, I should have worked out. She'd been a child in Nagasaki and on the day the Americans dropped the atomic bomb she'd been caught running. The bomb's heat had seared almost all the flesh from her back and only after innumerable operations had as much as I'd seen been restored.

Her story made me impotently angry. What was my pain compared to that she'd endured? How would I have coped with having my flesh burned away from my bones? Where did she get the bravery to endure? But, was physical pain somehow better? At least, there was physical healing.

The Japanese tour of 1970 was a watershed in my life. On the very positive side was the experience itself. We ended up being the most successful North American team to tour Japan and, of course, were by far the youngest, averaging out at 11.4 years. We'd played against the best Japan had to offer and even with an unfamiliar ball and a different net height had fought our opponents to a standstill. The girls had been excellent ambassadors for both their country and province. They'd made friends wherever they had gone and handled their semi-celebrity well. They were a credit to their families.

Given those successes, it's unthinkable that I opted out of competitive volleyball six months later.

The major reason was self-revulsion. Japan had given me a taste of fame and stardom. I, along with the team, had scribbled hundreds of autographs daily and, once I returned home, I was totally astonished when no one wanted my autograph. Social media hadn't been thought of. I'm sure that today the game we'd played in bare feet would have gone viral. But no one knew about us in Canada. It annoyed me that people didn't realise or appreciate who I was and what we had done. My reaction mortified me. Success had gone to my head and I despised myself for that.

For a couple of months, I maintained the regimen of my early years in Surrey – teaching, supper, then volleyball four nights a week. Gradually, though, I noticed changes. I would come home and, exhausted, sit in my sweats and stare at the television. At the time, the programme I watched most was Kenneth Clark's *Civilisation*. In this BBC series, Clark claimed to give "a history of life-giving beliefs and ideas made visible and audible through the medium of art." The time span was the fall of Rome through to 1969 and I was moved to tears of anger and moments of intense joy as Clark surveyed man's foibles and achievements. It was the perfect contrast to my life. The more I watched *Civilisation*, the more I wanted change.

I was bushed, totally exhausted. I should have taken a sabbatical after Japan, but no one knew of burnout in those days. After years of giving of myself, I had no self left and when people demanded more of me, I snapped. In giving myself to volleyball, I'd virtually shut off most of myself. All my dreams had become centred on that team.

I'd forgotten that the desire to learn was as much a part of me as life itself. Success in volleyball made me feel dirty. According to the men of the Japanese National Volleyball Association, it was an extremely good possibility that I'd achieve my goal of an Olympic medal. Fortunately, enough of myself remained to ask the one crucial question—what would happen afterwards? My reaction after Japan showed that I could easily succumb to fame and become totally egotistical. Was that what I wanted for myself?

Civilisation showed man's search for himself and the many ways he expressed humanity over the years. Some ways were despicable; others, noble. It showed that man never stopped learning and that one's yearning for that need not stop either.

Memories of the interpreter's back mocked those thoughts. Her pain haunted me as I wondered how it had affected her life. I knew my psychological pain crippled me. After attending church intermittently during the volleyball years, I still had a wistful concept of Christianity. I thought of Bernard of Clairvaux, of the faceless architects who had built Salisbury Cathedral and the anonymous monks who had lettered medieval documents. All those wonders, it seemed, had been inspired by their faith. Compared to theirs, mine wasn't even a mustard seed.

Yet, without it, how could my life go anywhere? No shops I knew of sold faith. My natural abilities and work ethic had given me a Midas-touch, except perhaps for my own healing, and I'd begun to believe that unless I could somehow deal with my past, my future was doomed. Night after night I lay in bed pondering this conundrum, wondering what on earth I could do.

Go to a shrink? I'd read enough psychology to distrust that process and was, in any case, too poor for a therapist. There were traditional remedies, such as churches, of course. But, most importantly, what use were gold medals and teaching awards when, at the core of me, a little girl still sobbed her heart out.

One night, as I lay awake thinking, a thought appeared from the blue. A question from my past. From the forbidden catechism classes: what is the essence of God?

Omnipotence, omniscience and omnipresence. Power, knowledge and time. It was a wonderful concept. God had the power to do anything.

Knowledge and time meant that God knew who I was and, far more importantly, who I could be. He was not bound to a finite existence. Suddenly, everything made sense. If God was beyond time's boundaries, he could see the thirty-year-old crying in my New Westminster bed, as well as the unloved child sobbing into my dog's fur in a Botany tannery garden. He knew the despairing teenager rebelliously striking out at anything and everybody. If God had absolute power, he could not only see the needs of those parts of me, he could do something about them. And so, I prayed like never before. God, I asked, go back to my young self. Stop the crying. Stop the hurt. Heal the abuse.

And then I relaxed and fell asleep. There was no appreciable difference the following day. I didn't walk around with a "whiter-than-white" Hollywood smile. But I had, finally, started to grow up.

CHAPTER 14

U AND E

U *stands for umbrage, uncharted, unequivocal.*

U also stands for University.

My decision to leave volleyball made, I applied to the Arts and Education faculties at both the University of British Columbia and Simon Fraser in the spring of 1971. The reply from UBC Faculty of Arts was swift and decisive. After looking at my motley record, it offered a little less than two years' credit for courses taken at the Teachers' College in Sydney, Cabrillo in California (for work done during the broken ankle summer), and UBC itself during summer school in 1964. Simon Fraser offered promised a quicker degree, but less interesting courses. That made the choice easy—UBC it was.

With a real sense of excitement and of burning bridges, I checked into residence in early July. Memories of Japan and volleyball had been ruthlessly suppressed, as had any thought of romance. To this point, my love life had hummed away sporadically, mostly on the back burner, but that was nothing new. I had a long-term friendship with Harry, an unhappily married man whom I saw sporadically. However, I'd known about his marriage from the beginning. He escorted me whenever I needed a date and we'd finish the evening with warm, funny, post-coital conversation. Like most unmarried women at the benchmark of thirty, I thought all the good men were married and my chances of a happily ever after resembled those of my finding a lasting relationship with God. Zero, in other words.

The night before summer school classes began, I thumbed through the UBC calendar reading about various courses and their prerequisites, particularly those in the history department, and in the back of the book found a description of its honours programme. It was a two-year programme and its twenty students received something like an Oxbridge education with seminars, rather than lectures. It sounded fantastic and something I wanted. When I checked the rules and regulations, I found I'd already qualified because of my grade in the Classics course of 1964.

The next day I went to the psychology and sociology classes I'd signed up for but found them unimpressive. Afterwards I made an appointment with the head of the honours programme and asked to join it. He frowned his way through my transcript and I got my first indication that there might be more to the prerequisites than the calendar advised. He cleared his throat a few times then told me the programme was full. The department had held a tea that spring for potential candidates and he was happy with the students selected in its aftermath. In any case, he added in a manner meant to be kind, my record was too spotty.

"But I've got a high A in a prerequisite course," I argued.

"Only in summer school and from a professor I've never heard of," he retorted.

"The calendar doesn't mention that you have the know the professors, or that I should have gone to a pre-selection tea. I've more than met the requirements it specifies."

The chairman was a gentleman from the Ivy League with little taste for confrontation. I, on the other hand, had just survived Japan. The more he talked out about the programme though, the more determined I became and seeing that I wasn't about to fold my tent he offered provisional acceptance. There were conditions: I'd have to transfer to a history course currently being taught, earn another high mark and, most importantly, be recommended by the professor teaching it. After that, he'd take my case to his committee.

It was a deal. I'd drop the boring sociology course, pick up one in history and work my ass off. Or so I thought. But after finding the classes I wanted were full, I realised I'd have to rearrange my schedule. I studied the course guide for hours, finally deciding that the only possible option was to add a creative writing course. To switch into it required the teacher's permission. "There's space," he said when I approached him, "but I need to see your work first."

"I don't have any," I wailed.

Besides being a brilliant poet, George McWhirter was extraordinarily kind. "Write something tonight," he said, "and let me see it. If there's enough promise, I'll sign you in."

Optimistically, I bought new history textbooks and began reading up on what I'd missed while trying to think of something to write. Finally, in deepest desperation, I hacked out a haiku. But when I showed the seventeen syllables to Professor McWhirter, he pursed his lips. "Well, indeed, you do have promise. You're too wordy though," he told me, eliminating several words and pointing to the result. "See? That's what you were trying to say. Now, try again."

That night, after reading the history assignment, I studied my edited haiku. The seven remaining syllables were indeed brilliant but they weren't my own work. I read the sparse beauty this master editor had created and suddenly wanted to learn from him with as much passion as I wanted to join the honours programme.

During the next two months, I gradually made the transition from international volleyball coach to mere student. The transition was far easier than the one I'd made when going from Australia to Wheaton. It didn't feel as alien and, sometimes, I didn't realise how different I was to the normal, blue-jeaned students ten years younger than me. One intimation came when I discovered there was a pool on when I'd wear a dress. Another emanated when a case of champagne was delivered in the middle of poetry class. George McWhirter took it in stride, rummaging around in several offices to finally emerge with enough mugs for everybody to toast me.

I had no idea who the donor was and, for at least a week, I was the most popular person in both my class and residence until the champagne ran out. Finally, after boxes of chocolates (which I had to share) and flowers that kept arriving, I discovered that one of the shy males in class was the culprit. I was not impressed; particularly since another pool had started with the entire class betting on the date I'd break down and go out with him.

Embarrassments aside, I loved both courses and when the marks came out, I cheered in jubilation. Sure enough, I was admitted to the history honours programme and I looked forward to September although it promised to be tricky. I would be taking the equivalent of six courses, one more than a regular student and, in my arrogance, I thought I could not only handle that load, but continue to teach full time as well.

And so I did. For three weeks. But something had to give and it turned out to be my voice. It was probably psychosomatic, but I developed a severe and long-lasting case of laryngitis. Not able to speak, I was unable to teach and thus given indefinite sick leave.

Laryngitis proved a blessing in disguise. Nothing I'd imagined prepared me for the history honours programme. My largest class had ten students; the others had five or six. Sometimes the total reading load was more than forty selected articles or books a week. There were no lectures, little note taking. The readings formed the basis of the seminars and we learned through discussion. It was exciting and broke many bad habits. I couldn't ignore my homework and bail myself out by writing brilliant final exams. There were no exams. My participation in discussions, the occasional seminar I'd present and term papers determined my grades.

At first, I had nothing to say, even if I could talk, and listened in awe as my fellow students discussed issues fluently. Some questions appeared simple but turned into quicksand. Such as, "What is history?"

"King's and queens," a somewhat flighty student answered immediately.

The following derision would have mortified me, but she remained unaffected and continued to offer quick answers to the many follow-up questions. As the weeks went by, we read various historians' views as we tried to answer that three-word question. By far, the most difficult philosopher was Hegel. I tried repeatedly to understand him.

By the time the next seminar rolled around, I had read through the required passage but hadn't understood much of it. Fortunately, every other student had the same difficulty and the professor allowed us another two weeks to work on it. During each of those fourteen days, I read the work diligently, paraphrasing every sentence, summarizing every paragraph. Then I wrote a *précis* of each section. When the professor next questioned us, there was still silence. No one wanted to volunteer an answer or venture a guess. The professor prodded, rephrased his questions and, after a while, I realised I knew some answers. So, finally, I began to talk, referring all the time to the summaries I'd made. My fellow students' mouths dropped, they looked at me and, for the first time, I felt at home in the programme. It was a very good feeling.

E stands for Eclectic, Ebullient, Elated.

It also stands for Evelyn.

While struggling with Hegel, I'd also wrestled with a strong urge
to go home to Australia during the Christmas break. I couldn't
put my finger on why I felt this urgent need but, after a time, I
succumbed to it and began saving money for my flight. I can't
remember how many jars of peanut butter I used as my protein
intake. Steak became a fond memory. Fortunately, I had plenty
of clothes from my previous incarnations as a teacher and coach
that were mostly in fashion – skirt lengths had dropped a little
but, as I'd found from the summer school pool, men preferred
mini-skirts to blue jeans any day. The one extravagance that term
was a phone call to Evelyn and Boy instead of my yearly letter.
If it was convenient, I asked, could I stay with them for the three
weeks I'd be in Australia.

I used a short stopover in Tahiti to acclimatize and adjust my
thinking. I knew I'd have to explain why I had thrown over both
teaching and my volleyball careers to Evelyn. I did not relish
the thought of being lectured by Boy, and being made to feel
as though I were still fourteen years old. Nor did I particularly
cherish the thought of another family Christmas.

The visit went mostly as I had expected. There were many
lectures from Boy, particularly when I didn't attend church with
them, and a general throwing up of hands because I was now
a poverty-stricken student and, a lot of silence. Many nights
I wondered why I'd bothered to come. Why did I have this
inchoate need to spend time with Evelyn? Most of the time I read
books I'd brought with me, readying myself for the second term
or exploring the grounds of their country home.

There was a zoo-sized aviary and Boy had created more magic. A
section in the back had various native trees and he'd recreated a

small forest featuring various ferns. This led into a large building for orchids. Everything had been done from scratch and Evelyn's orchid house rivalled many in botanical gardens. Although I didn't appreciate it at the time, Boy had worked out different watering systems to fit the plants' needs. His contribution made the beauty possible.

On the second or third last day I would spend in Australia, Evelyn sent him out to do a seemingly endless list of jobs. "Don't worry about us," she told him. "If Beverley can take a team to Japan, I'm sure she's able capable of putting a luncheon together."

Boy looked at me, didn't say a word, but I knew he thought Evelyn would starve. After he'd driven away, she called me into the sunroom. "Sit down," she invited, pouring a cup of tea from the pot Boy had insisted on providing before he left. "I want to find out exactly what you've been doing. Eighteen months ago, your picture was in Japanese newspapers. Now, you're just a student. What went on?"

There was no way I could tell her about Japan. I hadn't told anyone. But I could describe what had happened to me when I came back and I reminded her that going to university had always been my dream. It just had taken me an exceptionally long time and a very long way to get there. She said she didn't understand why I had left the American college, if that was so.

"Money," I replied, not wanting to go into the details.

She nodded. "I can understand that. I never thought you would try to go there in the first place without better resources."

I thought of saying that some of her resources might have made the difference between leaving and staying but I bit my tongue. Taunting her about their lack of generosity would have given neither of us satisfaction. So, I talked instead of Canada and how much the country meant to me. Like many others, she thought Canada a second-hand version of the United States and was fascinated when I elaborated on the many differences. And from there, it was an easy segue into my reasons for going into volleyball and how much work it had involved.

"Everyone said you were lazy when you were growing up," she replied. "I always knew it was a selective laziness. That you didn't care whether or not you had clean sheets on your bed, or a ton of dirty dishes in the sink. You knew someone would do that work eventually and so you concentrated on what you wanted to do – read, mostly."

She stopped to pour herself another cup of tea. I noticed that we'd run out of milk and fetched more from the kitchen. We made some small talk while she sipped the tea and after she'd finished, she resumed the conversation. "You know, it's funny. The only other person in the family who reads as much as you is me." While I absorbed that pronouncement silently, she reached for the book I had with me, Sir Isaiah Berlin's *The Hedgehog and the Fox*, a treatise on Tolstoy and his view of history. I watched in silence as she thumbed through it for several minutes, stopping occasionally to read a page or two.

"Take this book," she went on. "Nobody in the family would ever read something like it. No one would believe the amount of work you must have done to understand it. I have an idea, though, and I'm proud of you."

I think those were the first words of praise she'd ever given me. I know I sat slack-jawed, unable to take it in. It wasn't condescension or flattery. It had been a straightforward statement of fact. I felt ridiculously happy, and tears sufficient to fill the Pacific Ocean could have flowed, but Evelyn had a firm grasp on this conversation. Obviously, she had thought a lot over the years, trying to figure me out. Now she had her chance to question me, she was not going to let me escape into a maudlin cave. Her questions obviously demanded answers. And so, began a modified third degree.

"How long now will it be before you get your degree?"

"May, next year," I answered and then, before thinking too much about it, blurted out an idea I was flirting with. "If I do well, I could transfer into law school this coming May though."

"Law school?"

I nodded. A couple of law professors had discreetly taken me to the Faculty Club for lunch one day. I'd been amazed when I discovered they thought my volleyball background was the equivalent of a degree. "I'm being recruited," I told her and then had to explain exactly what that meant. "I can go into law school without finishing my degree."

Evelyn thought for some moments – so long, in fact, that I wondered if she'd dozed off until she suddenly snapped her eyes open. "Don't do it."

"Why not? I thought you'd be happy. It's far more money and prestige than I'd get in teaching."

"That might be. But it's never been your dream. If you'd wanted to go to law school rather than Teachers' College, I might have helped you."

In a pig's eye, I thought. Aloud, I said, "No, you wouldn't."

She laughed – another surprise. "You're right. I wouldn't. But, Beverley, don't compromise now. Get your degree. No one will ever be able to take it from you."

I pointed out that I might never have the same opportunity to enter law school. I knew I'd never be recruited again but Evelyn remained adamant. I'd wanted an Arts degree for so long. "You're thirty-two. I hope you realise that you only get so many chances in life. You're so close now. Don't let anything get in your way."

After she had delivered those pronouncements, I would have

thought she'd finished but it seemed she'd only started. "Tell me what you're doing," she ordered. "Don't tell me about your subjects, tell me what you're learning."

"To question," I answered simply.

She blinked. "Bah. You've always questioned. Always, always, always."

"This is different. I was like a shotgun before, popping off everywhere. Now, I ask questions to work out answers to problems."

"Like what?"

"Like why was Charlemagne crowned?"

"To be king, of course."

I laughed. I'd had the same thought when I was assigned that question. "No. You see he'd been king for twenty-five years before he decided on a coronation. Then, on Christmas Day, 800 A.D., he had the pope come to watch him put a crown on his own head. Can't you see that once I started asking questions, surprising details emerged. The questions led to understanding."

She nodded, her eyes alight with the excitement of learning something new. "Well, tell me. What did you understand?"

"That Charlemagne used that coronation to show the pope who had the most power. That, when he held that golden crown high, then lowered it slowly onto his own head, he was warning that the pope existed by his good will, not the other way around."

"Were you right?"

"I got a great mark," I answered and we both laughed. In the ensuing silence, I looked at Evelyn with new eyes. She was the first person I'd told about that paper and probably the only person I knew who'd show so much interest. The story of Charlemagne's coronation didn't sate her curiosity though.

"Tell me more," she demanded.

I told her I'd learned some practical tricks of the historians' trade. Like, how to sort out facts from conflicting accounts and then write a coherent summary. She wanted details and I gave them. Then I told her I was learning to withstand battering.

"Battering?" she asked with a hostile note in her voice. "From whom?"

I grinned. "My fellow students." She didn't quite know what to make of that. I let her stew in her own thoughts for a little before I explained. "You see, sometimes when we are asked a question, like Charlemagne's coronation and we have to give our opinion and our reasons for it, the other students try to pick us apart."

"That's battering?"

"You should try it. Having five or six people jostle for conversation space just to tell you that you are full of bovine excrement is something else." Fortunately, Evelyn lived in a world where such euphemisms were unknown and so I escaped censure. "After that," I went on, relieved that she hadn't followed up on the allusion, "they systematically take your opinion, your research and evidence apart. Sometimes, you're wrong and they let you know it. At other times, there's no clear answer, so you defend yourself and hang on for dear life."

She thought and looked at me for quite a while, then said, "You should do well then."

I smiled to soften the reply. "You gave me a good start. It's tough, though. I've never gone through anything like it. This marshalling of evidence, thinking everything out step by step. Of course, you've a hand in my success because you taught me to always hold back a zinger."

Evelyn looked fascinated by what she was hearing. I knew she also understood the subtext of the conversation – that I was letting her know what it had been like to grow up in her household. In this instance, she merely repeated my last words. "A zinger? Pray tell, what do you mean by that?"

"Well, when I give the reasons for my deductions, I always keep back one crucial bit of evidence, then, when the attack is hitting me hardest, I throw it into the discussion and by the time people have thought it through, the class is over."

She laughed, somehow picturing the scene and enjoying my tactic. Long after the time she would have been served lunch, I remembered Boy's taunt and managed to organize some food for us. When we finished, she asked about life after the degree.

"I don't know," I answered slowly and truthfully. "I love research so much. I love tackling historical puzzles. Maybe, I should go to London and find a job in the Inns of Court for a law firm specializing in those kinds of problems."

"Is that likely?"

"No," I grinned at her. "But it is a nice dream."

She didn't know what to think of that but neither did I, seeing that I'd never thought of going to England before. We continued talking about my life, what I learned and so on until we heard Boy arriving back. Evelyn knew our intimacy had finished.

"Don't give up," she told me urgently. "Whatever happens, never go back on your dreams, Beverley. Finish your degree, see where it takes you, but don't give up." We could hear Boy putting the car into the garage and, if anything, her voice became more hurried. "Beverley, I'm only going to be able to tell you this once, so listen. If I could live my life over again, the person I'd most like to be is you. You've made a lot of mistakes but, overall, I admire you. You've got guts, you stand up to people and best of all, and you chase your dreams. Don't change."

I looked at her and smiled widely. Nothing in the past had ever remotely indicated that kind of respect. Yet, I couldn't doubt the sincerity of what she said. Evelyn must have thought a lot about things while I'd been away, but it was so hard to believe. She wanted to be me! Sadly, it said so much about our poisonous past that I didn't hug her nor smother her in an extravagance kiss. Instead, as Boy entered the room and asked what we'd been doing, we merely looked at each other, smiled, and chorused, "Reading."

PART IV

AND THEN THERE WAS LOVE

CHAPTER 15

S AND M

S stands for *Stamina, Sumptuous, Supernatural.*

S also stands for Surprises.

That conversation and Evelyn's love and endorsement was the highlight that carried me through the next few months. Every now and then, I'd sit back and smile and let her words warm my life. One night, as I was drifting to sleep, I heard a voice say, "Didn't you know I answered prayer?"

God again, and not where he was expected or necessarily wanted.

"So, yeah," I said, "where were you when...?" I stopped, shocked. The little girl in the back yard of Botany wasn't sobbing anymore. Maybe, it had stopped right after I prayed. More likely, it had happened so gradually that I hadn't noticed.

But, once more, God had intervened in my life. I wondered if it was an overflow from that day with Evelyn. She'd told me then that she and Boy had never stopped praying for me and I'd thought, *Dollars would have been better.* But stopping that nine-year-old from crying was beyond value.

"Thank you" I said into the darkness, not knowing whether I'd said it to God or Evelyn.

When the academic year ended the following April, my head

felt crammed with knowledge. That's what I'd always wanted, but I'd never imagined such an extraordinary environment as the UBC honours history programme existed outside Oxford or Cambridge. To catch my breath and touch reality, I went back to Surrey to teach the year out and, when school finished in June, I applied for a year of study leave.

With my final pay cheque, I paid my summer school fees, together with a deposit to ensure a place in a residence, as well as the upcoming winter term's fees. Then, as I was expecting a very sizable tax refund, I splurged a little, giving myself a short holiday, and expecting the overdue refund to be waiting for me when I got back.

Instead, I found a letter from the tax people. As my income had dropped by more than $35,000 it advised me to ready myself for a tax audit. What a disaster! I had a grand total of $5.67 in my jeans pocket and that small sum had to last me until the tax refund arrived. Even worse, there was another letter. I owed a $5 fine to the UBC library and, if it wasn't paid, pdq, my university registration would be cancelled.

Initially, I was distraught. If the letters had arrived earlier, I would not have spent money on a vacation. I had one full week in residence that I'd paid for, but what next? I binned the library's letter and concentrated on living within my suddenly straitened means. I had friends in the same residence and we worked out a system whereby, once my week was up, they would take everything their prepaid meal tickets entitled them to and then share their extra food with me.

Food sorted, all I had to concentrate on, besides my studies in classical Greek literature and Latin, was the small problem of finding a place to sleep. Several people offered suggestions and Harry, my casual lover, gave me three nights in residence as an early Christmas gift. And, if things became totally desperate, there were always the banks.

As things worked out, I solved my sleeping problem relatively easily without having to see a bank manager. 1972 was a time of expansion and UBC erected a twelve-storey building called the Buchanan Tower to house the offices of several departments in the Faculty of Arts. Although formal occupation would take place later in August, the history floors were virtually finished by early July. Therefore, as there were plenty of empty rooms, I waltzed into the Buildings and Grounds office and with brass-faced effrontery and requested keys to the honours reading room and the Buchanan Tower's front doors.

A helpful cleaning crew helped me drag a sofa into the reading room and promised to wake me in time to avoid the nightly security sweep. Within days the reading room became my home away from home. A very good one too, for its isolation was conducive to much memorization of Latin vocabulary. Even after a couple of weeks the arrangement seemed perfect. No one believed that I could survive using absolutely zero cash but there I was, living proof that money didn't necessarily buy all things. I felt cocky, on top of everything. I should have worried about disaster or something untoward happening, but I didn't.

One day I read an urgent request for a cricket wicketkeeper in the campus newspaper. I can remember thinking, "Hey, that's me." I phoned the number, honestly admitted that I hadn't played for more than a decade but gave my previous experience. The voice on the other end of the phone convinced me that I was the closest thing to sliced sultana cake and I agreed to play the following Saturday.

What an arrogant fool! I spent the next day on the sofa in the reading room, unable to move, with my body and thighs a mass of bruises. The bruises seemed minor hurts when compared to the pain in my thighs. I hadn't squatted for years and my muscles let me know it. They protested every movement, no matter how small, and at times I thought wetting the sofa preferable to stumbling downstairs to the washroom.

I didn't go to classes the next day because I couldn't walk the distance to the lecture rooms. I needed some form of painkiller but there was the small matter of $5.67. Finally, I summoned enough courage to dress and shuffle to the history office (still in its old building) to see if, by some gigantic providential chance, my refund cheque might have arrived. No such luck. Groaning with disappointment, as well as pain, I moved towards the door, only to run into the honours chairman.

"Good thing I've seen you," he began jovially, "because I've been trying to contact you for a week now. We've a serious problem. It seems the university has decided to cancel your registration because you owe it a large fine."

"Five dollars," I muttered.

I tried to explain further but he held up his hand. "Stop. It's not my problem any more. I handed all the files over to the new chairman last Friday. He's in his office right now and you can clear it up with him. Come on, I'll take you over and you'll get to see our new digs because he's moved into the tower."

See the tower when I lived there? I couldn't tell him that, nor could I refuse the invitation. I followed in his wake, stifling screams of agony, and then rode the elevator to the eleventh floor. He misread the reason for my lagging behind because he almost pushed me into the room as he announced breezily, "This is Beverley Boissery, Murray. She's going to tell you why she shouldn't be kicked out of UBC. And Beverley, meet Murray Greenwood, your new chairman."

I groaned, literally and metaphorically as I stumbled forward to take his hand. Talk about making a good impression. But after chatting a little, Murray tipped some files from a chair onto the floor. "Have a seat."

Every one of my muscles screeched in protest at the mere thought. "No thanks, I'll stand."

Murray misunderstood. "It's okay," he said, smiling. "I'm not going to bite."

I gave up. Slowly and in infinitely small increments, I lowered myself to the chair. He watched, didn't say anything, and in turn I looked at him. He sported a six-inch beard, shoulder length hair and was dressed, incongruously, in grey flannel pants and a vile, mustard-coloured, polyester shirt. I couldn't remember seeing such ugly clothes on a man.

Good lord, I thought, *this guy hasn't realized that the hippie thing's over. What a loser!* But when I looked at his face and saw only patient kindness in his eyes, I slightly revised my opinion and decided to trust him.

So, I told my tale of woe about Revenue Canada, the library fine and my precious $5.67. He stood when I finished and I thought he was going to show me the door. Instead, he began fishing around in his back pocket. Eventually he discovered his wallet, opened it and pulled out a $100 bill. "Take this," he offered. "It should get you through the worse of things until that refund comes."

Taken aback, I must have looked like a guppy out of water. The urge to take that hundred dollars was almost overwhelming, but I knew myself well enough to know that I'd somehow fritter it away. Besides, existing without money had become a matter of pride. "Thanks," I said and smiled. "I can't take it. My cheque has to come soon but, if it doesn't, may I keep your offer in mind?"

"Of course." And then, as though offering one hundred dollars to a stranger was a regular thing, Murray sat down and produced my transcript. "It's a coincidence," he began, "but just before you came into the room I was looking at this and trying to figure out why it's taken you so long to get into fourth year when you've obviously got the brains. Most students have only used half a page by this point. You're already on your third."

I was far beyond being hurt by snide comments. I didn't answer, just tried to get out of the chair and leave the room, barely controlling my agony. Not too well because, of course, he noticed. "Pulled a muscle, have you?"

"No. Not one. Just a hundred thousand," I replied, my pride fighting against the primal urge to hang the consequences, take his money and buy painkillers.

"How?"

I told him about the cricket game the previous Saturday and how I was now paying for it. Interested, he told me he'd once tried to play cricket when he was a Rhodes Scholar at Oxford but couldn't get the hang of batting. From that point on, we talked about our athletic pasts: about the time I'd beaten an Olympian swimmer by false starting and of my softball exploits at Wheaton.

He had stories as well. He'd played on a hapless Oxford hockey team and once had scored all six goals in a 7-6 loss. One long ago Christmas he captained the combined Oxford-Cambridge team, which had toured Europe. He'd barred one player from their carriage for a ridiculous choice in the Botticelli game and bargained for the team's payments, once accepting bottles of Slivovitz, a Croatian plum brandy, rather than cash. My stories of volleyball were countered by his career as a sixteen year old college quarterback.

Somehow, we segued into jobs. He seemed interested that I was currently a teacher, albeit on leave. I was similarly intrigued by his decision to leave a fast-track job in the country's biggest law firm to do his doctorate in history, and by the fact that he'd turned down a scholarship offer from Harvard. Nothing in my life countered that, I told him, but he thought my getting out of volleyball similarly heroic. I argued and somehow that led into our backgrounds and the values they'd engendered. We had both been lonely kids and had learned early in life not to reveal too much about ourselves. At this stage, my stomach rumbled because I hadn't eaten all day and I looked at my watch. Only then did I realise that we'd spoken non-stop for more than four hours.

"Do you have to go?" he asked.

I shook my head. "Not yet."

Eyes are said to be the mirror of the soul. That day they were certainly the mirrors of our hearts. We looked at each and smiled – not the wide, teeth-showing grins so beloved of photographers – but quiet smiles of sheer delight. Murray's eyes had a lustre as he looked at me, and, I'm sure mine were the same. How could they not have been? After thirty some years, I'd found the missing part of myself.

Neither of us had the kind of disposition in which deep-seated happiness explodes outwardly, but that day I wanted to jump to my feet and stamp and yell with joy. Instead, I remained seated and, for goodness knows how many more minutes, we just smiled. At some stage, we began talking again and eventually my stomach reminded me that it really was empty. Like an arthritic octogenarian. I grabbed the chair's armrests and managed to stand.

"Look," Murray said, "I know you're hungry. I'll have to make dinner for myself if I go home, so why don't I take you out? My car's downstairs."

How could I refuse? I felt like I never wanted to leave him, and the thought of a good meal was icing on the cake. He took me to his club and helped me solicitously to a table. For the next couple of hours, we talked almost continuously, stopping only to put food into our mouths or to sip wine. For the first time that day, my muscles began to relax – that is, until Murray tried to work out when he could see me next.

"It was a fluke that I was in the office today," he began. "A lucky fluke, mind you. Normally, I'd be still at the lake. But my wife had forgotten something so I decided to come down to get it."

My muscles tightened and my heart stopped. Wife? Damn, blast and bloody hell. What was it with me and married men? A feeling of terrible betrayal replaced my joy as I carefully stood and asked Murray if he'd mind taking me back to the library.

"Why? What did I do?" he asked, as fleeting images of frustration and despair crossed his face.

"I've got a Lain test tomorrow," I answered, while hobbling to the door. "I really have to get some study in."

He followed without saying anything. When he reached the door, I realised that he didn't understand the abrupt way the evening had ended and was puzzling over our conversation. He drove to the library, as I'd requested, in silence. I couldn't understand the baffled look on his face for the life of me. How could I have opened myself up to a man, who was so blasé that he didn't see anything wrong in admitting that he couldn't see me because he had to go back to his wife?

When we reached the library, Murray shut off the motor. "Well, may I see you next Monday?"

I knew I'd cry if I said a word so I got out of the car as quickly as I could. "I'll be in the office from one to five," Murray called after me. "See you then."

In a rat's arse, I thought as I waited for him to drive off. What a monumental bummer! The man of my dreams turned out to have the proverbial feet of clay. Or was that mixing metaphors. Whatever. I really could not have cared less.

M stands for Magnitude, Maelstrom, Metaphor.

It also stands for Murray.

I'd been seriously in love with Mr. Darcy since I was old enough to read Jane Austen. Maybe he was to blame for the fact that I'd previously found real men so inferior. But in those short hours with Murray Greenwood I'd discovered the difference between fantasy and reality. I'd never felt so close to anyone in my life before. The proof was the fact that we'd talked almost non-stop for seven hours. That was new for me. Very new. So new that it had totally thrown my self-image out of kilter. I'd never used words to communicate the deepest parts of my life before.

I must have started thinking before I could talk because I sometimes find I feel the same frustration with them that I'd felt in math when I knew the answers but couldn't "prove" how I'd found them. Words are like that. The concepts or images are in my head and sometimes words are the ultimate hindrance. Sometimes, the search for them frustrates me.

Even more irritating, I am usually articulate and self-assured when teaching or speaking to crowds, even when they number into the millions as my Japanese experience showed. It's only privately, when talking about my innermost feelings or abstractions that I have the problem.

But, there had been no problem that afternoon. I'd told Murray Greenwood things I had never confided to anyone and somehow managed to string the right words together. It seemed, to me that, at long last, reticence and I had parted company.

Then he had revealed his wife!

I walked to my class the following day feeling as though I was in deepest mourning. Never again, I vowed, would I volunteer information about myself and I'd censor every word that came out of my mouth. No man would shred my defences again. Ever.

I was learning a lot about good intentions that summer and this crisis just added to that knowledge. Towards the end of the week

I took a break from classical Greek literature and Latin and spent the time rummaging around the Australian history section in the library. Part of my reason was pleasure, but there was also a work component. For my fourth-year creative writing project under George McWhirter's supervision, I planned to produce a collection of poems with the theme of discovering oneself in alien territory. He suggested I might want to include some "found" poetry, that is, reformatted prose. The pain and agony felt by convicts after they were sent to Australia could be part of my theme if I could find the right documents.

At least, that was my intention. But I found myself unable to concentrate and picked up a book I normally would not have looked at – a collection of historical stories published by one of Sydney's tabloid newspapers. The book, to my complete astonishment, fell open to a story about the experiences of Canadian convicts in Sydney.

Canadian convicts in Sydney? I'd thought I'd known my home city's history well but I'd never heard of such a thing. My fingers itched and I felt as though I'd struck gold. Suddenly understanding the Archimedes' bathtub story, I almost stood and shouted "Eureka" in the empty library for, as part of the fourth-year honours requirements in history, I needed to research and write a small (25,000 words) thesis.

The previous spring I had, after much thought, approached my favourite professor to ask if I could work under her guidance. She'd suggested I think about something to do with one of England's most obscure kings, Henry VI. Although finding documents would be difficult, she'd promised to share her private collection with me and assured me that the project was feasible.

But, boring. If Canadians had been truly sent to Sydney during the convict period however, I'd have a winner. After making a quick check through all the indexes of Australian books, I was discouraged. I could find no references to them and decided to talk with the history department's resident expert on Quebec history. His identity though dismayed me –Professor F. Murray Greenwood.

My heart fell. What a roller-coaster week. To have found a unique topic to write on for my honours thesis was akin to manna from heaven. To have Murray Greenwood as the reigning expert on the Canadian portion of it, however, was pure excrement.

I had truly intended to never see him again – that is, outside of getting necessary forms signed. I just couldn't begin another relationship with a married man. Harry was different. We'd been platonic friends until his wife moved from the province and our relationship, if it could be called such, had been about companionship and sex. Illogical as it might sound, I felt there was a huge distinction between having sex with Harry and dinner with Murray. Both men were married, but a relationship with Murray was taboo because it would involve my soul.

Monday came. I knew Murray would be in his office but I stayed away. The next day there was a note in my letter box saying that he'd missed me. I ignored it. I spent a lot of time now in the library, trying to discover whether the story on the Canadian convicts was fact or fiction. The Canadian references were so general that I got nowhere. I needed help if I were to go further and the deadline towards changing thesis supervisors loomed closer and closer. I had to find where to look. And who could give me that direction?

Murray, damn his married eyes, Greenwood.

It took another week of heart-searching. During that time Murray left various notes for me, some of which I put back into his letterbox unopened. That weekend, however, I realised that I had to see him. Now that he was officially back on campus after his sabbatical year, other students needed to discuss their schedules. I thought their presence would give me protection. I waited until there was a line-up at his door, and then joined it. Eventually my turn came and I walked into his office.

His face lit up immediately. "Hi there! I was becoming seriously worried about you, wondering if you had enough money, why you put those notes back into my box. How are you?"

"In top shape compared to the last time you last saw me," I replied, my voice friendly in a cool sort of way. I certainly didn't want to annoy him when I needed information so badly. Abruptly, I came to the point without further ado. "Murray, have you heard of a guy called Papineau?"

I found out later it was akin to asking an Australian about Ned Kelly, but all Murray said at the time was, "Yes."

"Well, then, did you know that his followers were sent to Australia as convicts?"

He looked startled and shook his head. "No, are you sure?"

"It's something I read. That there'd been a rebellion and when it was over some rebels were sent to Sydney."

He looked puzzled. "I know eight went to Bermuda."

"Well, the newspaper article I read said that fifty-eight went from Montreal to Sydney in 1839 as convicts."

He got up and began pulling books from his shelves. "I think you might be talking about the second rebellion in 1838," he said, flipping through indexes. "That's a pretty obscure topic. Most historians stop with the rebels' defeat in 1837."

"It would make a great honours thesis, wouldn't it?"

"An incredible one," he nodded. "Absolutely original. You'd be the first to work on the subject."

And that was what everyone – student or professor – wanted.

To get first dibs on a piece of history. I smiled at him, I couldn't help it. He smiled back, knowing what I was thinking. Then, he selected three books from those he'd scattered on his desk. "Look, I'm sorry I don't have more time to spend with you today. As you can see, everyone wants their timetable approved. Why don't you come in tomorrow? About 4:30?" He handed the three books over. "Now, here you go."

When I arrived the following day, Murray waited at the door. "Come along," he said cheerfully, "let's get a beer and talk this topic over."

"But…"

"No, buts. My car's downstairs."

I felt uncomfortable but I'd had tremendous luck that day. My long-awaited refund had arrived and I now had folding money in my pocket. Romance, though, seemed the last thing on Murray's mind. He was flat-out excited by my discovery. His research had turned up a treasure-trove of documents and it seemed no one had done serious work on the 1838 rebellion. He offered to be my thesis supervisor, obviously not envisioning a harder dilemma for me. On one hand, there was the chance to work on an original topic as a mere honours student; then, the propinquity to a man who was half-way to stealing my heart; and lastly, the opportunity for more encompassing conversations.

My scruples, such as they were, dominated the negative side. Even if we didn't make love on his desk or some place equally dramatic, and even if I could keep the relationship academic, I knew in my heart I'd be cheating his wife. And so would he. I agreed to think about it and left, again using my need to build my Latin vocabulary as the excuse. Work, however, was the farthest thing from my mind. I had a decision to make. The academic year would begin in a couple of weeks' time.

To turn the pressure even higher I received a formal letter from

Murray asking me to see him about my elective course at my earliest convenience. This worried me. The poetry project I had worked out with George McWhirter required the equivalent of two courses. This meant that my senior year would consist solely of three double courses: the thesis; my poetry project and one honours seminar. This, Murray wrote was against policy.

When I saw him, I argued that the compulsory seminar would force me to repeat work I'd done the previous year. I told him how torn I was between history and creative writing and how important the poetry project was to me. When I wound down and Murray finally got a word in, he promised his support if I wanted to fight my case. He'd talked with George McWhirter and received glowing reports.

In fact, Professor McWhirter offered to take me as an honours creative writing student if things didn't work out in history. I was flattered. While I absorbed this news, Murray informed me that his committee was prepared to battle for me against the rigid traditionalist who ran the history department at the time. If they were prepared to go to war, he went on, it would help greatly if I would decide on a thesis topic.

"I can't."

"Why not? Seems to me you've had a gift drop right out of the sky into your lap. Doing comparative history is difficult, but you have the Australian background already and I can easily teach you what you need to know about Quebec in my honours seminar. Talk about killing two birds with one stone. You, my dear, can bring down an entire flock."

And at what cost? In the following silence, while I thought about options, Murray produced a bundled sheaf of Xerox. "I did a tremendous amount of photocopying at the archives in Ottawa when I was on sabbatical last year," he continued. "Take them, they'll give you something to read until the seminar starts."

Suddenly a child's voice interrupted us. "I can give her something too, Daddy." In disbelief, I watched a small, blonde-haired boy clamber from a hiding place under his father's desk and gravely hand me a half-eaten apple.

Murray's face lit with a breath-taking smile. "As you can see, this is my son, Christopher. Chris, this is Beverley. Can you say hi?"

Damn, I thought, another Greenwood to fall in love with. Chris wriggled from one foot to another while he announced that his ambition was to be a frog when he grew up. "I'm a good jumper. See?" he boasted, and then proceeded to make his version of prodigious bounds around the office. I praised him, said he had a worthy goal in life and then turned as his father spoke.

"I think Chris is letting me know it's time to go home." He pulled his briefcase out, stuffed papers into it, and then looked at me, his heart in his eyes. I could see the hurt he felt because I hadn't responded to his interest in me, either personally or academically. I understood then that he had no idea why I was backing away. As we prepared to say good-bye, Murray made an awkward attempt to bridge the gap. "You've no more money problems, I gather," he ventured, smiling a little.

"Not for the next couple of days, at least," I grinned and tousled Christopher's curls.

It was one of the more uncomfortable farewells I've ever made. How sad, I thought, as I left his office, that we were now reduced to such. I could still read Murray's soul through his eyes and was shaken by the pain I saw there. I wondered if my eyes revealed a similar agony and if my scruples were worth putting us both through hell. Impulsively, and without giving myself a chance to think it through, I turned back. "Look. There's a lot of stuff I need to talk to you about. If you let me buy the drinks, you can name the time and place."

"Tonight's fine. Seven o'clock? Can I pick you up at your residence?"

I still wasn't prepared to let him know that I lived in the office tower. Instead, I said, "How about downstairs, in front of the main doors?" I walked across to the reading room, deep in thought. With any luck, I could also ask questions and get the answers I needed.

CHAPTER 16

B AND L

B stands for *Beverley, Boissery and Boisterous.*

It also stands for *Barriers.*

When Murray arrived, I immediately noticed that he'd modified his faux-hippie look for something more sportive. He later told he'd done this in a deliberative effort to somehow bridge the gap he felt between us, hoping I'd be more comfortable with this reminder of our joint athletic pasts. He was right. In another attempt to ease the constraint between us, he drove to a place on campus rather than an outside pub. His plan worked and I relaxed, knowing I could always walk away if things got out of hand. He watched moodily while I got a couple of beers and we sipped them for a while, talking about things in general. Finally, I asked about Christopher. Was he an only child? Was he going to school?

"He's going to start in a week or so," Murray answered. "And, I've one other son, Stewart. He's very athletic, involved in all sorts of things and he'll be in grade three this year."

"And your wife?" I asked tightly. "Does she work?"

As I watched Murray's face, he suddenly put the clues together and realised exactly why I'd backed away from the friendship he'd offered. To my astonishment, he laughed with relief. "She's fine. She knows I'm meeting you and she's comfortable with it."

"Why? I sure as hell wouldn't be."

As he started explaining, my eyes glazed over. Sweet lord, I thought, didn't he know that telling a woman that his marriage was defunct, that he was going to move out and therefore it was okay to have an affair was a cliché? As I listened to his variation on the age-old married man's theme, my lip curled in derision. How could he live with himself? He was intelligent. Didn't he know enough to invent something different?

He stopped halfway through his explanation, accurately reading my disgust from the look on my face. "Look," he said, grabbing my hand. "Let's get out of here. You're not believing a word I say. So why don't I take you home, you can meet her and ask her any question you want?"

He was either the most brilliant or the most stupid man I'd ever met. I let him take my hand while I stared into my beer and tried to figure him out. I knew he'd won a Rhodes Scholarship and that virtually guaranteed that he couldn't be stupid. Finally, after hemming and hawing for eons, I made the decision. "All right, you're on. I'll go."

As we drove to a leafy avenue mere minutes from campus, my stomach churned as I wondered if I'd called his bluff, or if he was on the level. When he rounded a corner and slowed down, I couldn't take it any longer. "Stop. It's okay. I believe you."

He did stop the car, but also indicated that he thought it was a bad idea. "I don't play games, Bev. Not with anything as important to me as I think you'll be. I'm quite prepared to let you meet my wife and have her explain our situation. Anything's better than the wall of silence you've erected around yourself. Besides, you'll have to meet her sometime."

"But not tonight," I blurted out, wondering why I had to meet a woman who might have every reason to hate my guts.

I was way out of my depth. Nothing had prepared me for this situation. I didn't know what to feel, where to go, whom to trust, or what to do. Only one thing was clear. Before I put myself through the agony of meeting a woman whose marriage was breaking up, I wanted to know the man a lot better. "Let's drive somewhere and talk instead."

We drove to Jericho beach, walked for some way and finally sat on the sand with our backs against a log. He put his arm around me and started telling me about his childhood in Westmount, an English enclave in the middle of Montreal. Leonard Cohen had been a year ahead of him in high school and had run for student council president with the slogan, "Vote for me and I'll buy you an ice-cream cone." I laughed and mentioned how glad I was that he'd since become a better poet. Finally, I felt sufficiently at ease and talked about my scruples.

"You're not cheating my wife," he declared. "My marriage is over. We decided that on my sabbatical in Ottawa. It's a horror story right now. We were once such great friends. Now we're coming to hate each other, and sometimes I feel so destructive that it frightens me. That's the main reason, besides you, that I want to move out."

"So, when will you do that?"

Murray sighed. "I don't know. It will hit the kids hard. Stewart's already acting up because of the tension. Maybe in a month or so. As soon as they've adapted to their new school."

I sighed as well. I now had to make a major decision that involved trust. I felt terrible hoping that one woman's marriage would dissolve so that I might have her husband. But a part of me countered that I should think about myself. Maybe it was my time for happiness. I thought about Stewart and Chris, of the adjustments they'd have to make and, finally, I thought of the bitter man Murray might become if he stayed with his wife.

Sensibly, he respected my silence and didn't push for any commitment that night. I don't know if I could have given one. But as we sat, absorbed in our thoughts, time passed and eventually I had to plead the truth about studying for a make-up exam in Latin. Murray didn't argue and drove back to the university. "Which residence? Or aren't you going to tell me yet?"

"Buchanan tower?"

"What?"

Laughing, I started telling him about the arrangement I had with the cleaners and how I'd be moving to a residence in a day or two. He pulled the car over and stopped. "Dammit," he exclaimed. "I've just realised something. I feel so stupid. You'd better say hello to Henry VI, after all."

"What?" I gasped. "I can't. I ran into my professor today and told her about the Canadian convicts. She wished me luck and signed me out. Whether you know it or not, I'm yours now."

"Oh yeah, that you are whether you know it or not," he said softly and smiled. "That's the only thing I do know tonight. But it's also why you're going to have to beg her to take you back. Because very, very soon I'm going to make love to you and, from that moment on, I cannot be your teacher or your thesis advisor. It's unethical. I'm sorry. I feel such an idiot for not recognizing this earlier."

L stands for Lackadaisical, Lugubrious and Lissome.

It also stands for Love.

Between his ethics and my scruples, Murray and I were a right pair, and we complicated my already convoluted situation by making love the following week. From that moment, I had to find another seminar and another advisor. But, I'd decided to grab for the brass ring in thesis topics as well. So, it was farewell Henry VI, again, and hello, Canadian convicts.

Once classes began I found myself enrolled in an urban history seminar taught by a professor who also volunteered to be my thesis supervisor. As for learning Quebec history, I was on my own. Murray tried to teach me the basics over coffee in September but this was squeezed into our very little free time. Frustrated by our schedules, Murray told me that wanted to spend as much time as possible with me but I still couldn't commit myself. My workload stretched me to my limits and I didn't know if I could handle more emotional upheavals. When he asked why I kept denying the strength of our love, I didn't know the answer.

One day I hid myself in the library and sat thinking about it all, wondering if I had the courage to go into a full-blown affair. If I committed myself and he rejected me in a couple of months, would I recover from the hurt?

My life had changed dramatically since I'd prayed to the God who was outside of time. I was healing. I knew it. I also knew that I'd hoped for love all my life. Now, Murray was offering me his on a gold platter. Did I have the temerity to refuse it? Would my God outside of time think I was disparaging him if I accepted Murray's love? I'd be a fool, though, if I didn't find out what it meant. So, when Murray left his wife in early November, I moved in with him a couple of weeks later.

Quite legitimately he was paranoid about anyone seeing us together. This was something I hadn't realised when I doubted his honesty. He'd had a lot to lose in career terms by having an affair with a student, even one of my mature age. So, on the days we both travelled to campus, he'd drive while I took the bus. In some ways, it felt like living in a closet, for only our closest friends knew the secret. Murray mostly ignored me if we happened to meet in a hallway and, as the following incident shows, went out of his way to prove he was unbiased when academic situations involved me.

As a history honours student, I was required to show literacy in a second language – the sole reason that I'd taken Latin that summer. When I looked at past exams though, I knew I wasn't competent enough. Therefore, in a moment of total idiocy, I declared French as my second language. It wasn't quite as far-fetched as it sounded. Murray had been giving me background articles to read for some time. I was beginning to remember a lot of my night school French, so it wasn't a total stretch.

But there was also one incredible complication – Murray was the examiner.

Nevertheless, after I'd written the exam I felt relatively good about my chance of passing it. All I needed was fifty percent and I thought I'd known at least half the words. When the list of successful students was posted, however, my name wasn't there. Murray refused to discuss the topic until I hid his car keys.

"Oh, you passed all right," he finally told me. "You did even better than a couple of other students I let through."

"So why wasn't my name on the list?"

"Caesar's wife, my dear. If you live with me, you'll have to get another fifteen percent if I'm to pass you."

Name-calling, threats and endearments proved useless. Murray had drawn his line in the sand and that was it. I'd have one more chance to meet his standard. If I didn't there'd be no honours degree after all. People writing about the cost of love, should include French literacy, I told myself in disgust. My love had added the equivalent of two additional courses to an already heavy load and I wondered petulantly if life would ever play fair with me. Nonetheless, I knuckled down, studied and began to feel reasonably confident as the day of the French exam approached.

The night before it, though, I received terrible news. Evelyn had died six weeks earlier. I felt so glad that I'd gone to see her the previous Christmas, overjoyed that we'd made our peace, but tremendously sorry that it had been for only one day. Somehow, as I tried to sleep that night, the thought of her decomposing body haunted me and I cried for the many chances to know each other that we'd missed, and for the fact that she'd never know Murray. Next morning I asked if I could take the exam some other time on compassionate grounds.

"No. I can't single you out."

"Bah, and humbug to you," I muttered and slammed out of the apartment.

An hour later, I listlessly took the examination paper. Murray gave the same instructions as I'd heard before. While allowed to use dictionaries, we were on our honour not to give or receive any other help. With that he left the room. When I turned the paper over, I breathed a sigh of relief. The passage to be translated came from an article on early Quebec. I'd read other material written by the same historian, knew some of his writing quirks as well as his style. With the dictionary's help, I felt confident of doing well and began writing busily.

Too busily. My neighbour, Peter, had looked at the exam and despaired. He was an interesting man. He claimed to be Australian but his Sydney seemed to have existed before the 1950s. He talked about walking through arcades that had been demolished, something that anyone who visited Australia as frequently as he claimed to do should have realised.

He'd also convinced various students and professors that he had worked for the CIA, been captured by the Viet Cong, and was on leave from an American television company to brush up on his grasp of international affairs. He gave guest lectures in various departments about his experiences and was treated as a colleague by some starry-eyed profs. What annoyed me most that the fact that he was writing his honours thesis on information supposedly picked up in an interview with Ho Chi Minh after he'd been released from a POW camp. I thought he belonged in creative writing, not history.

His stories, however, must have put him between a rock and a hard place when it came to the language requirement. As the department wasn't offering Vietnamese, he told us he'd reluctantly chosen to write the French exam. He wasn't quite sure, he went on with a deprecating little cough, how different Vietnamese French would be to metropolitan French, but he thought he'd do well.

Obviously, he hadn't expected Canadian French.

As I wrote, I noticed out of the corner of my eye, that his chair began easing its way closer and closer to me, and I soon realised that he was blatantly copying my work. I cleared my throat and looked at him but he refused to meet my eyes. I cleared my throat again and when the other students looked up, I rolled my eyes towards Peter's close chair. They rolled their eyes back sympathetically, distinctly implying that it was my problem. They weren't going to rat on him. And now, I was the one caught between the rock and the hard place. If Peter copied me, and our translations were identical, I knew Murray would fail both of us. Well, me at least. Now, not caring what other students thought of me, I looked at his exam and swore. He was not even paraphrasing me – he was copying my translation, word for word.

With that knowledge, I wrote as fast as I dared, not worrying if I had the most accurate translation, or if it was elegant. All I cared about was finishing. Then, I put my work to the side away from Peter and began again, this time trying to make it as different from my original translation as possible. This, of course, stymied him. He had no interest in rewriting and as I kept working, he began using his dictionary. Finally. He finished before me and left the room with a smirk.

Left behind, I wrote faster than ever but when Murray returned and pronounced that time was up, I had three or four sentences left to do. He would not let me copy them onto the new translation so I tore them off the old and handed them in with my revised translation. He posted the results the next day. I waited until everyone cleared away before I looked for my name. Sure enough it was there, but so was Peter's.

When I came home that night I stormed into the kitchen. "You passed Peter," I yelled.

"Of course."

"Was he that good?"

Murray looked embarrassed. "Bev, you know I can't talk about it."

"Well, you're bloody well going to," I erupted in coruscating rage. "I'm going to tell you something, Dr. Examiner, Dr. Professor, Dr. 'Let's make it hard on Bev' Greenwood. That bastard copied me word for word. Then, because I knew you flunk me and probably not him, I had to rewrite my entire translation. That's why I couldn't finish."

I went on in this vein for an embarrassing length of time, letting Murray know how angry I was with the whole situation of being cooped up, of having him scared to be seen with me. I was also furious at myself for not having the courage, or honour, to denounce Peter. It was the second time in my entire life that I had lost my temper. For thirty-four years I had kept a tight rein on myself, stifling any feelings of rage and anger. If I hadn't realised I was in love beforehand, that tantrum solidified the matter.

So did Murray's love. The following evening he told me to dress up. We were going out. I put a decent blouse on but remained in my jeans, thinking he meant to take us to the corner café. He disappeared to dress and when he emerged I saw that he wore a tie. That night I ate steak in one of Vancouver's finest restaurants. I drank the best red wine it had to offer and afterwards while we talked over liqueurs, Murray held my hand. Our love would no longer be a closet affair.

CHAPTER 17

F AND P

F *stands for Facetious, Fabricate and Flabbergasting.*

It also stands for Farm.

What a difference a summer made. In July 1972, I'd walked around with $5.67 clinking in my pockets. A year later I won one of the world's richest scholarships – $75,000 in 1975 dollars. Furthermore, in March 1974, I would become a doctoral scholar at The Australian National University and write my dissertation under the supervision of Australia's fabled historian, Professor Manning Clark, the absolute, number one authority on Australian history.

I'd met Manning through correspondence. Initially I'd written asking for any help he might be able to give on my convicts. He'd been fascinated by my honours topic, suggested that it would stand up to the rigours of a doctoral study, and, best of all, he'd loved my poetry.

It was a two-way love affair. I really liked the way he wrote history. He didn't poke away at things like a pedant. Rather, he painted his vision of the past with the abandon of an artist. That he might occasionally lose a few facts in the process didn't bother him or me. If I wasn't to be a poet, my goal was to make history both visible and accessible. He was my ideal teacher.

The summer of 1973 saw many other changes. Murray and I moved out of Vancouver and bought a small farm close to the American border in South Surrey. I wish I could explain our reasons in terms that make sense. The decision was more of a romantic dream than anything else. Murray was no farmer, in fact he was so impractical that he'd received three percent on a mechanical aptitude test. Even then he'd been lucky. He'd been able to identify a hammer, an axe and something else – probably his name. Definitely not light bulbs though, they gave him difficulty.

Therefore, it was fortunate that the farm was no longer a working one. Its most recent owner had been a movie producer who had tarted it up and grown marijuana behind the barn. That we found out courtesy of an RCMP raid. Murray's surprise and interest was too genuine to be faked and, thankfully, the police believed we'd been oblivious to the presence of our alien crop.

Some of our friends cursed Murray's other-worldliness, as well as the fact they hadn't bothered to explore every nook and cranny of the grounds. Thereafter there would be a steady parade of friends out to the furthermost reaches of the property, all hoping against hope that some undiscovered plants remained.

That aside, the farm was an ideal place for those first years in our relationship. We were sufficiently isolated that we depended on each other for sustenance of all varieties. I even became domesticated for that one summer, studying cook books, learning how to make jam from our orchard's plentiful supply of fruit, and cooking a few elegant meals. Murray spent endless hours contouring an island in the middle of a creek running through the farm, planting geraniums on it and lugging rocks onto it to his heart's content. With the help of a friend who did the actual work, he cultivated a vegetable garden. Towards the end of the summer he inveigled Chris and Stewart into picking blackberries for jam, pies and wine. We never did find out how good the wine might have been because it was drunk within weeks of its bottling.

Stewart and Chris, then aged nine and six respectively, loved the farm, despite the mandatory blackberry-picking excursions. As it had been the original farm in the area, all the outbuildings had been built from the huge first-growth lumber. Age and the weather had added a beautiful patina. The silo emulated Pisa's tower and was an octagonal piece of pioneer art. While the barn's milking stalls were intact and could have been made functional, the roof had long since succumbed to neglect and offered only marginal protection. But, the barn still had piles of hay.

It was only a matter of time before it served as a gymnasium with the boys climbing to the rafters and swinging down onto the hay, screaming in delight. There was also a strange outbuilding that we called the Basketball House. Murray, exhausting his mechanical skills, put up a basketball hoop and bought the boys an ABA tri-coloured ball. They spent hours in there, rigging old mattresses so that they could slam-dunk and learn the rudiments of the game.

More than anything else, the farm was made for parties. Murray loved croquet, and during the thirty odd years that I knew him he was never beaten. His version of the game differed considerably to that played on manicured lawns in staid clubs. He used the contours of the grounds, trees, and other hazards, inventing rules to help the game along and, invariably, the rules differed from one party to the next. One time, players had to drink a beer every time they knocked the ball through a hoop, and the survivors, after completing the croquet portion of the game, could only finish by driving a golf ball over the barn. Murray, in a fit of generosity, allowed the use of golf clubs.

These were indeed halcyon days – that is, until the arrival of my mother-in-law. Glady was the most beautiful woman I had ever met. Petite, outwardly gracious, very much the *grande dame*, she made me feel fifteen feet tall and so awkward that I constantly wondered if I had cow manure stuck to my shoes. She was a showstopper and, unfortunately for us, a plumbing stopper. No matter what time of year she came, or how important the occasion, she had only to plunk her aristocratic bottom on the toilet for the whole works to quit. At first we laughed, then after one memorable occasion, accepted that Glady's problems with our plumbing were immutable.

That visit had coincided with our back-to-school party. We begged her to arrive early to get the plumbing fiasco out of the way, but she'd already bought her ticket. When I picked her up at the airport and explained that we were expecting more than eighty people to the party that day, she almost had a heart attack. Then she moaned that she hadn't brought any clothes with her. As I had just stowed four pieces of luggage into the car, I knew that to be a patent untruth and, as soon as we reached the farm, she gave Murray a quick peck on the cheek and hustled to prepare herself. Unfortunately, that meant using the washroom.

"There's no water," she announced half an hour before our guests were due to arrive.

"Nonsense," Murray declared immediately. "I just washed my hands."

"No. I meant there's no water in the you-know-what."

She was right. Furthermore, there was now no water in the house. I went down to the basement and tried tinkering with the pump. It declined to work and I spent the next hour hauling water to the kitchen from the outdoor taps, which mysteriously remained unaffected. The guests arrived and soon Stew and Chris led a plethora of kids down to the barn to play Superman. Almost immediately, one of them returned to the house.

"I have to go. Where's the washroom?"

I explained that he was in the country now and that we didn't use washrooms. He shot me a look of disbelief. "You've gotta. I can't hold it."

I took him behind the old chicken barn and explained how men how survived similar emergencies throughout history. He wasn't impressed, but it was the first problem solved that day. However, there were seventy-nine waiting to happen. We eventually divided the farm into male and female only reserves, and our urban guests seemed delighted at this unexpected taste of rural, pioneer life. Glady was the only one who would not cooperate. She retrieved a bucket from the basement, carried it to her bedroom, and from that point I didn't want to know further details.

September 1973 saw further changes. Murray now drove to the university three times a week and spent the rest of his time researching and revising what would become his first authoritative article on the constitution's evolution. I'd been given a job at a nearby school, White Rock Elementary.

When March 1974 arrived, I should have been in Canberra, beginning my doctorate. But, because my thesis required further research on the convicts, I'd been given permission to spend the first year in Canada. Every afternoon I came home from school and spent at least three hours slogging my way through various documents dealing with the rebels' treason trials. Much of the material was in French, and it was only through Murray's help that I mastered the many depositions that had been written by barely literate men who used archaic spelling and expressions.

I studied the trial reports and, again with Murray's help, became familiar with the law of treason. As well I tried to write a small biography on each of the fifty-eight convicts, tracking down every reference I could find to help me understand their reasons for rebelling, and what they had done to merit transportation to New South Wales. One night Murray dredged a reference to them from the recesses of his mind. "You know," he remarked, "I think one of your men might have written a diary."

When I pointed out that two had published books about their experiences based on journals, he brushed my remark aside. "No, no, no. I don't mean those." His forehead knotted furiously as he thought for a moment or so. "I swear I've run across a reference somewhere to a handwritten journal. I'll see if I can run it down for you."

An actual handwritten journal, if it hadn't been published, would provide superb help. At the time, I thought the journal would be one of the men's reminiscences, written after his return to Canada. Murray came home the following day and with a grin of pleasure handed me a piece of paper. I looked, saw it was an archival reference and sent a letter off the next day asking the Quebec archives to send me a Xeroxed copy.

A bulky parcel arrived a few weeks later. Shocked, I opened it and looked at the ream of Xerox. The archives had sent a copy of the journal written by an obscure rebel named Basile Roy whose so-called rebellion had consisted of two nights of sentry duty guarding important prisoners in Beauharnois. That he was punished so severely seemed a miscarriage of justice but he lived in the wrong village, had just a little too much status to escape retribution. Hundreds who had fought the British in pitched battle escaped punishment altogether.

To this moment, he had been a minor figure. Now, he became important. When I looked at that package from Quebec, I wanted to turn the tape deck on and play "Proud Mary" at full volume while dancing naked around the farm. Because? Because the Roy journal had been written in Sydney during the man's actual imprisonment as a convict. It could be the cornerstone of my dissertation and I couldn't wait for Murray to come home so that he could see this treasure.

He didn't show any great enthusiasm. Rather, his brow knotted again as he glanced his way through the Xerox. Finally, he looked at me. "This isn't right, you know. It's not what I remembered."

"Well, then. Aren't I lucky because this is perfect?"

"No, Bev." He looked at the manuscript again, much more

carefully, and then turned to me. "Look. He didn't write this himself. It says here it was written for him by François-Maurice Lepailleur." At this, his careful nonchalance broke down and he smiled broadly. "Lepailleur. That's the name I've been trying to remember!"

I could hardly believe my ears. "Are you saying…?"

"There's another journal!"

We looked at each other as we realised the significance of what we'd just said. Then we smiled and this time I did put "Proud Mary" into the tape deck. After cranking the sound as loud as it would go, I dragged Murray outside and we danced till exhaustion. I remember thinking that I had to be luckiest so-and-so in creation.

And so, it was with renewed vigour that I worked on lists of references to research for my last research trip to eastern Canada before I left for Australia in March 1975.

P stands for Providence, Profundity and Propinquity.

It also stands for Propositions.

Sometimes, when I think about these early days with Murray, I feel as though we lived in a permanent state of "f…ing unbelievable." To prove my case, I bring up the insanity of my marriage.

I don't know when Murray began thinking of marrying me. He always pinpointed the date to the day I had stumbled into his office almost paralytic with aching muscles and bruised thighs. I'd pooh-poohed that, pointing out that he was already married to someone else at the time. As he never deviated from that position, I have to believe it. What I am sure about is that he had thought long and hard about marriage by February 14, 1975. For a romantic man, Murray was usually unsentimental, but on this occasion he booked a table at the finest restaurant in the area, sent me roses and even offered to drive – a sacrifice I politely declined.

When he'd first told me about this dinner I had put it down to little more than a special good-bye for I would leave the following day for Quebec and my time there would be very busy. After I'd (hopefully) located the Lepailleur journal, I'd pay Glady a short visit in Montreal, then spend a couple of weeks in Ottawa. I'd fly back to Vancouver, then after two days at the farm, fly down to Canberra. Therefore, after we'd eaten, it was no surprise to me that we settled in for some serious conversation. Murray began with the obvious. "I'm going to miss you."

"Me too," I answered.

I suspected our separation would be harder on Murray than it would be on me. I'd lived with loneliness for most of my life. He'd always been part of a group since he'd made the football team in high school. When I left, I'd be meeting new people, renewing old friendships and enjoying fresh situations. Murray would remain at the farm, be responsible for the many cats we'd acquired by some malicious form of osmosis. He'd sit at the kitchen table opposite my empty chair, go to sleep alongside my empty side of the bed – or so I devoutly hoped. His divorce would become final in early May, and several women had let me know already that they considered him fair game as soon as I was safely in the Antipodes.

To my surprise, Murray had thought long and hard about this situation, my impending departure, and what it meant to both of us. After our liqueurs had arrived, he reopened the conversation with what seemed to be a *non sequitur*. "The fact that your relatives are either step-this or adoptive-that bothers you, doesn't it?"

It did. At times I felt annoyed, frustrated or saddened, and sometimes all three at once when I thought of my family situation. I vividly remembered the irritation of being the only child in a school class without an Anglo-Saxon name, how I'd always had to spell my last name for people and correct their pronunciation. As well, I always had to explain my religion and who the Plymouth Brethren were. Later on, when I relaxed amongst friends and referred to my grandmother as my adoptive mother, I'd be asked to explain what I meant. At such times, Murray often made people laugh when he'd compare me to the mythical person who was his own grandfather. I'd laugh along with our friends, but Murray knew as well as I did that my hyphenated family remained an open sore.

When I sipped my liqueur and shrugged, he went on as though there had been no pause. "I've a proposition, Bev, for you to think about while you're waiting for documents, or missing me out east. I want us to marry but, there's a 'but.'"

If this was a proposal, I wasn't impressed. The other men who had importuned for my hand had known enough to bend their knees. They'd offered flowery speeches rather than this bald-faced proposition that Jane Austen's Mr. Darcy might have made. Stuffily, I replied. "What on earth's your but?"

Murray twisted his snifter a couple of times, letting his brandy swirl gently and almost seemed mesmerized by either its movement or the fumes. It seemed to take forever for him to string his words together. "I'll be honest, Bev. Getting married as soon as I get my divorce papers scares the hell out of me. I feel as if I'm being released after being in jail for twelve years. That, finally, in my life, I have the chance to be foot-loose and fancy free." He swirled his brandy some more. I waited for him to continue, thinking that even Mr. Darcy had done better. Finally, Murray looked across the table and smiled at me. "I love you, Bev, but part of me protests against giving up that freedom, and tells me that I'll be the biggest fool alive if I did so."

Strangely enough, I empathized. If anyone had been forced to tread the straight and narrow it was Murray. Since being enrolled in school at the ridiculous age of three and a half, he'd carried the weight of his family's ambitions on his then scrawny shoulders. He'd gone to university at fifteen, quarterbacked Bishop's University football team at sixteen, won the Rhodes Scholarship at eighteen. Even this evidence of a strong athlete with a fine mind hadn't satisfied his family. Instead his achievements had only fuelled its ambitions that he go on to become prime minister of Canada. For a while, after Oxford, he seemed to be following that path. His decision to bypass Harvard for UBC had been an early attempt at rebellion, his only one until the break-up of his marriage. So, I could well understand why Murray felt he'd never been free.

"That's only a small part of me, Bev," he went on, his eyes pleading for understanding. "A significant part to be sure, but a small one nevertheless. The other, more important, says you're the best thing that ever happened to me and I do not want to lose you. I don't want either of us to be hurt, and I don't want us to be torn apart. So, this is what I'm proposing.

"When you get to Canberra, make arrangements for us to marry there. I'll come down in mid May or so and, if you're willing, we'll be married quietly. Then I'll meet your family as your husband. They won't know we've lived together, and that way we won't get sermons about living in sin."

It sounded great. Too great. "Well, what's the but?"

"Oh, I'm coming to that. I want something in return. Your agreement that if a really gorgeous woman comes along, between now and the wedding, I can play around. Maybe even sleep with her. Without commitments, you understand. I'm not talking about that. I guess I just want some kind of guarantee that if I fool around it won't hurt what I have with you. That's what I'm asking for, I guess."

What could I say? I certainly didn't have words that night. On one hand Murray offered everything I'd ever wanted. The other hand, though, it seemed that nothing but heartbreak and disaster might lie ahead. I could also sense that Murray thought he was offering me a gift – that of legitimacy. Like Murray, I was torn in two. Part of me wanted to grab his offer with both hands, for I knew we were the loves of each other's lives.

Our love making that night had a desperation, and his proposition loomed like a grizzly bear between us. I left the next morning for Quebec City. Even finding Lepailleur's journal didn't raise my spirits. By the time I travelled down to Montreal I still hadn't made any decision. Of course, I couldn't discuss it with Murray's mom. She still hoped he'd become prime minister, so I pretended everything was well. I knew she was having secret fantasies about Murray's status as a divorcee, and thinking about well connected, beautiful women that she could cast as his wife. I thought of giving her a list of European princesses as a parting gift, but I don't think she ever understood the concept of tongue-in-cheek.

When I arrived back at the farm, Murray handed me a package. I tore it open, looked and gasped. While I'd been in the east, he had painstakingly translated the entire Basile Roy journal and now gave it to me as a parting gift. He'd obviously worked day and night on it, and if I'd ever wanted tangible proof of his love, I had it in my hands.

It made leaving for Canberra just that much harder.

CHAPTER 18

C AND W

C stands for Cacophonous, Circumspect and Consternation.

It also stands for Canberra.

By March of 1975 I'd been away from Australia long enough to feel a deep sense of coming home. The sounds of the birds, the shape of the gum trees and the sheer liveliness of Sydney mocked any thought that I'd forgotten my roots. I stayed with Mrs. Wark for a few days and slipped right into my old friendships. It was as though I had never left.

Canberra was new. I'd never been there before, and for a couple of days I felt a sense of alienation. But the Clarks invited me to dinner and I enjoyed renewing my acquaintance with Manning and Dymphna, his wife. They'd stayed on the farm the previous year when they'd swung through Vancouver as part of a world trip and, now, they anchored me. Gradually I met other graduate students. Unlike our North American counterparts, we did not have to attend courses nor pass the dreaded comprehensive exams. All the university demanded was a dissertation within three years from the beginning of the degree. In my case, that meant March 1977 was my deadline. All in all, a very civilized system.

I soon realised just how good the UBC honours history

programme had been. In terms of historiography and methodology I was light years ahead of my colleagues, even those who'd graduated from Oxford or Cambridge, the Ivy League schools, or top Australian universities. Two seminar presentations emphasised this feeling. One involved the editor of a series of documents who explained his task and its importance. I was more interested in what he'd left out because it seemed to me that an editor of documents always put potential users into his own way of thinking. What seem unimportant to him might mean a goldfield to someone else.

When was called upon, I challenged him, ending with, "Professor, in my honours programme, we were taught to always go to the original. Could the money have been better spent by microfilming all the documents and thus making everything available?"

There was an audible gasp. At the time, I had no idea of the man's high status, nor that he usually lined up opposite Manning Clark on various issues. He also controlled access to several post-doctoral appointments and that might have explained the aghast silence. There was no debate, not even a condescending smile in my direction. He simply turned to the questioner and went on as though I hadn't spoken.

Two weeks later, I found myself in another seminar twenty-four hours before Murray would arrive in Sydney. I daydreamed a little, thinking of the delights in store for me the following night. Suddenly the moderator asked if I'd comment on the paper, which had just finished. I gulped. I had listened at the beginning and knew it was about the convict system in the 1840s. I also realised that the presenter had tiptoed around certain conclusions that I thought he could have made, saying such things as, "They must have done" or "Probably they...." Trying to offer constructive advice, I asked, "Why don't you read some of the convict diaries to find out exactly what was going on? You'll make your case much more easily then."

There was that dreaded response again. Dead silence. Finally, another student spoke up. "She can't do that," he told me, his body language letting me know that I was a hick from the North American sticks, "no convict diaries exist. So, nobody knows their thoughts or anything like that. That's why we have to surmise."

"And, that's strange," I replied, "I know exactly what some convicts thought and how much money they made in illegal enterprises. I even know where they went to drink, who had affairs with prostitutes, what day the governor visited them and so on. I know which newspapers they read and what they thought about the daily news. You name it, I can tell you."

"You're joking."

I reached into my briefcase and pulled out a hefty folder. "No joke. Here's the proof. One of the diaries my convicts wrote while in Sydney."

It was an academic bombshell that reverberated as if shot from Big Bertha. The department head was the first across the room to see my Xeroxed copy. After looking at it, he jumped back. "It's in French."

"Of course. That was the language they spoke."

I felt the same way then that I had three years earlier in the library at UBC. I'd been lucky enough to have a winner for my honours thesis, I'd felt the same way when we found the Roy journal, and now I knew that the Lepailleur journal, which was far more detailed that the Roy one, would provide hard evidence on convict life that no one knew about. The two journals would make convict historians revise some suppositions. More importantly, I now knew that my doctoral dissertation would tell new stories. Elated, pleased with myself and the world, I flew to Sydney the next morning, arriving in time to meet Murray's flight from Vancouver.

I hadn't realised until I was in his arms how much I'd missed him. I wished I'd scheduled nothing but days of seclusion in our Sydney hotel. Instead, I'd agreed to a whirlwind of social activities as my friends wanted to meet him and I wanted to show him the Sydney I loved so passionately. We hit problems almost immediately.

"You have to play married," I told him as we wended our way to a dinner the first night.

"Bev. I've just got divorced. Give me a couple of days before I get shackled again."

I shrugged. "Well, I don't mind, if you don't. I'm warning you though, you'll have to listen to sermon after sermon on the virtues of the married state and the dangers of sin..."

He leaned across in the taxi. "I love you my precious, lovey-dovey wife." He smooched a little more, and then grinned. "Will that do?"

I grinned back, well pleased. "Um, you need a few more adjectives and less baby talk but, overall, it's a fair beginning."

He played the role well for the remainder of the night, telling me when we returned to the hotel it was just as well he had a role to play. My dear friends, knowing that neither of us was a professing Christian produced an excruciatingly large group of people who had, as their common goal, a compulsion to preach the gospel to us. Worse, they'd split us up so that eye contact was our only communication. I listened with bare civility to someone tell me that he'd pray that I wouldn't be seduced by that Bolshie-lover professor of mine, Manning Clark. Murray coped with something similar, an attack on all historians whom, his tormentor claimed, had to be Marxist – a philosophical position held by neither of us. Murray sought to deflect the attack by claiming he was lawyer but that only made matters worse.

"Don't you know what the Lord said about lawyers?" he was asked.

Murray knew. He looked around at his opulent surroundings then asked in reply, "And do you know the connection he made between rich people and the eye of the needle?"

Numbly, his inquisitor turned to harass someone else. It was not an auspicious beginning but worse was to befall us when we returned to our hotel. Boy phoned. Somehow, he had found out Murray was in Sydney and demanded a meeting. I negotiated, finally arranging a sightseeing trip for Murray, which would culminate in afternoon tea with Boy. Again, Murray played happy husband and things went surprisingly well. Boy was intimidated by Murray's size and intellect, his Rhodes Scholarship (which had made the family gossip line) and surprised by my happiness. What we didn't know for some years was that Boy had decided that Murray, with his beard and longish hair, had to be a counteragent with the CIA and thus, with Murray somehow validated, we escaped criticism.

Things turned rosy once we reached Canberra and Murray reconnected with Manning. After dinner, they drank wine and swapped academic tall stories until Dymphna stopped the conversation by demanding to know our marriage plans.

W stands for Wardrobe, Whimsical and Wondrous.

It also stands for Wedding.

"They'll be married here. Right?" Manning responded without hesitation.

"Right," Murray agreed and when he launched into another story, Dymphna and I went out to the kitchen to work out the details.

I'd done most of the paperwork by this point. Murray, of course, would have to sign various applications but these were trifling details. I explained this and Dymphna now asked how many people she should plan for.

"Plan for?"

"For the wedding breakfast."

I'd kept our impending marriage a secret. Most people assumed we already were married. I'd even gone so far as to use my pretend marriage state as an excuse to turn down one pressing offer for an affair from someone I couldn't afford to alienate. So, my answer was simple. "Just the four of us."

"No one else?"

I shook my head. "The celebrant?"

She nodded agreement but immediately voiced her disapproval. "It's not proper. Everyone should have a wedding breakfast with lots of people to toast their future." Then she brightened, "Well, where are you going for your honeymoon?"

"Nowhere in particular. As this is such a big trip for Murray, I thought we'd stay close to home."

"Nonsense. Why don't you spend a week at Wapengo?"

Wapengo was the Clark holiday residence on the south coast, about five hours from Canberra. It was fabled territory for us because Manning, in one of his more whimsical moments, had located a non-existent industry there in his multi-volumed *History of Australia*. Dymphna's offer, then, was a wonderful gift of friendship and I accepted it with gratitude. It was a good thing that I had, because Manning had made the identical suggestion to Murray.

Days later, I became sicker than I'd ever been. It turned out that

I was allergic to spring in Canberra. I bought over-the-counter medication for sinus problems and antihistamines by the score, but nothing worked. In total desperation, the day before the wedding, I finally went to the university infirmity. They checked me in immediately and began pumping me full of antibiotics for my infected sinuses. While I fretted, I wondered about Murray. Manning took the wedding seriously and was giving Murray his version of a stag night.

Next morning, I demanded to be discharged. The doctors argued that I needed one more day of treatment. I argued that if they didn't release me soon I'd be late to my own wedding. One more injection they told me, and then I had to wait for some medication to be delivered.

When I finally arrived at the Clarks, still in my jeans, Dymphna sniffed and reminded me that in her day women dressed up to be married. I told her that I'd dreamed of a traditional service for years, but knew that the celebrant would simply move on to his next appointment if I were late. It was either blue jeans or no wedding. Pacified by this evidence of my sensibilities, she gave me a small bouquet of flowers from her garden.

The Clark living room, where we would be married, was stark white. A huge painting of Manning and his dog on the rocks at Wapengo by one of Australia's greatest painters dominated one wall. When Dymphna walked me in, Manning sat beneath it talking to Murray who was, in turn, trying to bring the celebrant into the conversation.

The poor man was young and suffering, very obviously, from a case of celebrity-itis. Manning, at that time and at formal occasions, ranked after the prime minister, the governor general and the Anglican primate in importance. His name was constantly in the press and our celebrant was obviously awe-struck. Fortunately, he was also on a tight schedule, otherwise the ceremony might never have started.

The first few minutes went easily. His voice became stronger as he gained confidence and Manning kept blessedly quiet. Murray and I made our responses on cue. Then the celebrant asked whether a bar of consanguinity would prevent our marriage. Murray swore there was none and then it was my turn.

"I'm willing to accept Murray's word," I said after a long pause. "Though, honestly, I don't know what the word means."

That did it. Manning had been quiet for a record twelve minutes and I had unwittingly given him license to speak. He launched into a thirty-minute lecture on the abuses of consanguinity throughout history, ignoring every feeble attempt by the celebrant to shut him up. Finally, seeing him about to run down, Murray leapt into the breech. He now gave an impassioned speech on the legal side of the issue, or non-issue, dredging up doubtful precedent after precedent and, as he later claimed, giving the ceremony a Canadian perspective. The celebrant metaphorically threw up his hands in face of this verbal onslaught and shrank against a chair, shaking his head from side to side as though he could make the nightmare go away. It shook even harder when Dymphna, whom I suspected he thought was the only sane one, began an explanation of the word's etymological roots. I joined the celebrant in shaking my head.

Finally, the three of them looked at each other with congratulatory smugness. After I announced that I now understood the word and swore that consanguinity would not be a barrier to our marriage, the celebrant jumped to his feet and whipped through the remainder of the ceremony. Finally, he told Murray he could kiss the bride.

"No, thanks," my esteemed and very new husband said breezily. "She stinks."

It was true, of course. My infected sinuses did smell, but I've always felt that should have been a matter best kept to ourselves. The celebrant shot of look of loathing at Murray and, as though fearing a medical lecture, produced certificates for us to sign. With that done, I breathed a sigh of relief. Good-bye Boissery. No longer would I have to explain its pronunciation. Greenwood was so much easier.

Dymphna bustled out and came back carrying a tray of aquavit. She offered a drink to the celebrant but he gave her an anguished look. "I'm already late. If Professor Clark could just give me back my pen, I'll be on my way."

Manning's head jerked up. "Your pen? I don't have your pen, sir."

The celebrant shrivelled again. His nightmare had come true. He would have to confront Manning Clark after all. "Yes. You do, sir. It's in your front pocket." He reached as though he was going to take it until Manning slapped his hand away.

I surmised that the celebrant's wife, mother, or lover must have given him that pen. Nothing else that could have inspired him to tackle Manning. The effort he made to gather his courage for another attempt was plainly obvious. "Please, professor. After you signed the certificates, you put my pen in your pocket. I can see it. There."

Manning looked at the poor man as if he were an insect that had suddenly acquired strange verbal abilities. Then, he reached for the pen and we all collapsed with relief. But it wasn't going to be that easy. Manning held the pen up and examined it closely. "I'll have you know," he finally said, "that I wrote three thousand words this morningwith this pen. So, it could not be yours."

Checkmate – or, at the very least, stalemate. Manning clutched the pen, the celebrant clutched his chair. Murray and I looked at each other and I wondered if fate was punishing me for being married in blue jeans. Finally, Dymphna gave a great sigh of resignation and intervened. "Manning, look in your inside pocket, will you?"

Obediently Manning opened the jacket of his suit, examined the inside pocket and pulled out an identical pen. "Oh."

We were no closer to a resolution because now he had to decide which pen had produced those three thousand words. He held up one, then the other. It was like a shell game—now you see it, now you don't. At least, that's the way it seemed to me. But the celebrant was made of sterner stuff and he kept his eye on his pen. When Manning finally said, "Well, which is yours?" he made an undignified grab, pocketed the pen and almost ran from the room.

"Would you like to stay for the wedding luncheon?" Dymphna called after him. "It's jugged hare."

I'm sure he thought she meant jugged hair. His wailing, "Nooooooooooooooo," sounded forever as he fled from the house.

As Dymphna served aquavit, droves of people began arriving for some magical party in the middle of their work day that wasn't, of course, a wedding breakfast. Dymphna simply would not be cheated out of a party. I lost track of Murray and, not wanting to offend anybody with my toxic sinuses, found a quiet corner of the house and reflected on my wedding day.

Blue jeans instead of white lace. No sermon but three lectures. Two and a half hours rather than the twenty minutes I'd envisaged. By then my medication must have kicked in because I can remember laughing. Of course, my laughter might have had something to do with Dymphna's version of a wedding cake: sultanas, raisins and a dab of flour, all floating in brandy and held together by some magnificent icing. When Murray and I slipped away to head for the coast, our guests were still going strong.

My wedding was strange but little did I suspect that the honeymoon would make it appear perfectly normal.

CHAPTER 19

H AND V

H stands for Halcyon, Horrific and Harrowing.
It also stands for Honeymoon.

The five-hour drive from Canberra to Wapengo seemed anti-
climatic. I suppose I'd thought that the actual marriage ceremony
would have given me a sense of a beginning. Instead I'd been
amused by its farcical aspects. A virgin might have anticipated
the beginnings of a sexual relationship, but we'd lived together
for thirty months so there was no heightened excitement about
impending sex, or the sense of getting to know a beloved. I
remember thinking that maybe the old ways were best after all,
that familiarity wasn't necessarily a good thing. Then I asked
myself would I have voluntarily given up all the delights that
living with Murray had entailed in favour of waiting for a
traditional wedding night, and the honest answer was not.

If I'd thought there'd be no romance on my honeymoon, Murray
soon refuted that notion once we arrived at the Clark's cottage.
After spotting a huge wool fleece by the fireplace, he declared we
would not spend our first married night in anything as mundane
as a bed. So, we slept that night by the flickering light of an
ironwood fire with the fleece for a mattress. It had been a day
we'd talk about for years. Thus, it was with total horror that I
woke to hear someone prowling about in the kitchen. Disturbing

headlines ran through my head: "Naked Honeymooners Bludgeoned to Death," or, "Honeymoon Horror." I shook Murray awake and whispered, "Get up."

"Still dark," he muttered as he turned his back to me.

"Ssshh." I shook him again and this time he yawned. "Get up. Someone's robbing us."

As he reached for me, a pot clattered to the floor. Instantly, Murray came awake, and with the stealth of a rampaging elephant made his way towards the kitchen in naked magnificence. "Who the hell are you?" he finally shouted.

Another pot dropped and this time there was a squishing sound as well. "Geez, mate, don't creep up on a feller like that. I'm Roland. Roland Clark."

After this there was much mumbled conversation while the smells and sounds of frying eggs and bacon tantalised my senses. As Murray didn't come back, I guessed he was sharing Roland's breakfast. Finally, I heard Roland say, "Well, can you give me a hand, mate?"

"Sure," Murray agreed.

Roland was Manning's second youngest son and, as we found out, the manager of this coastal farm. He hadn't heard that we were coming and thought our arrival a lucky break for him as he had chores he couldn't put off. So, pressed into service, Murray dressed hurriedly, roared off in a truck and arrived back eleven hours later.

"Where on earth have you been?" I asked, already assuming the role of nagging wife to perfection.

"Don't ask," Murray groaned. "Just find some whisky."

I found Manning's liquor cupboard and from his array of

whiskies chose a rare single malt on the assumption that Murray must have done something to deserve it. I was right. Roland had taken Murray to an area of the farm that needed fencing. While Murray dug holes, Roland put the poles in and then they'd affixed strands of barbed wire. Deciding that Murray should have at least one treat on his honeymoon, he'd taken him for lunch with one of the area's pioneers who'd driven the teams of bullocks that had hauled the original trees to market. Then, had come the fun part of the day. They'd castrated a herd of young cattle. No wonder my poor spouse was so rattled.

Manning and Dymphna arrived the next day. So much for offering us a honeymoon retreat. Murray quit being the farm labourer and happily reverted to his familiar role of historian, arguing theories and facts with Manning. I helped Dymphna until she decided it would be far more efficient if I read and she worked. Other times, Murray and I explored the magnificent property. One evening after dinner, Dymphna surprised us by remarking that we should have a real honeymoon. "Why don't you drive down to Melbourne. There's a Dali exhibit there, and if you take the coast road Murray can see some glorious scenery."

It sounded great. Original works by Salvador Dali. More importantly, my favorite cousin Bruce, Vic's son, lived in Melbourne. I phoned, invited ourselves to stay and we set off the following morning.

By the time we reached Bruce's house, his wife had phoned all her friends and acquaintances. "Bruce's cousin Bev and her Rhodes Scholar husband from Canada," began every conversation — or so we heard from Bruce. She'd arranged a jam-packed itinerary with various parties given in honour of the Rhodes Scholar by her friends. We shrugged and went along with her plans. I didn't know Melbourne well, so both of us enjoyed sightseeing and Dymphna had been correct. The Dali exhibition was goose-pimply magnificent; the parties, on the other hand, were disastrous.

The last party was the most pretentious. I dressed three times before Bruce's wife pronounced me suitable. Only after Murray explained that he hadn't brought a suit with him was he allowed the informality of a cashmere sweater. Our hosts' house was large, but its dark brocades and velvets bordered on something you might see in a bawdyhouse, although some of its tawdry magnificence was diminished by wall-to-wall people. We pushed our way through to a large salon where we finally saw two free spaces on a sofa. Murray eased his way down, but when I tried to sit as well a woman's hand shot out to block me. "This space is taken. Your place is over there."

Feeling like Alice in Wonderland, I looked to where she pointed. There was an empty chair by the fireplace that seemed to have "Reserved" all over it. "There?" I asked incredulously.

"There. That's yours."

I'd never heard of pre-arranged seating at parties, but then I didn't know Melbourne well. Murray and I exchanged raised eyebrows and obediently I made my way across the room. I might well have been in purdah. No one spoke to me; no one served me wine or even offered *hors d'oeuvres*. I looked myself over, but everything seemed in place and what made my situation particularly galling was that everyone seemed to be salivating over Murray. Surrounded by women, he was in his element. As I watched, one popped a juicy oyster into his mouth while another handed him a glass of white wine. I hadn't even seen a glass of water. Worse, he was having a great time, telling stories about Oxford while I languished in my quarantine. As I heard him begin to talk about his favourite rpofessor, C.S. Lewis, I made up my mind. When someone left his side, I scrambled across the room and slipped into the empty space. But I'd no sooner wriggled my bottom into comfort than the woman who'd barred me from there before did so again. "Sorry," she said with acid cheeriness, "your place is over there."

"Why?" I exploded. "No one talks to me. The waiters don't even know that place exists. I'm bored, hungry and thirsty."

She was implacable and on her home turf. Like a whipped dog I scurried back to my designated place. Murray got up to follow, but he was pushed down as a voice admonished him, "Don't go. She'll be looked after. This is your place."

At this, he and I exchanged serious glances. It was too bizarre for words and if we'd had our own car, we would have left. "Had enough?" Murray muttered. "Let's find Bruce and go." As we began our way across the room he whispered, "Whatever happens, don't leave me. That's a man-eating shark here I've been tangling with."

We were fortunate. Murray's man-eater was repairing her cosmetics in the washroom, and so we safely navigated our way out of the salon. Our luck then ran out as we bumped into our host. "You're leaving?" he asked, not believing his eyes.

"Yes. Thank you very much for your hospitality," Murray murmured politely and unconvincingly.

"You can't go."

Murray and I looked at each other and I saw him square his shoulders. At that moment, obviously warned by someone, his man-eater arrived. "You can't go," she repeated.

"Why not?" we said in unison.

They looked at each other and finally Bruce arrived in a hurry. Murray turned to him in relief. "Just what the hell is going on here?"

Bruce blushed, something I would not have believed if I hadn't seen it. "Well, er," he mumbled incoherently. Then he turned to us and we saw he was a little shame-faced. "You, er, have to understand, this was the wife's idea. Not mine. I didn't know anything about it until ten minutes ago."

"Bull. You told us about this party when we arrived."

Bruce shuffled his feet, looking like his four-year-old self facing one of Evelyn's lectures. "Well, um. Yes, um. That I did. But what I didn't know then was that this was a wife-swapping party and these," he said in a rush and, then, pointing to the host and the man-eater, added, "these are your partners for the night."

If I hadn't been so scared, I think I would have dropped on the spot in amazement. What kind of knucklehead would have taken a couple on their honeymoon to a wife-swapping party? But what Bruce said made perfect sense and explained all the funny manoeuvres that had plagued us all evening. Murray obviously thought the same for, with a sophistication that I would not have expected, he said amiably in his best patrician-Canadian voice, "Well, I suppose in that case, it's only reasonable that we kiss when we say good-bye."

The man-eater smiled sensing, I thought, a chance to change his mind. She rushed forward, arms outstretched. But she hadn't reckoned on a champion quarterback. With a superb move, Murray ducked. When she stopped in amazement, he stepped right up to the host and kissed him full on the lips while groping the guy's ass.

Our host jumped back as though he'd been electrified, the look on his face searing itself into my memory. Bruce took the opportunity to find our coats and, not waiting to put mine on, I raced down the hallway as if running the Olympic hundred-metre sprint. No way was I kissing anyone in that house.

We arrived back at Bruce's house numb with shock. That dissipated after Bruce produced some bottles of wine rivalling those we'd been served earlier. Murray obviously had a considerable problem getting the night into perspective, and so he began probing into Bruce's life. Bruce was then working as a carpet-layer and when he heard this Murray raised his eyebrows.

"Did you finish high school?"

"Yes," Bruce answered and then added, "I didn't do well in my exams though. Didn't see much use in studying."

"But you're obviously very intelligent."

"What can I say? I was stupid but, at the time, I didn't care. I didn't realize that I was putting myself into a dead end. If I could do it over again, I would."

While Bruce stared at his feet, Murray and I looked at each other before he said very softly, "There's a spare bedroom at home and with Bev down here for the rest of the year, I could use some company when I go home. What do you say to coming back to Canada with me? I'll buy your ticket and do my best to get you into my university in Vancouver."

I saw Bruce swallow as though a mirage had become tangible. We sipped our wine as we waited for a response, both of us glad that it wasn't an immediate no. Finally, Bruce looked at us with tears running down his face. "I'm not a free man. I'm trapped into my marriage and I have responsibilities here. I will have to talk this over with my wife. I'm not going to say anything to her before you leave because, as I think you know by now, she'll probably try and tear your heads off. But, I'll phone you in Canberra."

We left early the next morning. His wife had not yet arrived back from the party, obviously enjoying her "partner's" company more than her husband's. On our way back to Canberra, I took Murray to visit Bruce's parents. After retiring from International Harvester, Vic and his wife Gene had settled in a small town in northern Victoria called Yackandandah.

V stands for Venerate, Versatile, Vicissitude.

It also stands for Victor.

I had loved Vic for as long as I could remember. He was a special man. Of all the family, he was the only one who maintained anything like a normal relationship with Girlie. More surprisingly, he stayed in the Brethren longer than any of Evelyn's children and even carried on Boy's tradition of going out into the community to preach. In Vic's case, he used his work connections to begin a radio programme to deliver the gospel to country areas. He became quasi-famous as "Uncle Vic" and several times a year toured remote towns in Victoria and southern New South Wales.

He knew that I'd worked out the truth about Girlie. After we'd washed the dinner dishes, I wasn't totally surprised when Vic began talking about the past and asked for my forgiveness.

"What on earth for?" I asked in amazement. I'd always thought he'd gone out of his way to help me.

"Because I didn't do what my conscience said I should," he responded haltingly. Slowly he explained that while the custody issue was being fought between Girlie and Evelyn, he and Gene had agonized about stepping in.

"We wanted to bring you up, but we couldn't."

I nodded. Everyone in the family knew how difficult it would have been to go against Evelyn. But Vic said that hadn't stopped them from adopting me. Rather, it had been the unforgiving nature of the Plymouth Brethren. "Everyone would have said you were the reason we had to get married," he finally admitted and the fact they he'd caved in to such pressure, I gathered, had eaten away at him as he had seen how increasingly unhappy I was.

Once he told me this, I felt devastated. I had only known love from them. One memorable Christmas, Bruce and I had somehow goaded Junior to the point where he lost his temper. Bruce was an athletic kid and tall for his age so Junior lashed out at me instead, punching my face and breaking my nose.

As several family members stood aghast, Bruce pommelled Junior, promising further retribution until Vic pulled him away. Evelyn and Vera rushed to console Junior, clucking over the damage Bruce had done to his face, but, Gene concerned herself with me. To staunch the blood pouring from my nose, she picked up some embroidered Irish linen handkerchiefs she'd just been given and administered first aid. I don't know if she was ever able to get the blood out of that fine linen. If not, I hope the handkerchiefs served to remind her of my admiration and gratitude.

This was just one instance that made me certain there would have been love in Victor's family. However, there was also a terrible sternness at times. I don't think I could have negotiated my problems or gained such early control of my life living with them as easily as I'd done with Evelyn. What's more, I shudder to think of Bruce and me in the same household and the havoc we would have unleashed on an unsuspecting world.

When I went to bed that night, I had the old nightmare where I couldn't seem to make people hear me. Although Murray consoled me, I felt desolate. For the first time, I'd sensed an ending to the dream.

"Five more minutes," I told him. "If I could only have stayed asleep for five more minutes, I might have known what it all meant."

"If you had stayed asleep for five more seconds," Murray replied, "you might have gone insane. Bev, you were terrified."

I'd thought, to that point, that I'd outgrown the dream. I'd told

Murray about it a couple of years before, never expecting that he'd hear my screaming.

On our return to Canberra, we settled back into my student life. Murray talked with Manning about a project he planned for his sabbatical – the translation and editing of the Lepailleur journal. Manning promised to talk his publisher and let them know he was willing to write a foreword for Murray.

A few days later, Bruce phoned. His marriage, to all intents and purposes, was over, and he willingly accepted Murray's offer. And so, when I drove Murray to Sydney to catch the plane to Vancouver, we met Bruce at the airport. He'd teach the following year and then come back to spend his sabbatical year in Canberra. Later, when I watched them disappear down the Qantas corridor leading to their plane back to Vancouver, they already looked like old friends, laughing and talking and slapping each other's back.

This time Murray was the one flying off to new adventures while I returned to Canberra and unbearable loneliness.

CHAPTER 20

R AND R

R *stands for Research, Repercussions and Ramifications*

It also stands for Reunion.

I also returned to hard work. Somehow my loneliness made it easier to write what I thought of as the boring parts of my dissertation and by mid-May, the following year, I'd finished the first half of my dissertation detailing why the rebels had been transported to Australia. It involved recapping a couple of chapters of Quebec history so that Australians would understand why Canadiens had felt that they no other recourse than rebellion.

As I drove to Sydney to meet Murray, I felt a sense of accomplishment and relief. We spent couple of weeks in the Sydney area as both of us needed to research at the Mitchell Library, staying with two of my friends, Rob and Moya Adams of Turramurra. Murray genuinely liked them, enjoyed furthering his acquaintance with them and they enjoyed telling him stories of my chequered past.

In such an atmosphere, I felt strong enough to do something I'd sworn never to do – I phoned Girlie. Her joy transformed the phone lines. When she asked to see me, I cautiously agreed. It had been more than twenty-five years since I'd seen her, and I didn't know if I could break through the barriers between us. Like a coward, I asked her to come to Turramurra, telling myself that if things went wrong, I could simply run away to the Adams's house.

We met at a restaurant and neither of us said much for a while. I can't remember what made the situation change but, suddenly, my mother began talking and it was as if floodgates had opened. When she told stories of her childhood, I understood them because I had lived through many of the same experiences. More excitingly, she seemed to have the same mental shortcuts that I'd thought unique to me. After we said good-bye, and I'd promised to keep in touch, I described the experience to Murray saying that it felt like trumpets had sounded.

I wanted her to meet Murray, so we asked her to dinner. At first the conversation was stilted, but gradually things became easier until Murray asked why she had "given" me to Evelyn when she obviously hated her mother and when her own childhood in that family had been so horrifying.

The resultant silence was deafening.

Girlie had made a new life for herself. My half sister, Caera, was doing spectacularly well and I think it had become easy for Girlie to forget about her early years. Now she bragged that she had a daughter doing her doctorate under Manning Clark to her friends, but they didn't know that she hadn't wanted me born, or that she had first sold me and then tried to kidnap me back.

I phoned her several times after that and flew up to Sydney twice to take her out to dinner. Unfortunately, the more we met, the more softly the trumpets sounded to the point where they became mute. Part of this can be attributed to the huge differences in our lifestyles and education, but those problems could have been worked through. What stopped the relationship dead in its tracks was her need to prove that she understood constitutional law better than Murray.

I have no idea why she became so evangelical about constitutions because she knew nothing about them. But, eventually, every time she began arguing, I reverted to my childhood's abhorrence of her became almost catatonic in her presence. Murray told me that at one point I'd almost curled myself into a fetal position and shuddered whenever she touched me. It was a sad ending compared to the glorious beginning at Turramurra.

To bring me out of what he called my Girlie-depression, Murray suggested that he head to the Thredbo area for a couple of days' skiing. He had brought our cross-country skis down with him and I soon discovered a huge difference between cross-country skiing in Vancouver and Australia. The Australian alps are some of the world's oldest rocks. Time and erosion have smoothed their peaks into plateaus so, that we needed to take a ski-lift to the cross-country runs on the mountaintops. That was fine until we realized that we'd enjoyed ourselves so much that we'd missed the last lift down the mountain. We'd have to ski the downhill runs to the bottom.

About half way down I felt exhausted and sick. I wanted to do nothing more but curl up in a ball under a goose feather duvet, but there was the small matter of survival. And so, I kept trekking, stopping once or twice to throw up. We reached our car as the last daylight disappeared. Murray took one look at me and offered to drive to the nearest hospital. I shook my head. I wasn't that sick.

I still felt sick when I drove home the next day. But once we arrived in Canberra, I forced myself to become energetic. We had a dinner party to give and my guests would eat one of my culinary experiments – carpetbag steak. I trekked to the market and after extensive consultations with butchers, arrived home with a steak that I would be able to cut open and fill with a mixture of crabmeat and shrimps. Then I'd sew the pocket up, broil the steak and top it with *Béchamel* sauce. It had sounded delicious when I'd read about it in a recipe book and my guests that night ate every bit.

I went to bed thinking that I might get a job as a chef if my dissertation didn't work out and woke to tremendous pain. Immediately I thought that I'd poisoned myself and my guests the previous night. But Murray was fine and so was one other friend when he phoned to thank us for the dinner. Finally, after hearing horrible sounds, Murray came into the bathroom and, after sponging my face, took charge. "Get a coat or a gown on. Something. Anything. I don't care. I'm taking you to hospital."

I was too sick to argue. While I made myself presentable, Murray looked up the hospital on the map and then carried me to the car. I didn't want to wear a seatbelt because I hurt so much, but he insisted and so we set off. The first corner was an adventure. He hadn't driven in Australia before and had trouble knowing which side of the road he should be on. With typical brilliance he muttered, "To hell with this," put the emergency flashes on and drove down the middle of the road, hand on the horn, scattering cars right and left. I could not have cared less as I had the passenger door open and was vomiting continuously.

We reached the emergency ward and Murray stopped the car with an alarming screech. The waiting room was full and we were given a number. I slumped a corner, thinking that surely my stomach must have emptied itself. Murray though was worried and, after we'd waited about ten minutes, he picked me up again and carried me over to a nurse's station. "My wife's seriously ill," he began before invoking his magical mantra, the one he used in all extraordinary situations in foreign countries, "I'm a Canadian and…" He didn't need to finish because I vomited over the nurse's desk and thus gained her full attention.

I stayed in hospital for twenty-four hours without any diagnosis. Doctors arrived periodically to poke and prod and, when they did, I'd involuntarily scream. I seemed to be passed from one specialist to another and finally I was told I'd be discharged the following morning. A nurse had a different opinion. No one could have been as sick as I without something being seriously wrong, she argued to the chief surgeon. He agreed and operated the next day.

By the time I regained consciousness late at night. I wanted to know what had been wrong with me but no one would say. I had to wait, they said, until the surgeon did his rounds. Convinced that they'd found something serious, I couldn't sleep. When the surgeon finally came, his demeanour that I blurted out, "Do I have cancer?"

"No," he said immediately and I breathed a sigh of relief, only to become apprehensive again when he continued, "but…"

"But what?"

"You've been very ill. We'd never seen anything like it before." Eventually I deduced from his hemmings and hawings that I'd had an appendicitis attack at the very time as my right fallopian tube ruptured because of an ectopic pregnancy.

It took months to recover from that operation. Murray was superb and Manning revealed an unexpected compassion and understanding. I couldn't concentrate, I couldn't work and to help my listlessness Murray decided to drive me towards summer – the far north coast of New South Wales. He'd made the right decision, although I suspect Dymphna Clark had a hand in it. Eventually we landed in a small community called Woolgoogla and there I sat on the beach for days on end, thinking about my thesis and slowly regaining a semblance of my strength – physically and mentally.

It seemed to me that all I'd done so far was write second-hand accounts of basic Quebec and Australian history. An idea, though, had rumbled around my brain for months. There was one incredible different between the Canadian convicts and their British counterparts. The Canadians were determined to reunite with their families. That was the real reason that they kept journals or paid their literate friends to write them. They knew their families and local priests were agitating for their pardons and return. Letters had arrived telling them this. But they also knew the Australian convict bureaucracy. If they couldn't go home, they would bring their families to Sydney, and, so they worked hard.

The British convicts could not have been more different. Only a handful of the 160,00 plus returned to their families. For the rest, it seemed there had been an emotional castration. They didn't write home, didn't keep journals and didn't save for familial reunions.

I knew what abandonment felt like and the damage it had done to me. To some extent I, as well, had lost touch with friends and family once I'd settled into Canada. I had become a "loner", much like the men who had worked to build Australia. That sense of aloneness explained the Australian ethos of mateship. Their mates helped them through life. I had Murray.

But what effect did that huge segment of men who had deserted their British wives and children have on the nation they help build? Was there lasting damage? Did it explain why women had to fight so hard for acceptance?

These questions went around and around my head as I sat on that Woolgoogla beach. I realised that I didn't have time to rethink my thesis. It was already May and I had less than ten months to produce an acceptable 100,000 words thesis. But, I kept thinking and pondering.

R stands for Replenishment, Restive and Ruminations.

It also stands for Return.

Stewart and Chris came for Christmas in 1976. We arranged for them to stay at Manly their first night, thinking they'd be jet-lagged. But they bounced from the plane and started running as soon as they'd cleared customs, chattering non-stop as we drove over the Harbour Bridge. The beach wowed them and they were silent for all of five seconds. However, they listened as I explained about the dangers of sun exposure, and agreed to wear their tee shirts when they swam that first day. I told them about swimming within the flags – a concept new to them – and how they must leave the water immediately if a shark alarm sounded. At this, their ears pricked up because one well-meaning friend had taken them to see *Jaws* the night before they flew down.

When the shark alarm sounded thirty minutes later, they scampered out of the water. Murray told them to look back and, sure enough, when they turned, they saw triangular fins moving just beyond the surf. From that moment, and no matter what else happened, their holiday was a success.

Sometimes I think Australia went out of its way to make sure Stewart and Chris not only enjoyed their time, but had lasting memories as well. They saw kangaroos, emus, koalas and the like in their natural environs. Chris was entertained by a blue-tongued lizard while playing cricket. Manning took Stewart fishing for salmon on the rocky point of Wapengo. They enjoyed our friends and watching their dad play baseball. Most of all, their visit meant so much to Murray and after they returned to Vancouver, we felt the void they left behind. One night after talking about it, we decided to sell the farm when we returned home. We'd buy a house in Vancouver, as close to the boys as we could find.

Our own time left in Australia now seemed minuscule. I concentrated on writing, trying to catch up on the months I'd missed through illness. After Murray and I decided to sail home on the P&O ship, the *Oriana*, we'd induced Glady to fly down to Honolulu to meet us, and then travel the final stage together. As the *Oriana* would sail from Sydney April 4th, 1977, that became the absolute deadline for submitting my dissertation.

Murray flew to Sydney on April 1, to say goodbye to Rob and Moya Adams and to make sure that all of our thirty-four pieces of luggage were safely stowed in the cargo hold. On the morning of April 4 Canberra friends drove me to the printer's where I delivered the dissertation for Xerox and binding, and then to the airport. After arriving in Sydney, I took a taxi to Circular Quay reaching the dock about an hour before the ship was due to sail. Unfortunatley, it looked for a while as though that might well be as close as I got to the ship.

I'd applied for Canadian citizenship on my last research trip to Ottawa and my application had been approved only after I'd returned to Canberra. Therefore, I'd entered Australia as an Australian citizen and, as such, had no need for a visa. However, I had to surrender that passport when I became a Canadian and my new Canadian passport, issued in Canberra, had no entry stamp or visa in it. I explained this circumstance as well as I could but the emigration officials seemed disinclined to believe me. For a while it seemed I might be held in custody while they checked my story.

Fortunately, I had the sense to resort to every woman's friend – copious tears. My friends were having a farewell party without my being there. My husband wouldn't know how to rescue me. The ship would sail without me and I had no money, I sobbed. It was all on board with my luggage. Finally, common sense prevailed and they let me board.

The seventeen-day trip was an excellent hiatus, although Murray became bored after Honolulu. After a day's rest, we entered into various activities with gusto – particularly if a bottle of champagne was the prize. And so, I saw a side of Murray I never expected to find. Amongst strangers – people who had no preconceptions about him, who didn't know that he'd won the Rhodes or was a professor – Murray became an extrovert. He entered Hawaiian dress and hula competitions, dressed up as Gilbert and Sullivan's admiral of fleet, and enjoyed general knowledge contests. All told, between the two of us, we won a grand total of sixteen bottles of champagne, a very respectable haul that ensured we had plenty of friends for the trip. Even Glady seemed mellow when she came on board at Honolulu. She'd been away from Montreal long enough to adjust to a different cultural environment and she was overjoyed to see Murray again.

The night before our arrival in Vancouver, experienced travellers had warned us to get up at dawn, so that we would not miss the ship's progress down Georgia Strait and Burrard Inlet. I'd thought nothing could rival the entrance to Sydney's harbour, but that morning convinced me otherwise. It truly was as magnificent as we'd been told. There was another surprise as well. Both of us had been away long enough to experience "foliage shock".

Our life changed once we landed. Murray's counter-revolution days were behind him. He'd represented the Canadian government in Australia when touring several universities, speaking on the constitution and discreetly evaluating them as possible sites for Canadian Studies programmes. His beard had become short and very stylish, and once the facial foliage disappeared I discovered he had dimples. My blue-jean days were also temporarily left behind in Australia. As befitting these new images, we bought a house close to the boys' home and the university, in an exclusive area of the city. We were professionals now and expected to act as such.

We joined various clubs, played bridge with friends and altogether became as respectable as I think it was possible for us to be, which was, as we found out, not quite as much as other people.

Glady had a chance to see the new house before she left for Montreal and, after checking its plumbing, she fell in love with it. She was so happy her son was finally living in something fitting that she even helped finance it. When we took her to the airport and said our good-byes, she promised she'd not be a stranger. In fact, she looked to spending many Christmases in the new house.

I thought about trying to get a university position, but had learned enough about university politics to know I just didn't want to work in such an environment. Therefore, I returned to Surrey and, with my Ph.D. in history, was rewarded with a junior high job teaching English. It took a while to adapt. I missed the freewheeling, philosophical thinking of a university environment, although I did make a lifelong friend from among the students, such as Chris McBride, Des Reddick and Megan Paterson. As well, I'd taught neither English nor junior high before. A third factor almost made the situation unbearable. While Murray could walk to his job, I had to drive more than fifty kilometres each way to reach mine. As I taught five days a weeks and ten months a year, there many times when I wished university politics weren't quite as intense or catty. However, when I looked at the reason we'd moved into Vancouver, the proximity to Murray's sons, I thought the sacrifice well worthwhile.

Chapter 21

W

___

W *stands for Wallow, Wince and Wayward*

It also stands for Wounded Wing.

Of all the seasons of the year, Christmas was by far Murray's favourite and the new house gave us space to entertain. Shortly before Christmas 1977, Murray decided to begin a tradition. Henceforth, our parties would be known as the "Annual Tasting of Dr. Samuel Johnson's Excellent Recipe for Mulled Wine". He'd unearthed the recipe from goodness knows where and, before I had a chance to say my two bits, had invited a few friends to his First Tasting. It was such a success that he couldn't help boasting about it to Glady, foolishly telling her, "You'll have to make sure you come next year."

Fine words. The following year was one in which school lasted almost through to Christmas Day. This made for kids bouncing off the walls and short-tempered teachers as they tried to combine professional and family responsibilities. Murray decided on December 23 as the date for his mulled wine party as school would be finished. With the date set, I consulted with caterers and Murray phoned to tell Glady the news. She booked her flight and arrived on December 22.

When I picked her up at the airport on my way home from

school, we were both exhausted. Immediately she began quizzing me about the party, subtly letting me know that I was being too lackadaisical towards it. She loathed the fact that I was relying on caterers, and when we reached home she made that unhappiness known exclaiming, "Forty people, Murray. I'm not sure Beverley understands just how much work she has to do. But, she needn't worry. I'll look after the food."

Murray and I looked at each other in horror and vainly tried to convince her that we had everything under control, but the more we talked, the less she listened. Finally, I drove her to the supermarket the next morning where she bought various supplies. Just in case, she told me. I bit my tongue. Later that afternoon, I went to pick up the many trays of food from the caterer and when I arrived home Murray and the boys met me at the door.

"Bev, you've got to do something about Mom," Murray announced.

"Me? She's your mother."

"Well, she's driving us bananas. She won't believe that a man can cook. She doesn't understand that I have to simmer my mulled wine for ages."

I sighed. Glady did have a problem sharing kitchens. Not just her own. Any kitchen. And not with just a daughter-in-law, but all women and all men. "Glady," I called as I entered the house. "I need your help. I'm afraid the caterers didn't do a good job. Will you help me rearrange the trays? I think we should use our own, not theirs. Don't you?"

Murray breathed a sigh of relief as his mother and I began working in the dining room. After rearranging the food onto our platters, we put them into the fridge, then fed the boys their supper. Already exhausted, I went upstairs to have my bath and relax. Suddenly a bellow of pure anger rent the house.

"Bev!"

I hustled from the bath, whipped on a robe and raced downstairs. Murray had a wooden spoon in his hand and stared at his pot of mulled wine with horror and anger. He held the spoon out to me. "Here, taste this."

I took the spoon, sipped and spat. Seawater tasted better. "What happened?"

"It wasn't quite right," Glady answered from the back of the room.

I hadn't noticed her sitting at the table by the window. Now, I wondered if she sat there to get as far away as possible from Murray's anger. "What's not right?"

"The mulled wine," she replied as Murray made a strangled sort of noise. "It wasn't sweet enough."

"Because I hadn't finished adding all the ingredients," Murray shouted. "I asked you not to interfere."

"Well, I just added a little bit."

Murray turned to me with an empty salt carton in his hand. "A little bit? She emptied this into my wine!"

Glady rose to her feet, every inch the Montreal *grande dame*. Slowly, she poured herself another glass of sherry and walked past both of us. "I thought it was sugar, refined sugar."

Murray threw his hands into the air. "What can I do? I'll have to make another batch and the liquor stores are shut by now. How the hell do I find a bootlegger?"

"Try Peter," I said, referring to a restaurant owner. "Surely he's got a few gallons of grog he'll let you have for a king's ransom. Or, see if anyone else will take pity on you. If not, we'll just have to limit people to a glass of the mulled wine, then steer them to other drinks. Don't worry, it'll be all right."

Just as I said those words, a crash and a startled cry sounded from the stairwell. We ran from the room and found Glady in an undignified heap at the bottom of the stairs, blood everywhere. We picked her up and found that she'd been taking one of our crystal sherry glasses up to her bedroom. When she'd tripped, she'd fallen onto its rim and now blood poured from a deep, circular cut in her palm. Murray rushed for a towel while I tried to apply a tourniquet as best I could. Then he and I looked at each other.

"I'll take her to the hospital," I said and Murray nodded, preoccupied again with the problem of his mulled wine.

Glady, though, was made of sterner stuff than either of us. While I'd been prepared to brave the emergency ward with a coat over my robe, she would not budge from the house until she had taken the curlers from her hair, put on makeup and an elegant dress. Impatiently I waited ten minutes before she pronounced herself suitable to be seen publicly. Only then was I able to get her into the car and to the hospital. Three hours later, she had about thirty stitches in her hand, still looked immaculate, and had three doctors promising to come to her party when they went off shift. Once we reached home, she exchanged the hospital sling for a silk scarf and danced one-armed with virtually every male, receiving compliment after compliment on her bravery for the rest of the night.

That incident went into family lore as the "Wounded Wing" Christmas and was the harbinger of other, equally memorable, Christmases, ones that would make us laugh when remembered.

PART V

THE QUESTION OF FAITH

CHAPTER 22

U AND P

U *stands for Ubiquitous, Unattainable, Unfathomable.*

It also stands for Ultimates.

Every intelligent person asks the big questions at one time or another. We and our friends were no different. We often met for dinner and, after dessert, the discussion flowed as freely as the wine. Was there life after death? Was there similar life anywhere else in the universe? What was the purpose of life, anyway?

I'd always trot out the answer from the Westminster Catechism that I'd learned so many years earlier – to worship God and enjoy him forever. People sometimes laughed until Murray explained my deep-seated belief.

At this, everyone relaxed and after a while I became their go-to person about God. Nobody wanted anything to do with church. Or, Christians. Everyone seemed to know people who claimed to follow Christ, but who showed nothing of his friendliness, much less his love and compassion. I often thought that if Christ was a country that he'd fire all his so-called ambassadors because they brought nothing but discredit to his name.

Our after-dinner discussions ranged far and wide. None of us accepted the sacred cow of science as truth. There were far too many historians in the group who recalled the various wrong positions science had taken in the past. We accepted that scientists, like us, searched for truth and we, rather sanctimoniously, thought ourselves less dogmatic than they were.

These were good times and, after one of them, Murray asked a truly astonishing question. "Why don't we go to church next Sunday and find out if it's all rubbish?"

But, which church? Murray asked around and was told that Harry Robinson, at an Anglican church, St. John's in Shaughnessy, was the most interesting preacher in town. I bought a church outfit, Murray rummaged around and found a tie, and next Sunday we went to church and slunk into the back row. Harry Robinson was as advertised. Very interesting. Maybe five hundred people crowded the church and all seemed to know each other. We didn't know anyone.

As soon as the service ended, Murray rushed outside for a cigarette and in doing so, I suppose, marked us out as beyond the pale. I had feared that we'd be mobbed. After all, we were two sinners who needed to be saved. Over lunch, we discussed the morning. We'd looked respectable and it seemed inexplicable that we'd been ignored. "Do you want to go back?" I asked Murray.

"Yes. I like the preacher. He's got an interesting slant on things."

And so, we went to church amidst much ribbing from our friends. Somehow, and I'm not sure how, and it had nothing to do with St. John's, Murray was persuaded that we should join two other couples in a Bible Study. The males were strong personalities. One was a leading evangelical figure in Vancouver; the other, a prominent dentist. We bought Bibles and wholeheartedly committed ourselves to this new venture.

Maybe, too wholeheartedly for our own good.

The group suggested that we begin by reading the first eight verses of Paul's letter to the church in Colossae. I'd memorized them in my Sunday School days and thought I had no homework. Wrong. Murray told me I wouldn't be so lackadaisical if it was a seminar and I was to read the whole letter while he went off to the library to read everything he could find about the book of Colossians.

During that first meeting, I came to understand the vast difference between academic and Bible Study. The other couples seemed happy to dissect small segments and had problems with Murray's initiative. It was almost as though he'd indulged in some unauthorized reading. I think they also had a distinct problem with the smell of liquor on our breaths. But we didn't pretend to be anything other than sinners searching for God and, when their disapproval became obvious, I wished I had the courage to remind them that Jesus socialized with publicans.

We stuck the study group out for about two months before it disbanded. On one level, I felt nothing but relief. On a far deeper level I felt betrayed, yet again, by people who claimed to know Jesus Christ. That short group study had made both Murray and I read our New Testaments rather thoroughly and there seemed such a disjunction between the charismatic person of the first century and the didactic, gloomy Christ that his followers portrayed in the twentieth.

We attended church almost every Sunday for eighteen months. With a couple of exceptions, we had yet to be spoken to, much less invited anywhere for drinks, dinner or even for coffee. I must say in the church's defence that we weren't particularly accessible. Murray sat in the back row and scuttled out as soon as he could.

When the World Council of Churches held its meeting in Vancouver in 1983, we were appointed as hosts for one delegate – John Australia, the Australian Anglican primate. I felt nothing but apprehension about this. We couldn't get along with our local Anglicans. What would this primate, the head of all the Australian Anglican churches, make of us?

I need not have worried. An hour after we met, the bond between Murray and our guest was palpable. John had been a chaplain during World War II and loved to tell stories of his army days. Murray also had stories, dating back to his officer training stint in the early 1950s. As well, both could swap tales about Manning Clark. One Saturday night they went out together and when he came home Murray announced that he'd take communion from John the next day at our church.

I don't know why things didn't work out for us at St. John's. Murray quit going for good a couple of months after taking communion. I lasted a little longer although I did not attend regularly. I felt ridiculous. I was flunking church once again.

In 1987, it became obvious that Glady's heart was giving out. We worried, feeling that the distance between Vancouver and Montreal rendered us impotent in terms of helping her. We asked her to relocate to the west coast, but readily understood her refusal. Her remaining friends were in Montreal, and she felt too old to begin making an entire set of new ones.

At the same time, Murray became increasingly frustrated at the university. As he took his teaching seriously, his research and writing suffered. Although he was now accepted as an authority in his field, he had yet to publish a major book. As we talked these problems over, a radical solution occurred. Why didn't Murray take early retirement, even though he was only fifty-two? We'd move to Quebec, oversee Glady's health and Murray would be close to the archives in Ottawa. The university accepted his retirement, granting him emeritus status.

My school board was less amenable, and for a while it looked as though I would have to resign. But one morning, while driving to school, the inevitable happened. After ten years of driving one hundred kilometers five days a week, I was caught in a traffic accident. A rather severe one. I was the third car in a five-car pile-up. After I recovered somewhat and knew that I had an indefinite number of months in rehab, I applied for and was granted indefinite sick leave.

P stands for Pertinent, Pliable, and Portentous.

It also stands for Penultimates.

It's impossible to say what would have happened if Murray had not taken that early retirement. In the short run, it proved ineffective and disastrous. Glady died just before we left Vancouver and I estimate the decision to move east cost us easily a couple of million dollars. For example, when we returned from the east three years later, we could no longer afford our old neighbourhood.

On the other hand, and thank God for other hands, neither of us would have been as happy if we had not followed our hearts. Murray published his definitive study on the effects of the French Revolution on Canada, *Legacies of Fear.* It pinpointed the moment when French and English-speaking residents in Quebec began their linguistic divorce.

I became extremely proficient in delving into arcane legal records, particularly those of the late eighteenth century, and came to know the Canadian and British National Archives very well. The highlight of my research career came the day I discovered a legal opinion that others had missed for a couple of centuries. It had been partially hidden in a group of papers containing plans for mazes, amongst other things, and my inveterate curiosity caused me to stumble over it.

At the Toronto launch of Murray's book in 1993, I made polite social chit-chat with a fellow guest. He seemed fascinated by my dissertation and asked to read it. Incredibly, I left Murray's launch party that night with two publishers suggesting that I turn it into a book. Fate had obviously decided it was payback time. I had never dreamt of writing the book that was published in 1995 as *A Deep Sense of Wrong* and much less becoming a respected legal historian in my own right.

Although we were considerably poorer than we would have been if Murray had not taken early retirement, neither of us ever regretted the decision. Our bonds became stronger than ever, life became happier.

In late August 2000, I spent two weeks by myself in Maui, attending the Maui Writers' Retreat for six of those days. I had the extraordinary experience of trying to switch from academic writing to a more popular style through working with the acclaimed author Elizabeth George. Riding home in a limo, I knew I'd meet Murray and then we'd head towards our favourite bistro in Crescent Beach, where we now lived. We'd dissect my holiday, I'd tell him what I'd learned, show him what I'd written and receive a hefty chunk of his own work in exchange. Then, we'd talk about the upcoming publication of a book we'd co-authored, *Uncertain Justice*, plan some publicity for it, and relax in our love.

Shortly after the limo turned off the freeway and headed over a bridge on its way to Crescent Beach, I asked it to stop. I got out, walked over to the river, and thanked whatever being there was for the way my life had turned around. I was loved, respected and happy. It was an extraordinary feeling. While I gave thanks for it, I thought life could not be better.

Irrationally, I believed Murray and I would live like that forever.

CHAPTER 23

D

_____

D stands for *Desolation, Despair, Disconsolate.*

It also stands for Death.

Murray turned sixty-five on 29 November 2000 – an eagerly anticipated occasion. At long last, he would get something back from the government, a pension. As well, not being a lover of understatement, he looked forward to not one, but three, birthday parties: one with Stewart and Chris, watching that emblem of Canadian football, the Grey Cup; a dinner party on the actual birth date with friends; and another, two days later at a local golf club.

I simply looked forward to December.

As it turned out, that last week of November 2000 was a wretched one. We'd gone to Toronto for the launch of *Uncertain Justice* and I'd caught the flu, spending most of my time in bed, trying to recuperate from it between Murray's various parties. When Murray announced that he had my flu, I believed him.

But I began thinking he might need medical attention when he asked for aspirin. He looked terribly ill and, as he rarely took any medication, I offered to phone for an ambulance, but he begged to spend the weekend at home. He loved our place in

Crescent Beach, about four miles from the American border and an hour's drive from Vancouver. We lived right on the waterfront and he'd spend hours outside, watching the passing walkers and enjoying the scenery. Besides this, he'd had an irrational fear for a couple of years that if he went to hospital he wouldn't return home. As matters proved, his fear was more premonition than irrationality.

Even after I'd called for an ambulance, he almost blustered his way into staying home. He was diabetic and he half-convinced the paramedics that he had a low blood sugar problem. Or, if not low, he blustered, then it had to be too high. As they carried him out of the house, he still protested fate as best he could. Catching my eye, he winked. "Give me a beer, love. A couple of sips for the road."

Sometimes I wish I'd given him those couple of sips because, already, he was beyond further hurt. Diagnosed at our local hospital as having an aneurism, he was immediately sent by ambulance to Vancouver General Hospital and there, the waiting surgeon found no aneurism but an ulcer that had ruptured some days previously. When he broke the news, Chris, Stewart and I stared at him in utter shock.

"What are his chances?" Stewart asked after a minute or so.

Clichés abound – even in times of crisis. When the surgeon cast a harried look around the intensive care waiting room before answering, we realized the news had to be bad.

"Less than fifty-fifty."

"How much less?"

When he sighed, we steeled ourselves for the answer. "Maybe, twenty percent."

Murray's sons, desperate for more information, immediately peppered him with technical questions while I absorbed the shock. Twenty percent? None of us had known Murray was that sick. So many people had remarked on the tremendous form he seemed to be in at his various parties and at the book launches for *Uncertain Justice*. The news that he had an ulcer, much less that it had perforated seemed unbelievable. We knew of his diabetes and its various complications, but an ulcer? A perforated one?

Like other families in similar straits we waited, talking desultorily. Chris and Stewart, unable to accept inaction, occasionally prowled the room. "Dad's a fighter," one would say. We'd agree, somehow gaining a measure of reassurance from the thought. Then, remembering the look in the surgeon's eyes, we'd relapse into silence. Minutes stretched to hours. When they finally allowed us into intensive care it took just one glimpse at the banks of machines and drips for our bravado to seep away. In a kind of paralytic shock, we needed every ounce of energy just for hope.

A fighting chance.

As I drove back to Crescent Beach, these words became my mantra. Murray was a fighter. He'd proved it time and time again. Yet, once I'd reached home after the hour's drive, I knew beyond doubt that Murray's fighting spirit wouldn't be enough. He needed help this time. Numbly I opened my email and scrolled down my list of contact names. I highlighted most as I set up a circular plea, asking everyone to add their will to Murray's. Please send positive vibes, best wishes, whatever, I begged. To those whom I thought might believe in a god, I asked for prayer. Tears cascaded as I hit the keys that sent these messages worldwide, because the person I needed the most as I struggled for personal strength was no longer accessible by email.

Nor was God.

That night, try as I might, I couldn't remember the last time I'd prayed. Fifteen years? The last time I was at St. John's church? I had no idea. Furthermore, as someone imbued with Australian values, I firmly believed in fair play, and I asked myself if I could approach God. Was it right? Would he listen? Why should he? I hadn't bothered about him in years.

Curling myself into a ball on the daybed in my workroom, I began this debate. My cat, Lillie, sensing distress and offering comfort, tucked herself as close as possible while I fought for words. As I questioned the propriety of approaching God, long-forgotten Biblical verses flooded my mind: "Him that cometh unto me, I will in no wise cast out," together with the admonition to call upon God in my day of trouble. That made sense. As I struggled, trying to sort fact from hope, another text, "Call on me in this day of trouble," became a constant refrain.

What is prayer? The words Jesus suggested to his disciples that we have institutionalized into something called the Lord's Prayer? Formal collects read aloud in church? Prepared words, or inarticulate calls for help?

It had been such a long time since I'd thought about these questions, much less known with any degree of clarity what I thought about God. That night in my desperation, I finally blurted out, "God, I know I'm a foul-weather friend." For the next few hours I didn't try to philosophize or answer my own questions. As I thought of Murray's fight, my entire being vibrated in inchoate communication.

Murray had always talked a lot about dying. He feared it and his finely tuned, logical brain found faith in an afterlife difficult. There was no doubt that he wanted to believe both in it and in God. When Glady died, he spent months waiting for a word, a sign, or anything that might convince him of life after death. I tried pointing out that God demanded faith – whatever that meant. If Murray needed a sign, I argued, he negated God's requirement. Murray replied he didn't believe in faith.

But, a sign? If it came, how would he recognize it? From my

younger days, I remembered stories of Thomas, the disciple, and his disbelief. If Thomas, who had known Jesus intimately for three years hadn't recognized him after the resurrection, why did Murray think he might detect a supernatural guidepost? God had made faith a prerequisite for a reason. It was the only quality available to anyone. Just think about it, I told him. If God had set a logical standard, how much intellect would be required? As it was, anyone, regardless of his or her brain power, could believe.

"In hobgoblins or the validity of faith?" he scoffed, before asking how he could know that the God of the Christian church was indeed the true god. Yet Murray had a bedrock faith in something, and that was my steadfast belief in God's existence. "She's the only Christian I know," he'd joke, "who doesn't believe in Jesus Christ."

When our friends laughed and looked at me, I'd shrug, but never deny it. None of them admitted to believing in a god, much less a personal one. But what Murray said about me was half-true. I did believe in God, although all I knew for sure was that my god wasn't the one of my childhood.

My belief made life difficult at times. While Murray might publicly declare himself an agnostic, privately he'd say time and time again that he'd trust my faith. I believed in God. Murray believed in my belief and thus, the responsibility for Murray knowing God was mine. He didn't see anything abnormal in this. His trust in me to get him places or solve various problems was a cornerstone of our marriage.

These thoughts and Murray's fear of death dominated my mind that December night in 2000. If he was the least bit conscious, I knew he'd be petrified. And so, as I "talked" with God, I introduced him to the Murray I knew, beginning with his flaws. That was the easy part. They were so obvious. Murray had always drunk far too much and everyone knew it. But his other qualities far outweighed this. Murray's innate morality would shame many Christians. As well, he put no qualifications on his love.

The only other being I knew who loved similarly was God himself. This shared quality made introducing Murray to God dead easy.

I am so very grateful God didn't demand words that night. How could I have put so many conflicting needs, wants, thoughts and confessions into anything approaching a coherent form? And, as the hours passed, I found everything distilling into two pleas. Give Murray peace, I asked, and flood him with love. I didn't dare ask for his life. Somehow that seemed too selfish and that night wasn't about my needs or me.

When Lillie, my cat, woke me three hours later I blinked myself awake, thinking everything must be a horrible nightmare. Only after I checked the clock did I understand. It was seven-thirty a.m., well past the time Murray usually let her go outside. And so, reality returned. I phoned the hospital, and then let her out. Gradually I became aware of words running through my mind, like a crawler on a television screen: "Peace I leave with you, my peace I give to you... Let not your heart be troubled and don't be afraid."

I knew who had said them. Jesus. I also knew where they had come from, the gospel of John, chapter 14. I'd learned it as a thirteen-year-old for Mrs. Wark. John 14 had been one of my favourites, although I doubted if I could have remembered any of it the day before Murray's hospitalization. But that morning as the words repeated themselves time and time again, I became sure of two things.

One was that God had listened to my prayers the previous night and given Murray peace. Secondly, and more surprisingly, he'd given it to me as well. From that point on I knew that whether Murray lived or died, God would look after him, and when I visited the hospital later that day, I told Murray that I knew God had him in His hands.

For the next three and a half days, Stewart, Chris, and I were confident that Murray would live. Each time we visited, the nurses complained about the latest manoeuvre he'd done to rid himself of the life support tube in his mouth, or how he'd managed to work his hands free to pull it out. We'd laugh; telling ourselves this was vintage Murray. Seeing their outrage, we'd tone our laughter down and agree it definitely was not a good thing. Underneath the tut-tutting though, we were delighted.

Murray was fighting for his life and the fact that he was so ingenious with the tubes proved this. We knew he'd hate anything that stopped him from telling stories. So, partly to appease the nurses, but more to give him reassurance, we'd each sit down beside him and explain what was wrong, and why he needed to keep still. It's just a perforated ulcer, we'd say with dire understatement. But we couldn't escape our joy because we knew his mind was working. Carefully and guardedly we began to talk about Christmas, hoping that he'd be discharged by then.

On the fourth day, everything changed. Several operations had not reversed the toxic flow throughout his body, and moments of consciousness became increasingly rare. As his condition changed, so did our hopes. Sometimes hour by hour. Gradually we came to accept that Murray would not be home for Christmas. Then we adjusted to the fact that he'd not be out of intensive care and, finally, that he might not be eating solid food by then. One terrified day I checked out funeral homes and costs.

At the family conference that night, the doctors offered a ray of hope but even that dimmed the next day when we realized that only an industrial-strength miracle would save Murray's life. His doctors and nurses fought hard, and sometimes the battle lasted throughout visiting hours. The family adapted as best it could. Stewart, in a new job, visited as much as possible after working hours. Chris, a federal prosecutor, managed to book out of court and spent most of his time in the cafeteria, fine-tuning his case and waiting for the precious few seconds we were allowed in to see Murray.

And me? Desperately hoping for a positive outcome, I adhered to my daily routine as much as possible. I kept Murray's night light on, wrote during the mornings, printed the pages out, and brought them with me to the hospital. Then, when permitted, I read them aloud to Murray. When I finished, I read him the emails that were flooding in from all over the world. Most of the time I knew my voice meant something for occasionally, especially when I read a funny part or best wishes from a particular friend, Murray's eyes blinked or his fingers tightened.

By now, the daily deterioration was obvious. Even to us. On Thursday, December 14, I made little attempt to read and spent most of my time simply holding his hand and rejoicing in the warmth and love I could still feel coming from it.

During the time I was by his bedside a couple of doctors dropped by to ask if I'd sell them copies of *Uncertain Justice*. My instinct was to give them the books in gratitude, but I could sense Murray's hackles rise, as he was an unabashed huckster when it came to his writing. So, I set a price that garnered a modest profit. It was just another way of keeping faith with Murray, and I wonder if he ever understood that on the second last day of his life, while lying in an irreversible coma, he managed to sell two books.

He would have been extraordinarily proud!

Around 3:30 a.m. the next morning Lillie yowled. Immediately I knew something had changed. It took little time to understand that for the first time in thirty odd years I could not feel Murray in my mind. Desperately hoping that my suspicions were wrong, I phoned the hospital. Instead of the usual platitudes suggesting no change, I was asked to come in at three that afternoon for a conference. When I arrived, the doctor took me aside into a private area. She had just begun talking when Chris and Stewart came through the door.

Her news was devastating – Murray would die later that night or early the following morning. She advised us to go home, to rest and prepare ourselves for the end. Though I'd been expecting such news since the cat cried, I was still shocked. Stunned, we hugged each other and then departed, by choice, to our separate homes. I could have saved myself the hours of driving by staying in Vancouver. Certainly, Chris and Stewart offered their homes and company. But I needed my familiar places.

So, dry-eyed, I had a bowl of soup on my lap and was desultorily watching the evening news when the phone rang. The doctor's voice was soft and sympathetic. Murray, as usual, had done the unexpected and slipped away peacefully, thus sparing us a death vigil and the terror of waiting for a screen to flat-line. As the doctor calmly explained a few details, I felt a bleakness beyond words,

Murray Greenwood died on December 15, 2000, during the coldest spell of winter, ten days before Christmas, his favourite season. It was just seventeen days after reaching the milestone of sixty-five, and being able to cash in on his government pension, and six weeks after the launch of *Uncertain Justice*, the book that he had the most pride in. He was more, far more than my husband. He was my best friend and the only person I knew who loved me completely– warts and all.

Thus, it was understandable that many others and I myself thought his death might mean my destruction as a person. Before November 2000, I'd tried to imagine life without Murray several times and found I couldn't. Where would my sustenance come from? If anyone had pushed me on the subject, I would have answered that I'd probably either commit suicide or run back to Australia.

Neither happened.

CHAPTER 24

C

C *stands for Confirmation, Causality, Confidence.*

It also stands for Christian.

David Short's sermons are usually memorable, but I can't remember one word he spoke that Sunday. I do remember bobbing and weaving around the back pillar in an effort to become invisible, but I defeated that purpose by filling out the visitor's card that churches place so optimistically in every pew. I've always had a problem with forms. As, for example, naming my father. That Sunday though, I filled in my name and address, and then tried to check the right boxes. The first selection asked whether I was a visitor or a newcomer. Being neither, I declared I was a "prodigal son". I also filled out another card indicating my willingness to attend discussions centred on "Discovering Christ". And that, I thought, as I slunk out through a side door to avoid David Short, put the ball squarely into St. John's court.

It was lobbed back immediately. The Discovering Christ programme director, Karli Baldwin, phoned the next day to tell me the next series of discussions would begin in a month. As we talked, she described her own discovery of Christ. Raised in a Buddhist home, she'd come to Christianity through reading the Bible. In contrast, I'd grown up in a Christian home, had known the Bible well, and yet had been driven from Christianity.

David Short's letter reached the house a day later. After welcoming me to the church, he added a postscript reflecting his inimitable sense of humour. He'd been delighted, he told me, to see a prodigal daughter in the back row. So much, I thought, for the bobbing and weaving around the pillar.

I went to church the following Sunday and, after, the initial feeling of being at home, I began to feel uncomfortable. Because I didn't believe in much of it, I could only mumble a few words of the Creed and I stood or knelt mutely when various collects were said. When the time came for communion, my backside remained firmly planted in the back row.

I thought constantly about Christianity. The intense joy and the feeling of love had not faded or disappeared although, mercifully, my tendency to break into song was diminishing. Believing in Jesus Christ, though, and acknowledging myself as a "going to church on Sundays" kind of Christian scared the pants off me. I'd only ever enjoyed the company of a handful of Christians, and had always found it very difficult to get along with the rest. If I succumbed to Christ, I'd be lonelier than ever now that Murray had gone.

As I grappled with these issues, I slowly adjusted to life as a widow. At first, living by myself was extremely difficult. Forcing myself to make proper meals took weeks of adjustment. Somehow, it just didn't seem worth the effort to cook for one. Shopping habits changed as well. I could now buy most of the month's groceries in one trip to the supermarket but setting priorities and re-establishing a structure in life seemed impossible. Gradually, as the raw hurt of grief faded, some mundane routines returned.

I suppose, at this point, I could have thanked God very much for getting me through the first, so difficult, months of widowhood without drowning out the joy and love that now dominated my life. I could have explained that I'd never been able to find my niche in a church, and why I didn't believe that could change.

My whole life proved that the Christian church and I were incompatible.

But such thoughts mocked what had happened to me in the weeks after Murray's death and, if I believed anything, I believed that God had sustained me. Therefore, I wasn't averse to talking more with Karli Baldwin. Her story fascinated me, though her reiterated requests that I read the Gospel of John did nothing for me. I'd learned several chapters as a kid, and if the memorised words hadn't brought me closer to God, why should reading them do so?

Then fate intervened. A Canadian philosopher whom I'd wanted to hear for years was giving a series of lectures at the University of British Columbia. Once I'd decided to attend one of them, several things clicked into place. I would drive into Vancouver early, go the bookstore of Regent College, a Christian graduate school affiliated with the university, and buy a stand-alone copy of the Gospel of John.

I phoned the college. "Do you have a bookstore?"

"Yes."

"Does it sell Bibles?"

I heard the person's curiosity in the monosyllabic answer. "Yes?"

To my great delight I found a passport-sized gospel and remembering that C.S. Lewis had described his conversion from theism to Christianity in his book *Surprised by Joy*, bought that as well. Then, I took myself off to a local restaurant, ordered half a litre of wine, and told the server to hold my food order for at least an hour and settled down to read.

Lewis's book surprised me. Somehow, over the years, I'd thought of him as an easy read. Mainly, I suspect, because since the late 1950s the only works of his that I'd read were The *Screwtape* Letters, the Narnia Chronicles and his science fiction.

Surprised by Joy is far more abstract and deals mainly with Lewis's journey towards theism. In it he described the emotion joy evokes as so intense that anyone "who has tasted it would never … exchange it for all the pleasures in the world." To him, joy was distinctly different from either happiness or pleasure and, eventually, his quest for it would lead him to God.

My own case was different. The joy I'd experienced I knew, beyond a doubt, had come from God. My quest would be my response to it. Like Lewis, I knew that joy was rare and could not be conjured up on demand. I could never ask God for a repeat of that Monday morning after Murray died. It had been a gift, pure and simple. My response, however, was complex.

As I read more of Lewis's quest, I began to see some similarities. God, in the personae of Love, he wrote, had opened "the high gates to a prodigal … brought in kicking, struggling, resentful, and darting his eyes in every direction for a chance to escape." That described me, especially if the high gates opened to reveal Christianity. But the gates had only brought Lewis to where I was – theism. I sipped my wine slowly as I tried to follow his conversion to Christianity, hoping for a yellow brick road, or at least some guideposts to follow.

He gave none. In fact, he almost glossed over the experience, describing it as being akin to a man "lying motionless in bed" who slowly becomes aware that he's awake. That was it. As opposed to his account of the careful, methodical path leading to theism, and the many philosophical references and conversations guiding him there, the final step to Christianity seemed to have been something he couldn't analyse or describe.

He said that one day he decided to visit London's zoo. He got on a bus to Whipsnade, and when he got off he was a Christian.

I shook my head. If Lewis were still alive, I'd go over to England and shake him. How dare he gloss over something that important? Then, I remembered my own words to Murray –

God didn't make it necessary for us to use our intellects to find him. The philosophers and other great men that Lewis bandied about were of no help. In Søren Kierkegaard's idiom, they could lead us up the craggy heights by reason, but it still took a step of faith to reach the top.

Without enthusiasm I turned to *The Journey*, as my pocket-sized Gospel of John was called. I knew I was going to read: "In the beginning was the Word and the Word was with God...." But something happened on my way to the end of the sentence. Since memorizing those words, I'd become a writer. Subconsciously I always look at style when I first open a book. So, my first soul-shattering experience that day in the restaurant was that John's style was right. Its simple, uncluttered prose fitted what I remembered of the gospel perfectly. Moreover, the lack of sentence complexity was exactly what a semi-literate person, like John, might have written. Prejudices dropped by the wayside as I began reading: "In the beginning...."

Instead of words that I could have parroted, I had the image of an unsophisticated man talking directly to me, telling me what he'd seen and why I should trust his words. These careful qualifications only made John seem more believable. As a trained historian, they were exactly what I would expect from a historical record. Suddenly, I began taking the booklet seriously; making comments in its margins and treating it like any other book that had engaged my mind. When I reached the description of Jesus meeting John the Baptist, and the Holy Spirit's descent from heaven, I stopped. I knew I believed in God, and now I realised this belief extended to his spirit. That's okay, I told myself, this spirit might take different forms. God needs an interpreter. That's understandable. It's how he communicates.

"So?" I thought I heard a voice say.

In Sunday schools and listening to innumerable sermons, I'd heard a lot about God speaking to men in a still, small voice, and I'd never questioned the veracity of those who claimed to hear it. For one thing, they were long since dead and their stories belonged in the Old Testament. For another, I never imagined that God still spoke directly to us. And if that still, small voice existed I never, ever, in my wildest dreams thought it could take on the characteristics of a Brooklyn teenager's cynical drawl.

I looked around, but no one else was in the restaurant. I sat sipping wine and heard God speak again.

"So, two outta three ain't bad, is it?"

Two out of three wasn't bad. In the less than immortal words of Yogi Berra, it was like batting five hundred. But, for me, hearing this voice seemed another indication of insanity. Was I really going mad? God did not speak directly to people. And if He did, and it was a big "if", he surely didn't assume teenage attitudes, did he? Or speak in Brooklynese?

For some moments, I floundered. Lewis had written about God closing in on him. Now, I began to realise there was no escape for me. Metaphorically, I flown to the farthest reaches of the earth, I'd plumbed its depths, suffered the greatest loss I'd ever have, and been rewarded with love and joy. Now, I knew, God wanted more than debate from me. If I hadn't realised it the first time, that voice returned to reinforce the message.

"So?" it questioned.

"So what?" I snapped back, making a server glance over her shoulder.

"So," the voice responded with barely concealed impatience, "if you believe in God's spirit, how does that show itself in your life?"

"Galatians 5:22," I answered quickly, before wondering exactly what I'd said. I didn't have a complete Bible with me, and I seriously doubted if the restaurant ran to one. But I vaguely remembered that in the fifth chapter of Galatians, the apostle

Paul wrote about the Holy Spirit's impact on our lives. There was a checklist, and I slowly enumerated it in my head – love, joy, peace, patience…

"So?" my monosyllabic guide interrupted.

Then something happened. That series of exasperating questions made me realise that God had been in my life for years, changing me slowly, until even I could see the qualities Paul had mentioned in Galatians 5:22. There was little trace any more of the sullen teenager who had trailed despair after her.

I now understood why Lewis had glossed over the process by which he changed from theism to Christianity. He'd set out for the zoo and, amazingly, arrived with a belief in Jesus Christ. He says he didn't think or experience any great emotion on the trip.

I turned back to John's gospel and began reading again. I sped through the intervening chapters until I reached the fourteenth, the one I remembered when Murray first went into hospital. My reading slowed and I began thinking about the words I'd memorized for Mrs. Wark so many years before.

"I am the way, the only path of access to God the father," Jesus declared. I was still puzzled. I couldn't doubt that God had intervened directly in my life. Did Jesus's assertion mean that my interaction with his father could only be through him? For a few seconds, while I sipped my wine, I felt discouraged. Then, I read of Philip's plea to Jesus to be shown his father and pondered the reply. "If you've seen me, Philip, you've seen my father." Maybe, it went both ways, I thought, and then some follow-up words simply leapt off the page.

Jesus had gone on to say something like, "If you can't believe in me in any other way, believe in me because of the work I've already done in you."

What more did I expect of God? That he would put flashing neon signposts in front of my house? Once more, I ran through my list of what he'd already had done for me – he'd accepted the fierce bitter longing of a wounded child; he'd saved my life in Chicago; he'd shown me what altruistic love was like through Murray; he'd stopped the little girl's sobs; and, lastly, he'd taken away my greatest treasure and given me back immeasurable love and joy. Could I doubt any longer?

When C.S. Lewis climbed onto a bus to go to the London zoo, he did not find faith in Jesus Christ. When I entered a restaurant on West Tenth in Vancouver, I did not find it either. In both cases, God found us. It is the central promise through the Bible. If we hope for God, He will find us and offer us faith. As I told Murray, faith does not require wealth or intellect. It's available to anybody everywhere.

In Hebrews 11, the Bible says that faith is being sure of what we hope for. It's why we must have the temerity to hope.

CHAPTER 25

Q AND A

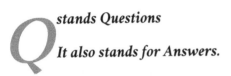

stands Questions

It also stands for Answers.

Questioner: Thanks for the book, Bev. I really enjoyed reading it but I still have questions.

Bev: So, do I. I've had to become reconciled to the fact that I'll never find any answers for some of my own questions, much less anyone else's.

Q: Well, what about your birth father? Did you ever find out anything about him?

Finding out who my father was became the great game amongst my cousins and, together, we've deduced certain things. One, that he was rich and that either he or his parents were powerful. Reason 1: the records of my birth were burnt by an act of the NSW legislature. Therefore, I can never get a birth certificate. Reason 2: the kidnappings and Boy's status and income as a plumber. Why was I kidnapped, if not for money? When I look back at my life I can see three huge infusions of cash coming into the family: shortly after my birth, when I was about six; and later when I twelve. We think this was blood-money from my father and that whoever had me in their possession got the cash.

Q: Couldn't Girlie help you, tell you something?

It seems to me that Girlie spent most of her life pretending that I didn't exist. She told me various names and religions over the years and then claimed to remember nothing. So, my father could have been Catholic, Jewish, Protestant, whatever. I once spent two weeks in the N.S.W. archives reading through the exam results of every boys' school for the years 1928-1936 and found nobody with the names Girlie had given. It's something I live with. I'll never know who he was.

Q: Well, talking about Girlie, how would you describe your relationship with her?

Zero. Nonexistent. She held Evelyn and me responsible for wrecking her life and thought I'd had everything handed to me on a silver platter. Her hatred was corrosive and spewed out whenever I was around. On the other hand, she was a good mother to Caera and a doting grandmother.

Q: Let's talk about something else. Are you still a Christian? How has that worked out?

Yes, indeed, I'm still a Christian. I go to St. John's where people have been incredibly patient with my ups and downs. I started with the intention of not flunking church again and never expected to find most of my current friends there. I am loved by many among the St. John's community and so grateful for their support, especially through my prickly Christian "toddler" years.

Q: Does God still talk to you?

Has God stopped talking to me? No, but nowadays, it's more likely to be through the Bible where he encourages and sometimes admonishes me.

Q: *Why did God talk to you one-on-one? I don't know anyone else who claims to have heard God directly. What makes you so special?*

I'm not special at all. God is the ultimate in universality. He loves everyone, not just me. Jesus died for everyone. I've thought hard about this, though, wondering why certain things happened. A comparison that might explain what happened to me is the story Jesus told about a shepherd who had one hundred sheep. He cared for his sheep, kept them warm and safe, and knew them well enough to know when one was missing. And so, he searched until he found the lost sheep, then lifted it up and carried it home on his shoulders.

That lost sheep would have had a slightly different perspective of the shepherd than the ninety-nine that were safe in the pen. On his shoulders, it might have felt his pulse or heard his heart thud. But, once home, the lost sheep was indistinguishable and treated the same way as the rest of the flock.

So, I am not special, just someone who was lost with no one to help me except God Himself.

Q: *Is there anything you didn't mention that you'd wish to pass on?*

The importance of prayer. I've realized that I've talked to God most of my life. Most of the time, it was somewhat scurrilous because I was so angry with Him and with life. And so, one piece of advice for people with hard lives and those who find hope almost impossible. Talk to God. Don't pull punches. Tell him your thoughts, your despair, your anger and ask for hope and rescue. He promises that if you search for Him, He will find you. In any case, you have nothing to lose, do you?

Second, I'd like to encourage the parents, grandparents, aunts, uncles, friends etc. who pray for lost sheep. Like many in my case, you may not live long enough to see your prayers answered. But, as my story proves, God will respond in His own time. Whatever you do, don't give up hope.

And lastly, on the topic of prayer, I'd like to talk about healing from abuse. I remember being the little girl who sobbed into her dog's fur in my back yard. Seeing the perpetrator go to jail would not have stopped my tears. Compensation may have made me richer and counselling may have helped me get on with my life earlier, but the only sure-fire way I know to stop those tears flowing is to ask the God who is all-powerful and outside of time to love that abused child and heal you. If you're a person stuck with that gnawing, angry, violated ache of a wounded child, please think about asking God for complete healing. You have nothing to lose. It may take time, but it certainly worked for me.

Q: You've emphasized hope throughout your book. Why is it so important?

Hope hurts. It hurts much more than fear. It means going beyond rationality, going against the evidence of our eyes, thoughts and experiences, to hope in something we cannot see or prove.

Yet, without hope we live in dreary futility and fear. That's why suicide becomes so attractive. Novelist Greg Iles describes hope as "faith holding out its hand in the dark." William Faulkner is a little more bracing when he says: "You cannot swim for new horizons until you have courage to lose sight of the shore.

If you are a person who cannot see tomorrow, who cannot swim for new horizons, you have to hope for them. But, if there's no possibility of hope in you, pray. Tell God how you feel. Use whatever language you want to, but above all, ask for hope. And, if you cannot find anyone who will listen, reach out to me.

Q: Who is God? You asked David Short and he said "holiness". What's your one-word description of God?

Friend.

ACKNOWLEDGMENTS

Like an Academy Awards speech, this list could go on for ever, but I will limit it to people who have supported and helped me during the past seventeen years. Michael and Lesley Bentley have taken me into their family and David and Bronwyn Short nurtured me during the first tricky years of being a Christian. And, as well, I'm grateful to the community of St. John's for putting up with me as I grew in my faith.

My personal roll of honour includes: Ed and Anita Bowes; Ali Cumming; Leonor Cumming; Rod and Irene Douglas; Cynthia Friesen; Kathy Gillen; Mandy Johnson; Jeanette and Joseph Jones; Ed and Bettina Konrad; Anna Kwan; Ruth Matheson; Jim and Karen May; Kristina Nilsson; San Nolte; Sally Palm; Susan Pieters, Wes Pue; Eddie Rittinger; Ian Robertson; Karl Rose; Deb Sears; Dave and Bron Short; Peggy Smart; Neil and Sylvia Stopforth; Laura Spruston Darrell Thomas, Amy Tippett; Irena Tippett; Adele Voth; Adena Waffle; Theo Wending; Ewen Wilding.

Thank you, Valerie Gray, my brilliant editor who trimmed fat and gave structure to the book. Three wonderful women helped with the proofreading — Denise Rumble; Heather Williams; and Katie Drysdale, who read and reread. I take responsibility for any remaining errors.

And lastly, I am grateful to Concert Properties and Tapestry (especially Avril, Doug and Greg) where I live and thrive.